PAPERBARK

Jack Davis has been active as a Black writer and spokesperson since the 1960s. He was editor of the Aboriginal magazine *Identity* (1973–79). His works include the poetry collections *The First-born, Jagardoo* and *John Pat,* and wellknown dramas such as *The Dreamers, Kullark, No Sugar, Honey Spot* and *Barungin: Smell the Wind.*

Stephen Muecke teaches at the University of Technology, Sydney, in the area of communication studies. He has edited *Gularabulu: Stories from the West Kimberleys* by Paddy Roe, and is co-author with Roe (and Krim Benterrak) of *Reading the Country.* He also runs a small publishing house, Local Consumption Publications.

Mudrooroo Narogin is the author of four works of fiction: *Wild Cat Falling, Long Live Sandawara, Doctor Wooreddy's Prescription for Enduring the Ending of the World,* and *Doin Wildcat.* He has also written the poem sequences *The Song Circle of Jacky, Dalwurra,* and a critical study, *Writing from the Fringe.*

Adam Shoemaker is the Canadian-Australian author of *Black Words, White Page: Aboriginal Literature 1929–1988* (UQP, 1989). He has published widely on Black literature, and is currently assistant professor of literature and communication at Bond University.

UQP BLACK AUSTRALIAN WRITERS

Editorial consultants: Jack Davis
Oodgeroo Noonuccal
Mudrooroo Narogin

Forthcoming titles:

Graeme Dixon, *Holocaust Island*
Joe McGinness, *memoir*
Mabel Edmund, *life story*

PAPERBARK

a collection of
Black Australian writings

edited by

Jack Davis   Stephen Muecke
Mudrooroo Narogin   Adam Shoemaker

University of Queensland Press

First published 1990 by University of Queensland Press
Box 42, St Lucia, Queensland 4067 Australia
Reprinted 1990

The typeset text for this book was supplied by the editors in camera-ready form
Printed in Australia by The Book Printer

Distributed in the USA and Canada by
International Specialized Book Services, Inc.,
5602 N.E. Hassalo Street, Portland, Oregon 97213-3640

National Bicentennial Aboriginal and
Torres Strait Islander Program

The financial assistance of the Aboriginal Arts
Board of the Australia Council and the National
Bicentennial Aboriginal and Torres Strait Islander
Program on the first printing is gratefully acknowledged.

Cataloguing in Publication Data

National Library of Australia

Paperbark : a collection of Aboriginal writings.

   Bibliography.
   Includes index.

   [1]. Australian literature — Aboriginal authors. 2.
   Australian literature — 20th century. I. Davis, Jack, 1917-

A820.8089915

ISBN 0 7022 2180 5

Contents

Note by Oodgeroo Noonuccal   *vii*
Foreword   *xi*
Acknowledgments   *xiii*

Introduction   *1*
JIMMY PIKE   *Kirrkirr (Chicken Hawk)*   7
ARCHIE WELLER   *The Legend of Jimmy's Axe and Other*
                            Verses   9
DAVID UNAIPON   *Narroondarie's Wives*   19
                            Wondangar, Goon na Ghun
                            (Whale and Star Fish)   33
Testimony To Gawler   53
Letter from Nepabunna   55
TILLY BAILS   *A Good Thrashing*   57
JIMMY PIKE   *Jilji Kurmalyi (Sandhills)*   59
PADDY ROE   *I Went to Perth Once Too*   61
NGITJI NGITJI   *"Cuppa Tea" Song*   64
                            The Possum Woman   65
ROBERT CHURNSIDE   *Goanna Hibernating*   67
SNOWY HILL   *A Story of Wongawol Station*   69
JIMMY PIKE   *Purnarra*   77
SALLY MORGAN   *The Letter*   79
GLORIA BRENNAN   *Unwritten Policy*   82
JIMMY EVERETT   *Waterdogs*   84
ELLEN DRAPER   *Old Cobraboor*   90
M. THORNE   *Mission Truck*   104
JACK DAVIS   *White Fantasy — Black Fact*   107
                            My Brother Harold   113
                            Pay Back   115
TRACY BUNDA   *Bidjibub*   118
HYLLUS MARIS   *The Way Forgotten*   121
                            The Concrete Box   124
                            Joey Comes to the City   126
ARCHIE WELLER   *Stolen Car*   128

RUBY LANGFORD   *A Letter from an Aboriginal Mother*   141
                The Trials of Nobby   144
GORDON LANGFORD   *Nikky's Story*   149
LYDIA GEORGE   *Gelam*   151
BANJO WORRUMARRA   *Pigeon Story*   158
ROBERT BROPHO   *The Great Journey of the Aboriginal
                Teenagers*   164
LEANNE HOLLINGSWORTH   *Reflections on a Black
                        Childhood*   173
WILLIAM FERGUSON   *Nanya*   175
JIMMY PIKE   *Mirnmirt*   197
MUDROOROO NAROGIN   *Struggling*   199
JIMMY PIKE   *Mirnmirt*   291
JIMMY CHI   *Black Girl*   293
HERBIE LAUGHTON   *My Finke River Home*   295
BOB RANDALL   *Brown Skin Baby*   297
GERRY BOSTOCK   *Here Comes the Nigger* (extract)   299
JIMMY CHI AND OTHERS   *Bran Nue Dae* (extract)   311
JIMMY PIKE   *Ngurra Wanjulajarra
             (Land All Over The World)*   319
ROB RILEY   *Aboriginal Land-Claims Not Excessive in the Land
            of the Great Fair Go*   321
PAT DODSON   *Restore Dignity, Restore Land, Restore
             Life*   326
GARY FOLEY, REVEREND CHARLES HARRIS, GALARRWUY
YUNUPINGU, TIGA BAYLES AND KAREN FLICK
  The Year of Mourning   330
NIMBALIMAN   *Still You Keep Asking Asking*   343

List of Abbreviations   345
Bibliography   347
Notes on Contributors   364

Note

Oodgeroo Noonuccal

As a tribute to one of the most respected elders and artists of the black community, the editors have included the following note by Oodgeroo Noonuccal, with her permission. In this autobiographical account, she explains how she came to adopt the name of "Oodgeroo" which means "paperbark tree".

I was born Kathleen, Jean, Mary Ruska, on the third day of November, 1920. The second youngest of seven children. My father taught us to uphold our Aboriginal identity, by teaching us about our tribal way of life.

I am of the Noonuccal tribe, my totem, Kabool, the carpet snake, my tribal land, Minjerribah, which the European invaders renamed Stradbroke Island.

We all went hunting for our natural foods. As we lived on an island, sea foods were in abundance. Our sea spirit Quandamooka, which the Europeans renamed Moreton Bay, kept us well supplied with food. Fish, oysters, crabs, quampee (pearl shell), eugaree (pippy) and dugong (sea cow). Also, we trapped and ate bandicoots, wallabies, kangaroos, flying foxes and larrakeets such as the blue and green mountain parrots.

Our Aboriginal diet kept us happy and healthy.

My father worked as a foreman with an Aboriginal gang at Dunwich. He received three pounds a week. He worked six days a week. He worked for the Queensland Government's Dunwich Benevolent Asylum for the Aged and Infirm on the island.

The Aboriginal gang did all the menial tasks around the island. Wood gathering and cutting, making roads, sweeping out gutters, and unloading cargoes. The European Australian staff ran the institution.

Draught horses were harnessed to heavy drays. The State Government ship, *Otter*, brought cargoes, needed for the institution, from Brisbane, twice a week.

I went to school at the Dunwich State Primary School. I left school at the age of thirteen to work as a domestic for two shillings and sixpence a week.

The Queensland State Government paid the Aboriginal workers a small wage plus rations which consisted of rice, sago, tapioca, matches, flour and one bar of soap which was handed out per fortnight. On the Queen's Birthday, we were issued with blankets and one plum pudding.

Aborigines were never allowed to join in any of the social activities of the European Australian staff.

We were banned from their dance floors and when we went to the theatre we were made to sit with the "inmates" of the institution, on long hard seats, while the European Australian staff sat on cane chairs at the back of the theatre.

We were expected to go to church regularly.

When World War II broke out, my two brothers joined the army and without firing a shot, were transported to Singapore, where the Japanese took them as prisoners of war. They returned home after the war ended — one minus a leg. Both died of war injuries and are interred in the Dunwich Cemetery.

I joined the Australian Women's Army Service and trained as a switchboard operator in LHQ Area Signals at Chermside, Brisbane.

I married Bruce Raymond Walker whose tribe came from the Logan and Albert rivers. I had two sons and ten years after my marriage, I divorced my husband and reared my two sons alone. I took in washing and ironing and went back to domestic work, until I applied for a soldier's rehabilitation course.

I went to college and trained as a stenographer. I passed my shorthand, typing and bookkeeping without much difficulty.

In the early '60s there was a group of people in Victoria, trying to raise interest in helping the Aborigines, with Pastor Doug Nicholls and Gordon Bryant spearheading the move. When they decided to hold a conference in Queensland, at the Queensland University, I became interested.

When the Federal Council for the Advancement of Aborigines and Torres Strait Islanders (FCAATSI) conference was held at the university in 1960, I joined them and became Queensland state secretary and held that position for ten years.

In 1970, Queen Elizabeth II came to Australia to "celebrate Captain James Cook's discovery of Australia". The members of the FCAATSI movement met at La Perouse, Sydney, to hold a service to the dead tribes who had been wiped out by the early English invaders and to throw wreaths into Botany Bay as a protest against the "celebration".

At the meeting, Pastor Don Brady was sitting with me awaiting the arrival of the rest of the members of the FCAATSI movement.

He remarked how surprised he was that my poetry books were being bought and read by European Australians as well as Aborigines and Torres Strait Islanders and he said to me, "Kathy, you must be a tribal sister to the paperbark trees because you write so good. You couldn't do what you do without their help. Your real name must be Oodgeroo, which is our name for the paperbark trees."

Foreword

Work on this collection first began in 1983, as an outgrowth from the First National Aboriginal Writers' Conference held at Murdoch University in Perth. It has always been shaped by the conviction that there was a need for a comprehensive text of Black Australian writings, restricted neither by genre nor geography. Thus, *Paperbark* includes material from all the states and territories of Australia, from a wide range of age groups, and from both urban and rural environments.

Largely because of this goal of representativeness, it has been impossible to accept for publication all the contributions which were submitted. We would like to thank the many Black Australians whose submissions were not in the end published. There is at least another book's worth of writings which, unfortunately, cannot appear here, but we firmly believe that there will be other opportunities for those voices to be heard in the future.

The editorial process was a communal one, which took place over a period of six years in various locations. Each editor collected submissions independently and then we had round table discussions—with manuscripts spread before us—in Perth, Sydney and Brisbane, in order to arrive at the final product.

The genesis of *Paperbark* has also paralleled moves towards the establishment of a literary award for new Black Australian writing. This idea was mooted in our original manuscript proposal to the Aboriginal Arts Board and the publisher of this collection—the University of Queensland Press—has now taken up the idea enthusiastically and administers the David Unaipon Award, which includes a guarantee of publication for the winning entrant. As a measure of our own enthusiasm, part of the grant money for this volume has gone towards the establishment of the Unaipon Award and has funded the inaugural prize won in 1989 by Graeme Dixon for his manuscript, "Holocaust Island". The Unaipon Award is presented annually for a book-length manuscript of any type, either in English or Aboriginal or Islander languages, written by an Aborigine or Torres Strait Islander who has not previously had a book published.

We are delighted that this idea has been realised, and that the spirit which informs *Paperbark* will live on in this award.

Acknowledgments

The editors would like to thank many people and organisations for their help with this book. The Point McLeay (Raukkan) Community Council provided us with the first authorised publication rights to David Unaipon's work and the Mitchell Library, State Library of New South Wales, allowed us access to his original manuscripts for this purpose. We are indebted to Isabelle Kent for making available the manuscript of "Nanya", written by her father, William Ferguson, and to *CAAMA Music* for permission to republish the lyrics of Herbie Laughton's *My Finke River Home*. We are grateful to Jimmy Pike, Patricia Lowe and David Wroth of Desert Designs for permission to reproduce original prints as well as to Trevor Nickolls for permission to utilise his painting as cover art.

We would like to thank the Koori Oral History Program of Koori Kollij, Melbourne for permission to reprint its transcription of "The Year of Mourning". The Museum of South Australia, through John Moriarty and the Department of Aboriginal Affairs (Adelaide) authorised us to reprint the historical texts "Testimony to Gawler", "Letter from Nepabunna" and "A Good Thrashing". Pru Black, Johanna Dykgraaf, Clare Forster, Bob Hodge, Peter Kerans, Phillip Morrissey, Douglas Muecke, Craig Munro, Shane Rowlands and Celeste Warren have all helped in a variety of ways.

Oodgeroo Noonuccal's article first appeared in full length in *Australian Writing Now,* ed. Manfred Jurgensen and Robert Adamson (Ringwood: *Outrider* and Penguin, 1988). Snowy Hill's "A Story of Wongawol Station"; Gloria Brennan's "Unwritten Policy"; Jack Davis's "White Fantasy — Black Fact", "My Brother Harold", and "Pay Back"; Hyllus Maris's "The Way Forgotten", "The Concrete Box" and "Joey Goes to the City"; and Raymond Chee [Archie Weller]'s "Stolen Car" were all originally published in *Identity*. Banjo Worrumarra's "Pigeon Story" was first published in *Aboriginal History* and Leanne Hollingsworth's "Reflections on a Black Childhood" is from *Black Voices*. Rob Riley's *Aboriginal Land-Claims Not Excessive in the Land of the*

Great Fair Go was first published in *The Canberra Times*; Pat
Dodson's "Restore Dignity, Restore Land, Restore Life" is from
Justice Trends and Robert Bropho's "The Great Journey of the
Aboriginal Teenagers" was originally printed in *Limit of Maps*. Sally
Morgan's "The Letter" was first published in the *National
Aboriginal Day Magazine*. Jimmy Chi's song "Black Girl" is from
the cassette tape *Kuckles* and Nimbaliman's "Still You Keep Asking
Asking" was transcribed from a videotape of the same name
produced by the Northern Land Council. We would also like to
thank Bond University and the University of Technology, Sydney
for the use of facilities.

Introduction

A comprehensive collection of Black Australian writing is long overdue.

Since the 1960s, Australian Aboriginal traditions have been transformed from oral to written forms more than ever before. For good or ill, the bicentennial events of 1988 focused more attention upon First Australians, their grievances, their protests and their creative works than any year since the invasion 200 years ago. In this context, the need for a nationally representative selection of black writing has never been greater.

Work on this collection first began in 1983. It has always been guided by the belief that Black Australian literature, while largely unknown and unheralded until the past three decades, is not a new development. Many of the stories, poems and dramas published in these pages have their roots in the oral traditions which for centuries have been the lifeblood of the Aboriginal and Islander cultures spread right across this continent. These cultures provide a kind of black unity which spans Australia, and this is the first book which brings together a comprehensive range of their writings or texts. Just as Australia was not discovered by the British in 1788, black writing was not "discovered" in the 1960s: what appears in these pages is only a fragment which indicates what has always existed and what can exist in the future.

Oral "literature" (or "verbal art") is transcribed here. It is reproduced on the page according to a technique first used in Paddy Roe's book, *Gularabulu* (1983). This technique is designed to retain the rhythm and pace of the oral narrative, as well as the special formal style of Aboriginal English. But this can only be a partial representation of the complex of gestures, inscriptions, melodies and intonations which characterise Aboriginal storytelling and singing.

In this collection there are also writings which follow the generic conventions of Western literature: poem, dramatic script, novella, short story and so on. These forms are of Aboriginal content, but paradoxically they wear the formal "Western" clothing of established genres. This sort of writing is of relatively recent origin. Oodgeroo Noonuccal published her first volume of poetry in 1964, while Mudrooroo Narogin published the first Aboriginal novel in 1965. Since then there has been an upsurge in Aboriginal literature and it is now included in many school and university syllabuses, while Aboriginal people are publicly making more and more explicit policies for their arts and traditions.

In 1983 the first National Aboriginal Writers' Conference was held at Murdoch University. Over forty Aboriginal delegates from all over Australia discussed their work and the outcome was eventually published as *Aboriginal Writing Today* (1985) edited by Jack Davis and Bob Hodge. This conference consolidated the political basis for Aboriginal literature, a literature or a set of writings which has never been divorced from the Aboriginal struggle for economic freedom, legal recognition and reforms of basic living conditions. It is as if aesthetic questions have taken a back-seat compared to the politics of literature. Put another way, if one accepts the proposition that all literatures are political expressions, then Aboriginal literature is one of those which has not yet succumbed to the rhetorical ploy of saying that "politics gets in the way of literature". It asserts the contrary: literature is one of the ways of getting political things done. Accordingly, this collection makes no claim for an Aboriginal literary aesthetic divorced from rhetorical writing. Its aesthetic, if anything, lies in the force of the political statements that it makes, a force which makes much contemporary Australian fiction look tame and parochial by comparison.

The writers in this volume will profit most by being placed firmly in their own contexts of production—their own Aboriginal families and communities. While some of the pieces are by well-established Aboriginal writers, others represent more popular forms of writing emerging from experiences at work, home or school by writers who have no pretentions to literary grandeur. These examples represent the experiences of people who write because writing is one way of coming to terms with the struggles of daily life. But black literature is proactive as well as reactive. In this sense, Black Australians often feel the necessity to communicate effectively on behalf of their people so that political gains can be won.

Many authors are appearing here for the first time in print, or have only been published in obscure places, like in the journal *Identity* of which Jack Davis was the editor for a number of years. *Identity* published for the first time Aboriginal writers like Archie Weller and the poet Aileen (Louise) Corpus, and was thus an important part of the development of Black Australian writing. It has been closed down and without a successor for a long time now. In its stead a few specialist places for Aboriginal people to control their own means of literary production have emerged. Magabala Books in Broome is producing most original Aboriginal texts. Other Aboriginal writers are finding "mainstream" publishers increasingly eager to profit from the local and international interest in Aboriginal literature.

Aboriginal writing can often be seen as a *community gesture* towards freedom and survival, rather than the self-expression of an individual author. These examples are closely related to *the petition*, for which the ultimate aim is often land rights. For example, the "Testimony to Gawler" in the first section of this book is about an attempt to control the government of a community. In including writings of this sort we were inspired by Bruce McGuinness and Denis Walker who observed in *Aboriginal Writing Today* that most early writings by Aboriginal people were in the form of petitions and similar documents which were examples of people writing literally for survival.

In the same vein, there was a famous bark petition sent to Canberra by the *Yirrkala* people of the Northern Territory in 1963. It also indicates that what we call "writing" need not always be defined by the Gutenberg tradition of script on paper which has been reproduced by the printing press. In a broader sense writing is definable as any sort of meaningful inscription, and in the case of Aboriginal Australia this would include sand paintings and drawings—like Jimmy Pike's graphics in this volume—body markings, paintings as well as engravings on bark or stone. To the extent that these markings are called sacred, it is worth recalling that prior to the invention of the printing press, scribes and iconographers were engaged in Europe and elsewhere in the task of copying sacred texts and illustrating their manuscripts in ways that stressed the importance of the text as a culturally significant artifact in its own right, not as a way of reproducing and disseminating information or ideas on a mass scale in commodity form.

However, the first Aboriginal "writer", in the European romantic sense of an individual expressing his or her own ideas, was David Unaipon from Point McLeay, South Australia. Born on 28 September 1862, Unaipon was in a sense a scribe for his people as well. His little-known but extensive manuscript and typescript, "Legendary Tales of the Australian Aborigines" (1929), preserved in its entirety only at the Mitchell Library in Sydney, is a rare and intriguing cultural artifact.

It is also one which, historically, has been appropriated by Europeans for other ends. In 1930, the anthropologist William Ramsay Smith published a collection of Black Australian stories entitled *Myths & Legends of the Australian Aboriginals*, which was reprinted as late as 1970. It included, without credit or reference to Unaipon, the majority of stories which are contained in his 1929 manuscript. The case of David Unaipon therefore cries out for further research, investigation and publication, focusing not only on the content but on the context of his work. As these factors are so central to Aboriginal literature, we are conscious of the responsibility which we have assumed by choosing to print only a selection of Unaipon's writings. Those stories which do appear in the pages of *Paperbark* present, for the first time in acknowledged form, a creative insight into a fascinating and influential Aborigine who was equally at home with Victorian theology and Black Australian mythology.

The selections of "oral literature" are intended to provide samples from the continuing tradition of the *oral* production of Aboriginal culture. This tradition is so important that many Aboriginal people are suspicious of the written word. They are conscious that the adequate transmission of an oral culture involves the maintenance of the means of communication, the specific techniques of storytelling and the contexts (family, ritual) which involve person-to-person contact and the warmth and liveliness that always go into keeping cultures alive. In that sense putting an oral culture into books is like "embalming" it for posterity, and even this book enters into that paradox (paperbark is also a material used for shrouds in some parts of Aboriginal Australia). However, books do have their uses, and to the extent that education of and about Aboriginal people is going to demand more and more written documents, then books will continue to contribute to the various institutions that are training the next generation.

As this indicates, *Paperbark* is more than just the title of this collection. The term is a multi-layered one, referring both to the traditional and the contemporary and the continuing links between the two. Eucalyptus trees provide the canvas for the Arnhem Land bark-painter just as pulped and processed European trees provide the neat white sheets on which much contemporary black literature is written. "Paperbark" is also the term chosen by Aboriginal authors such as Oodgeroo Noonuccal (literally, "Paperbark of the Noonuccal tribe") to indicate both their representative role and their traditional affiliation. Finally, it suggests a continuum of natural and environmentally-based values and of the true Australianness which can be found in the pages of this volume.

Kevin Gilbert has made the point that non-Aboriginal writers have often sought the refuge of their predecessors in order to establish the sense of a White Australian literary tradition. As he stated eloquently in the introduction to his 1988 anthology of Aboriginal poetry, *Inside Black Australia*:

> Of course there will be many who, not wanting to reveal any overt or covert racism, paternalism, condescension, misconception, self-deception or otherwise to the value of the contribution, will dart like a prawn in a barramundi pond to the safety of antecedents. To us it is like seeing a saga of these British Boat People returning to the wreck to salvage a plank and, holding it aloft, try to make comparisons with the indigenous tree and twist it to a semblance of the 'tree back home'. (Gilbert 1988: xviii)

Gilbert's book not only establishes the independent paradigm of Black Australian verse but also demarcates the wide-ranging talent of Aboriginal poets. While *Inside Black Australia* is specific to one genre, *Paperbark* ranges over many and, in this sense, the two collections are complementary. This anthology is underpinned by the conviction that Aboriginal writing, like Uluru—two-thirds of which is hidden underground—is still largely unknown to most Australians. It is our hope that this collection will contribute to the process of "learning the country" for the reader, both in this nation and overseas.

KIRRKIRR
(chicken hawk)

JIMMY PIKE

Sometimes they kill a snake when they are landing. They kill a big one or a small one.

The Legend of Jimmy's Axe

Archie Weller

Here is the legend of Jimmy's axe
that scarred the country with ochre red blood:
as red as the flaming hair on his head
or as the fire that writhed in his cold eyes,
green like the trees and the grass of his home and the swift
parrots that flew through his skies.
Here is the story of a cruel axe.
Sometimes its ringing singing tones would roll
across the wheat-heavy hills on which he worked,
as he crowned the land with wooden fence-posts.
In the year this Federal country was born,
toasted in champagne and praised in loud song,
Jimmy, lost in these new lands,
with his axe held in half-caste brown hands
came stumbling and bumbling, sullen and wild;
came like Ned Kelly, maiming and killing
women and children old men and babies
with his brother, who laughed like the Devil,
and like storm-filled rivers blood was spilling
until at last they shot him dead.
Shot-gun pellets tore through his head
and ripped to shred his dreams of war
then Jimmy and his axe were no more.

Yet,
did his wife,
as white as he would have liked to be;
white like the flour those squatters never gave him
and for which he took up his bloody axe
to smash the white eggshell complacency.
His wife as white as the day he was born;
she as white as the baby that was not his—
all so white on that gruesome awesome night...
Did she mourn?

Manteena

Archie Weller

And from Manteena's dreams he came
as beautiful as the rising dawn,
yet his body was like the fog
that clings and still escapes pleading hands:
for can you tell me, what are dreams?
She dies; her heart it fades away
so he also goes.
From the ground Manteena rises
as beautiful as she was in life—
but her dream lover is like a cloud
and she sleeps alone.

For Kath Walker

Archie Weller

My words are like the banksia.
Men pick the full sweet cones
for their hungry children
and suck on the honeyed flavour
that comes from this crooked old tree
so old and wise, knowing
the ways of her country
the ways I leave to you.

Ngungalari

Archie Weller

I go. I go. I go.
I, Ngungalari,
last of the Kaneang tribe.
I leave my brown-skinned brothers
sitting like frogs by the river,
waiting for tomorrow's princess.
I leave my sisters with their ghosts
of the pale-eyed wadgula men.
Croaking like a crow I go,
shaking like a wind torn tree
and I not yet a woman.
Keep your Nellie Strongfellow
for Ngungalari is my name.
I am last and lost in this strange land
that once was mine.
I leave fathers with their hopes
and too-young mothers with their tears
and unborn children with their fears.
For like a chicken-hawk I soar
I fly
away
so free.
Cry not for me,
Ngungalari.
I leave you with your dreams.

The Hunter

Archie Weller

I sing a song to the kangaroo
whose blood turned the green grass red.
He who danced a last agonized dance
black against the setting sun.
Gladly I sing for happy am I.
Tonight the hunter's belly will be full.
And hear my children's laughter;
like sparks to the sky it soars.
The rain comes over the hills,
like fluttering birds it comes.
I stand in my brother's tears
happy as the running stream.
Ho! Brother.
Tread upon the wide plains.
Lonely rugged mountains
rule the land.

The Hunters

Archie Weller

Outside the weather-boarded hall she stands
poised, half in flight, like a bird
and two drunken white hunters
fall down the old stairs
whispering the things she always has heard.
Arm in arm they all giggle and stumble
into the darkness of the sad trees
breathing no-one will love her
they only will use her
and she is so pretty yet easy to please
Did they bring you promises of things to come?
Did they buy you some beer or wine?
As the hunters devour you
with rough caresses
do they still smile and say you are divine?

Noonkenbah

Archie Weller

My mother's breast
that nourished me
with legends and with songs
gives out a milk as black as I
so from her heart it comes.
Now in their trucks the whiteman comes
to squeeze my mother dry.
They take our laws.
They take our lives.
and now they take her too...
The earth heaves. The skies' rain falls down.
The old men sing their songs
but my mother weeps rich black tears.

The Last Songman

Archie Weller

Alone I sit.
I wait.
I wait.
My country cries red tears
for there are no more songs.
No more stories around
the everlasting fire.
No more young men here
to dance and leap like flames.
I am the last of the song men.
I go.
I go
to join Purpupriki
amongst the stars.
The stars,
flowers
of my country.

Untitled

Archie Weller

Our songman is a flashing silver king
who will always please and never die;
whose vibrating songs are new all the time:
honeyed lips, love and soulful eyes.
In our Boora rings, on the corners of the roads
we, the young men of our tribe, gather
for initiation ceremonies again.
Our scars are not from flint but are from knives.
We are the drunken stumbling warriors
of our tribe—our dissipated tribe.
We shout out the legends gathered from our back-roads
and our kangaroos we kill from behind the bar.

He reclines upon his shabby throne:
his broken-backed
bursting springs throne
and watches his soldiers coming home
youths swaggering—
staggering—home.

Narroondarie's Wives

David Unaipon

Narroondarie is the name of one of the many good men that were sent among the various tribes of the Australian Aborigines. Now the name Narroondarie is better known among the Narrinyini tribes of the Lower Murray, Lakes Alexandrina and Albert, and the Encounter Bay, South Australia. Before he came into South Australia he was known or called Boonah, hence the initiation ceremonies. Narroondarie and Boonah are names by which he is known as a good man, as a Sacred Man who is endowed or guided by the will of the Great Spirit, the Nhyanhund or Byamee, the Our Father of All, His messenger and teacher. After coming from the Northern part of Australia down into various parts of New South Wales and Victoria, he found his way into South Australia, dwelling mostly in and around the shores of Lakes Alexandrina and Albert, and he would visit various camping grounds where the people lived permanently. Some of them would run into the water and hide among the reeds and water plants, and when he saw that the people fled from him he would call Young Hund and they would remain silent and he became annoyed at the people's attitude. He would say to them "Well, children, if you will not answer me: Pooljarra Wallul. This is a command and a curse. Now you shall all become birds and shall remain thus for ever." And they suddenly became birds at the command of Narroondarie. And while there were others who summoned sufficient courage and came at his call, these were or are the tribes that remain this day around Lake Alexandrina.

Now this should have been the completion of his mission, so he chose two bald hills, which were free from trees with only low shrubs and grass trees growing, as his last home on earth, the surrounding country being dense growth of Mallee and Honeysuckle and the Oak, and a few species of Gum-tree and other shrubs. He made the choice of these two hills because he was able to have a view of both lakes, and it was his intention to rest here until the Great Spirit should call him to take his place in the heaven among the other Great Company that had gone before him.

On one of his fishing expeditions he was passing on his way to Lake Albert when he saw in his path two grass trees, young and tender, swaying gracefully in the Kolkamai South Wind, and his attention was so arrested that he stood for a moment looking upon these two stems of grass trees, and then from the She Oak's bough came the weird note of song—not of pleasure or joy or happiness, but of sadness. The song was that of the two bound up in the stem of the Grass Tree. The Selfish Spirit of the Grass kept these young maidens bound thus because they were so sweet and he delighted to invite the nature Bee and Ants and Honey-birds to come and dine with him. And his heart was moved by their pitiful cry. Now these two maidens have captivated many and many good men, who have fallen victims to their wonderful charms, on their way to the Spirit Land. These two maidens have been passed on from stage to stage, sometimes into the form of a butterfly with beautiful colours, sometimes found or imprisoned in the Karldookie, the flower-tops of reeds. Various trees, shrubs and plants have gone forth with the endeavour to keep these two maidens prisoner because their chief delight was to captivate all the great men. So it was at this time an effort of the Grass Tree to keep them bound up; it was the last of the Vegetable Kingdom and all were wondering whether it would succeed. So that is why when the Great Man Narroondarie stood looking at the Grass Tree's stem that the boughs of the She Oak began to wail as the wind was passing through the wiry leaves. Now the sounds seemed to come from the She Oak, but were coming from the Grass Trees. These cunning maidens knew that if they were at this moment to try to use their charm to win this Sacred Man they would fail. But to touch the cords of pity—surely this good man would pity them and release them. On this move they were sure he would set them free. They were conscious the Grass Tree was not a good medium through which they could send their message on the Narroondarie, so when the Kolkamai South Wind breathed upon all nature they caused their sorrowful cry of distress as if some loved one had died and they were mourning. Then Narroondarie stood and being a Great Man heard the cry of the two maidens and said: "Yaka

Yakatumburra. Oh, I pity! Oh, I pity you both! Mackcunda Ngool Purpe. Why do you both weep, or what makes you weep?"

"Menpeel Nullum. They have placed us into this Grass Tree and our flesh with its sense of taste, smell, hearing, and touch is dead, and it is only this subconscious state which is still alive makes us accept this prison home. Our bodily form and human flesh have become the form of vegetable flesh. Oh, Great One, take pity upon us and release us and we shall become your servants." And Narroondarie thought and thought. And these two maidens with the cunning of many and many years' experience began to use it upon this Sacred Man. And he listened and then he began to think within himself how nice it would be to see what would be the form of these two spirits enclosed in this Grass Tree. It will not be any harm for me to look upon them although I am forbidden to associate myself with women. I will assist them and cause them to come forth and thereafter look upon them for a while. So he bade the Grass Tree body to give the fair maidens their liberty. In the twinkling of an eye the maidens stepped out of the Grass Tree a picture or Punerrie of beauty. Their perfect form and their wonderful Peel langga eyes so captivated the Great Man that he fell a victim to their charm. And he decided that he would make them both his wives. So he told the maidens that now he had given them their freedom he would ask them to. Instead of going a-fishing as he intended he returned to his home and asked them to be seated, and then he gave them something to eat. After they had enjoyed their meal he began to tell them of the various laws and customs that he gave to the people, and that some of the laws were very drastic, that is to say when broken would result in the death of the offender. For instance, in the making of the youth in men no woman is allowed to look upon them or to give or offer them food, or their portion of the flesh of a kangaroo and emu, or fish such as the Pondi (Codfish), Tcherrie, a fresh water bream, and especially the Tookerrie, a silver-scaled fish and extremely bony. No woman is allowed to eat this fish under penalty of death. Now this fish is much sought after by the aborigines.

As time went on they were passing through new experiences and the whole woman's tendencies began to exert themselves, and there began to arouse in the mind of Narroondarie some coming trouble. He would not allow them to remain at home by themselves, but would ask them to accompany him on his fishing expeditions. One day they were out fishing on the Lake Albert; he was in his canoe whilst the maidens were wading in the shallow water along the shore, with a net made from the rushes that grow on the bank of the lakes, made in a cone shape constructed after the fashion of the old style candle extinguishers only a great deal larger. They would place this at the opening of a dense growth of reed; one would go along the bank and enter the water and reeds at the other end and splash the water causing the fish that were between her and the one with the net to escape so that the fishes would swim toward the entrance and enter the net and be trapped. And they would take the net to the bank and empty the contents, and they would be fishes of different kinds—a Tcherrie, Pillulkie, or Kumarrie. Unfortunately on this occasion there were three beautiful white silver Thookerrie, and they looked around trembling with excitement. They covered the fishes with weeds and rushes and went on their way with the net, feigning fishing, but they were so overjoyed with their catch that they payed no attention to what they were doing. They could not stand the strain much longer and so decided to go home, and looking out into the lake their attention was attracted by a column of smoke that rose against the clear sky looking north-west. So they called their chief and husband, Narroondarie, and he came to them, and the elder of the maidens pointing towards the smoke said "Look! a message to be sent." So he sat down waiting for an impression. Suddenly he arose and told them that Nebullie sent a message asking that he would like him to come to his Nawondie, his home Rowhokkun Point Macleay Mission Station now, so he would leave at once and they should make themselves comfortable at home; so they parted. The young maidens said "We will stay here and watch you cross over to the other side of the lake and then we shall go to our home." So Narroondarie got into the canoe and paddled across the lake. When the maidens saw that he had landed safely and was on his way to Rowhokkun they turned around and went toward a heap of weed and rushes and removed from beneath the coveted prize and food and they sat looking and looking, turning the fishes over and over and after they had finished admiring them they rose and walked toward home; in fact they ran all the way until they reached the camp, and then began hurriedly to make a fire of She-oak tree bark.

When the wood had burned and nice red coals were left they placed the fishes beside the fire. First they place a layer of soft grass—a grass that retains the fat of animal bird or fish (no flesh food is cooked without it)—and then they take two thin dry, or sometimes green, sticks about a foot or sixteen inches long and about half an inch in diameter or less and place or take these two sticks between the thumb, first and second finger lying between the thumb and index finger on top, and by a trained manipulation of this thumb and two fingers take a coal of fire, as you would with tongs, and place upon the fish, then cover the fish with live coals and allow it to remain for a while, and then they remove the coals from the fish over the cooked side which they lie upon the grass in the first instance, and the fishes are repeatedly turned over several times, and when cooked thus the fat comes out and explodes like fat in a frying pan. And Narroondarie heard the fat of the Thookerrie sizzling and he said to Nebullie "Do you hear that sound as if some one, a woman or women, is cooking the forbidden fish? I shall not sleep here to-night but I shall leave you just before sunset." After the fishes were cooked the maidens sat down on top of the hill so that they would have a vision of the surrounding country and should anyone be passing or come to their camp they would have plenty of time to hide the remaining portion of the fishes so that they should not be accused of having eaten a forbidden fish. They sat in the sunshine eating and chatting, expressing their delight of enjoying such sweet food, "Ah the men are clever! They know what are the nicest foods, and so they make laws to prevent and deprive us. But we have been too clever." So they ate and laughed and made merry.

Now they had completed their meal and were reclining on the grass enjoying a rest, listening to the song of the birds in a valley not very far distant, but just as the sun was half way down the western sky they came to themselves, and rose to a sitting position, looking into each other's eyes enquiringly, then spoke: "Oh what have we done! We must not stay here any longer. It is very strange, do you not smell the oil of the Thookerrie? The grass shrub and tree have retained the smell. Come! We cannot stay here and be asked questions when our lord and master returns." They awoke to their sense of guilt, so the elder said: "Come, let us flee." "But," said the younger, "whither shall we fly? Let us stay and face the wrath of Narroondarie. Stay and be placed back and embodied in a tree-shrub plant lest when we are caught fleeing he may cause us to be into something more dreadful than these." "Come!" said the elder, "there is no time to discuss the matter; we may go into some strange land and win the affection of Mookumbulli, become his wife, and no one will dare to interfere with our liberty."

So without another word they both gathered a great bundle of grass-tree sticks and carried them to the waterside and bound them together, forming a raft, and they shoved the raft into deep water and sat upon it and paddled across the western side of Lake Albert, and slept at the point near the estate of the late T. R. Bowman. Now this happened during the night, and it was late in the evening that Narroondarie arrived home. When he was about a hundred yards or more from his mia mia he was struck with the smell of the Thookerrie fat. "Ah!" said he, "those silly and frivolous maidens have eaten the forbidden fish and now they must be punished." When he entered his mia mia there was no one about, then he called Young who Nhod "Where are you both?" No answer, only the screeching of the night owl, which was a sign that there was something wrong. The culprits had fled. So he lit a fire and sat down for a while pondering over the misdeed in his two young wives. He was thinking deeply what excuse he should make to the Great Spirit for releasing those maidens from the prison of the grass tree into which they had been placed by the last victim—the Proolgie, the Spirit Native Companion. He must have had an excuse. "Now to what form of punishment or prison shall I put them? Well, before I can decide I must capture them."

So he lay down to sleep and before the sun rose he took his Plonggee, a weapon about eighteen inches long with a nob at one end the size and shape of the smallest child's football and a handle at the other end about a foot long and about an inch in thickness. Now this is a weapon for the bruising of the body of a person who transgresses a law, and it means a slow, painful death which will give them time to think and repent of the misdeed. He also took a boomerang and his Opossum skin bound around his shoulders, and set off walking slowly down to the shore of the lake, and then the sun rose and he began to walk faster, still casting his eyes upon the ground looking for footprints. When he got to the lake side he made for the place where they left their net, and saw that there were the scales of the Thookerrie upon it; and now he was satisfied of the reason of their absence from camp. He got into his canoe and paddled across the lake and landed at the same point, and saw the Kindie or raft made with a bundle of grass trees, and he walked around among the bushes that grew on the bank of the river and saw a fire and a place where they had slept. Then he began to follow their tracks leading toward the Coorong—that is a strip of water between a strip of land hummock lying northwest and southeast in the Encounter Bay, South Australia—and he saw again where they had constructed another Kindie and had just gone across a few hours before his arrival. So he thought he would rest and make the attempt of fording the Coorong in the morning.

When the sun arose he crossed over the Coorong and began his search for further tracks of his wives. But in this he failed and stood wondering in which direction he should go. Never before was he baffled; and so he had to decide which way he should go, and he chose to go South-east, following the Coorong. He walked with great speed, covering about seventy miles, then rested awhile, thinking that he must have come before the maidens if they had come in this direction, but no one passed; so he built a small camp made of the boughs of shrubs and grass, and at midnight he went to sleep. He was so tired with the previous day's journey that he slept soundly long after the sun rose and would have slept on but he felt a touch and heard a voice calling: "Awake, sleeper! Beware! Thine enemy is near." So he rose and looked around, but saw no one.

But the visitor was Puckknowie, the Grand Mother Spirit, the Guardian Angel of good people, that is ever beside them and warns them of danger. So he broke his fast and made preparations to meet the unseen enemy. Then he began his search for his two wives. Now away among the Punbbaalee tribe there lived a very cruel man who had become a disciple of the Crow and like his chief caused a great deal of mischief; and he was transformed from a human being into a Wombat, and this Wombat wandered among the sand hummocks all alone and, as Narroondarie was walking along, he saw it and throwing his spear struck it in a vital spot—right into the heart. He withdrew the spear and allowed the blood to flow from the wound upon the white sand, then he picked up the Wombat and carried it to his mia mia and tied it upon a pole. And just as he was about to sit down he missed his spear, and remembering that he had left it where he had speared the Wombat, he returned, and behold, he saw that the blood of the Wombat was developing into a man, so he sat and watched it.

Presently there was a man lying upon the ground breathing as if in a deep sleep, so Narroondarie, instead of taking his spear left it, thinking perhaps it would become of use to this man. So he went away among the ti-trees and made several Yundi spears and returned a third time to his mia mia. And this time he pondered over the man that had developed from the blood of the Wombat. As a servant of the Great Spirit he was aware that there were spirits of good and bad men embodied in tree-shrubs and plants, but this discovery was something new. A spirit to be within the life blood of an animal! He began to experience an uneasy feeling, as if something unpleasant was about to take place, so he returned to see what the person was like—whether he was a friend and would assist him in the discovery of his two wives; and he began to cautiously wend his way until he came to the spot but the person had disappeared, so he looked around, hoping to see footprints which would lead to him, but there were no footprints and now he was convinced that the strange person was an enemy. A friend will always leave a footprint—this is the teaching of the aborigines. So he thought to himself, like all wise men do, that he would be always upon the alert; and during that day he was not seen.

On the second day of this event Narroondarie sat upon the peak of a high sand-hummock looking first Wolkundmia (north), then Tolkamia (west), Kolkamia (south), and Karramia (east). There was no one to be seen. Then he sat down and debated within himself as to which direction to take. Presently he heard the voice of someone laughing. It was not the laugh of joy or amusement, but a laugh of scorn, so he leapt to his feet and immediately his eyes caught a vision that almost froze the blood in his body, and cold chill ran down his back; for there before him stood the arch enemy of the Good Parrimparrie, the Evil One. So Narroondarie grasped his Rarrarburr, standing erect with the weapon held firmly in his hand ready to hurl it at the approaching figure. Parrimparrie stood about two hundred yards away from the base of the hill on which Narroondarie stood, and, calling, addressed him thus: "Yar Raa Rongundd Ta Now ind Glan im un—Oh brother-in-law of mine do you not recognise me?" So when Narroondarie heard this friendly salutation he came down to where the deceiver sat, but about twenty paces away he stood and said: "Oh Roongundun, was it yourself that I released from the body of the Wombat?" "Yes," said the Deceiver. "Now, brother-in-law of mine," spoke Narroondarie, "do you claim to be my Roongie (brother-in-law)?" "Yes," replied the Deceiver. "Then perhaps you may be able to tell me the whereabouts of your two sisters. I am in search of them." "Nou, hie um run un. No I shall not tell you, oh mine enemy. I have waited long and patiently but during your sojourn among the people in various parts of the country I was prevented by your followers, those who have gone above, the Peenwingie, Proolgie, Hawk and Native Companion. They have placed me into the body of the Wombat and you have released me, and now you shall die before you reach Wyerriwarr, heaven." Now all Great Men have been given the privilege to go to heaven without death. "Mack kundun Yun Krook, Roongund. Then why did you call me: oh brother-in-law of mine. Why have you deceived them now. Kunthun itch Me wee. Are you not pleased that I have been the means of your release? Were you not at my mercy? Do you realise that I could have slain you? I allowed you to take your present form. Come, let us not quarrel. Nup Ghie ell lung, I leave you now." And Narroondarie turned and was making in the direction from whence he came, Nor'west. Then the Deceiver began to laugh and sing a song.

And Narroondarie kept walking and, thinking that he had gone a certain distance, he stood and looked about, and still hearing his enemy singing thought that he was following, but he saw that he was in the same place and had not moved an inch. He looked round and saw the Parrimparrie was dancing and brandishing his spear in a threatening attitude, with spear raised and poised ready to send on its mission of death. Narroondarie stood awaiting results. Suddenly the spear was hurled with lightning speed and would have entered a vital spot had not Narroondarie seen it delivered in time. With a downstroke of his Rarraburr he quickly smote the spear and its point tore a flesh wound on his thigh. Then Parrimparrie began dancing and singing because he had drawn the first blood.

So Narroondarie took his spear and placed it into the Ghyrulgie (the throwing stick) and poised it well above his shoulder and, like all warriors, uttered a prayer, and speaking to the spear he said: "Thow, tack," which means, "Oh, my trusted spear, art thou not my handiwork; have I not made thee for my purpose. Come, now, behave thyself favourably to thy master and do his bidding." And with muscle and mind he hurled the spear with lightning speed, and it entered the body of Parrimparrie and pierced his heart. He fell lifeless to the ground with the life-blood trickling into the ground. So Narroondarie began, as he thought, his journey.

He walked and walked, taking no notice of the things around him until the presence of a Rich er Rookitty (Willy Wagtail) that seemed to be continually in his path drew his attention. He looked about and saw that he was still in the same place, so he said within himself "I have met a great and powerful enemy; although his life has left the body, he is influencing the conditions around that are preventing my escape." So he sat down to rest himself awhile before making another attempt to depart and as he sat he noticed that the bird or animal that came near the body was unable to go from it, so he came to the decision that the only way out of it was to burn the body. He rose and gathered a great heap of grass and twigs and piled log upon log until he had a heap twice his height and then he took the body of Parrimparrie and placed it upon the huge wood heap. Next he took two grass trees; in one he punctured a small hole and into this hole he put the point of the other, which he held between the palm of both hands and began rubbing and rubbing until a spark was produced, then he set fire to the wood and so burned the body of Parrimparrie. And once again he began his journey. He walked and walked, then looked to see how far he had come, but he was still in the same place. And he said to himself "I must see whether I have burned everything that belongs to him" and turning round he found the congealed blood of Parrimparrie upon the ground so he made another fire upon the blood and stirred the hot ashes until there was no sight of blood. Then he began his journey and this time he was able to pass on without any hindrance. He walked so fast that he covered about seventy to eighty miles in an hour. Now he found soon he was confronted by the Murray flowing into the Southern

Ocean, so he spoke to the Great Spirit asking him to make it possible that he should be able to walk across. His prayer was answered; the ground came up and fo.med a bridge across the river. Now when he had crossed to the other side of the river he saw the footprints of his two wives that had been made three days ago and following their footprints he came to where they had camped for the night. He noticed that the cold ashes had the stained appearance of a Tararrie, that is a lump of fat inside a Mullowie or some call it King. Now this fat of the fish Mullowie a woman is strictly forbidden to eat, and when Narroondarie saw this evidence he was so greatly grieved and sorrowful in heart that he sat down beside the camp and wept bitterly for the sins of his two young wives. He spent the night there weeping, because he loved these maidens very much. To think that it was he who delivered unto the people the word of the Great Spirit, that those who broke these laws would receive the full penalty—Death! and that he who had brought them out of bondage and given them the feel of living a human life should now bring about their destruction. And this punishment must be greater than the first.

The thought weighed heavy upon his mind that he must punish them and set them up as an example that the way of the transgressor is hard, and that the coming generation would look upon these two as the well beloved wives of the Greatest of Prophets among the Aborigines. He prayed for their forgiveness but the answer came: as a person chooses to live, so shall he die. And now he set out to overtake them and mete out the punishment. He followed their tracks which led him to what is known as Port Elliot, S.A., and he came to where they had camped two days before him. He saw and examined the ashes and saw that they had cooked cockles and periwinkles and mullet (fish). Again he wept; this time beside a huge rock; and his tears trickled into the sea. He wept so much that to-day some of the old folk will point out the place and say "This is the spot where Narroondarie wept bitterly for his two wayward wives." It resembles a soakage of fresh water by the side of sea, and that which was liquid of salt bitter tears and a narrowing heart comes as a sweet, cool and refreshing water to journeying souls to the land of the spirit. And when the Aborigines visit this spot you will see tears trickling down their cheeks, the result of their thoughts of their

Great Leader, the Messenger and Teacher of the Will of the Great
Father of All.

Now Narroondarie, after spending a restless night, rose early and
walked rapidly until he arrived at the Bluff, Victor Harbour. He sat
there with his eyes turned toward the West and he saw them in spirit,
and again he wept because he saw in a vision what was to happen
and that it would be he who should bring them to their timely end
before they reached the Spirit Land, Kangaroo Island. So he hurried
on once more, while in his bosom waged a great conflict. His
lovable nature was willing that they should reach this island and be
free for ever of all punishment for their wrong-doing. Now the
maidens arrived in the afternoon opposite to Kangaroo Island. At the
time of the story the Island was connected with the mainland but
during a severe southerly storm the sea would cover the connecting
strip of land and the maidens, instead of going across that afternoon,
spent the time in collecting honey, with the intention of crossing on
the morrow. And another reason: there was a keeper on this strip of
land on the mainland side who was in charge, and he was known as
the Khowwallie, the Blue Crane, and no one would attempt to cross
without his permission. He was a very austere person and a very
dangerous one with whom to dispute because he always had beside
him on his person a very sharp-bladed spear that would cause a very
nasty and severe wound.

Now Narroondarie was just four or five miles behind or away
from the maidens; he could see them standing on the cliff looking
across to the Spirit Land, so he made a little mia mia and went into
the bush and procured a Possum and roasted it, and allowed it to
cool before eating; and the maidens did the same, they made a
comfortable little mia mia and also a large fire whose blaze
Narroondarie was able to see. Narroondarie was awaiting a message
which would instruct him how to punish the disobedient girls, and at
midnight the Kroolthumie carried the instructions that these maidens
should be allowed to walk the strip of land that acts as a bridge to all
pilgrims to the Spirit Land and when they should arrive half way
across then should Narroondarie chant the Wind song. First he must
chant the Tolkamia—the West Wind—and sing its Song of Fury to
bring up the waters of the mystery land and let them roll with
vengeance; then he must sing the song of Kolkamia—the South

Wind—to blow and bring the water that comes from the unknown land; then they may wish to return to land; then he must sing the song of Wolkundmia—the North Wind, and the waters shall all come together and toss and toss them until they become exhausted; then he must command that they shall become rocks. So Narroondarie rose early in the morning and came near unto the maidens and sat upon the cliff to see them begin their journey of death. They came to the Knowallie and asked his permission to cross, which he willingly gave, and the maidens began laughing and chatting, anticipating the joy and pleasure and happiness that awaited them when they arrived upon the Spirit Land, but most of all they would be free from the Law from which they were trying to escape. Little did they realise that within a few moments they would meet the full penalty of their disobedience.

Now Narroondarie came a little nearer to the strip of land that led to Kangaroo Island and sat upon a vantage spot, watching and waiting until they were half way over the distance. When they reached that point Narroondarie began singing the Wind Song: "Pink ell lowarr. Mia yound Tee, wee warr, La rund, Tolkamai a, ren who cun, Tinkalla. Fall down from above, oh thou Mighty Wind; swiftly run and display thy fleetness! Come thou down from the Northern sky, oh water of the deep! Come up in a mighty swell!" and the Westerly wind burst forth in all its fury and came screeching overhead, while the maidens were pressing forward struggling against the storm. Then presently the waters were churned and welled and rose just over the way. Then Narroondarie sang a song of the Wind, and the South Wind blew, and the waters from unknown land came tantalisingly on, raising themselves like miniature mountain peaks, and the waters closed upon them, lashing them and tossing them about like corks. They struggled first toward their goal, Kangaroo Island, then it seemed as if the Spirit were against them and they turned themselves and began swimming toward the mainland. But the Wolkundmia, answering the call of Narroondarie, was willing to do its duty in bringing these two maidens to pay the penalty of their sins; as they sped on they called "We come, we come!" and the maidens sank with exhaustion and were drowned and sank to the bottom. And the Winds suddenly ceased and there was a calm. Narroondarie wept bitterly, although he hated everything that was displeasing to the Great Spirit, and he felt within his inmost consciousness that he loved those youthful maidens with all their faults and errors. And again a voice whispered to him: "Command that the maidens' bodies be turned into stone to stand out as a warning to all women not to eat of the forbidden food."

He spoke, and it came to pass as he was told. These two rocks can be seen from the mainland as well as on passing vessels and are known to-day as the "Two Sisters". Before the coming of the White Man these stones were called and still are to the few remaining aborigines "Rhunjullang"—two sisters. Many were the pilgrimages taken by the aborigines in days gone by to see these stones and view and contemplate the way of the Great Teacher, Narroondarie. After this had happened, with tears still welling in his eyes and a broken heart, Narroondarie commanded that the waters should go back, to allow him to walk upon dry land to Kangaroo Island. And on the Eastern side of the Island was a huge Gum Tree and under its shade he rested until the sun sank into the western sky, the Land of the Spirits. He walked to the West of the island and plunged into the sea and sank into the deep, and was there a long while, seeking in the depths of the sea the spirits of his two wives, and he rescued them from the watery cold grave and arose with them clinging on both sides of the Great Teacher, and he flew upwards and upwards until he came to the Land of Wyerriwarr to join that bright and happy group Nabulle, Whyoungarrie, Jeeveelang, Munjungie, and to look down to cheer and comfort and encourage the Komnukalda to press on to fight all the evil desires that are within, remembering always to obey the will of the Great Spirit.

Wondangar, Goon na Ghun
(Whale and Star Fish)

David Unaipon

Now some of you will have already read of the great philosopher
and astronomer, Koala (the Teddy Bear), of his discovery of the
Thousand Isles away in the eastern sea, also of his wonderful
achievement and skill in the navigation of a large fleet of canoes
bringing many strange beings, inhabitants of those lands, to the
shores of Australia. There were the representatives of the animal
tribe, the Whingamie (Kangaroo), Barraal (Wallaby), Wombat and
others; the bird tribe, Peewingie (Eagle Hawk) with all members of
that family, the Muldarie (Magpie) and members of that family; the
Lyre Bird, Kookaburra, Peenjullie, and other members of the
feathered tribes; then there were the Lizard and Reptile family
represented by the Thooyoungie (Goanna), Frilled Lizard, and other
members of that family; the Snakes, the Rock Python, Carpet Snake,
and other members of that family. And there were among this
multitude of strange beings, two beings who were more strange than
the others—Wondangar (the Whales) and Goon Na Ghun (the Star
Fishes).

Now when they arrived at Shoal Haven they all landed safely,
unloaded their canoes, and pitched their mia mia and rested for
seven sunrises, and on the eighth sunrise the Koala sent the
Peenjullie (Emu) to go among the beings to inform them that at
midday he would instruct them what they should do. So the
Peenjullie hastened in and out among the strange company, with
sign and gesture asking that no one was to leave the camp to go a-
hunting, but to remain until they should receive instruction from the
Koala. So these beings just sat and ate their breakfast, whiling the
time away chatting to each other in many strange languages.

Now as soon as the sun was overhead again the Peenjullie (Emu) gave a sign, "Silence the Great Munkoobullie comes." Then the Koala mounted upon a stump formed like a pulpit and with sign and gesture called each of the heads of the families and asked them to choose where they would like to live. The Peenjullies came forth, and, pointing and giving signs, expressed their wish to travel beyond the mountain, Tolkamia (Sou'-west). The Koala, nodding, gave his consent. Then he beckoned to the Whingamie (Kangaroo) and inquired where he would like to make his home. So the 'Roo, pointing and with gesture, expressed his wish to travel and make his home with the Peenjullie, that is, if they had no objection. The Koala called the attention of the Peenjullie, and inquired if he had any objection to the Whingamie accompanying him, and he said "We would enjoy their presence on our journey." So all the marsupial tribe followed their chief, the Kangaroo, with the exception of the Platypus, who expressed a wish that he would probably go west for a time, but would like to return and travel Wolkund mia (North). Then the Koala beckoned to the Peewingie (Eagle Hawk). The Eagle Hawk said "We do not wish to ask for any particular part. Will you allow us to travel just where we can find food." The nodding Koala gave his consent.

When all had expressed their wish where they would like to live, the Koala was just about to close the meeting when the crow called his attention to two strange beings—the Wondangar and the Goon Na Ghun. "Oh," said the Koala, "come along up here beside me, and tell me where you would like to make your home." They both said in sign and gesture, "Let us stay here awhile and we shall choose later on. Will you grant us this request?" "Oh, you are all at liberty to do just what you think would suit you best. But before closing this meeting I would very much like you all before taking your journey into these unknown and unexplored regions, to let us all spend six moons with each other to give some of you time. Perhaps you may change your mind and select some other place. And let us understand each other better before we part." So the animals, birds, reptiles and insects gave their consent to remain at the pleasure of the Koala.

Now the Wondangar, before the departure of the Koala, beckoned the Peenjullie, so the Emu very obligingly came to him and said, "What can I do for you? I shall be pleased to be at your service."

"Very well," said the Wondangar, "go to the Koala and plead with him to allow me the sole right and use of all the sand hills or hummocks that are along the coast-line, and also to give instructions to others that no one shall live or rest upon the white sand unless with my permission. This I ask of him as a temporary favour, until I shall decide as to my permanent abode." "I shall do as you wish," said the Peenjullie. So he went to the Koala and asked him whether he would be allowed to present a request from one of the party. "Oh," said the Koala, "speak and I shall listen." So the Peenjullie began, "Oh Munk Koorebullund (O thou great and clever) One; The Wondangar would like your permission of all sand beaches and hills or hummocks that are along the coast-line for a short period until he shall decide definitely at a later date what he intends doing." "Go," said the Koala, "and tell the Wondangar that they have found favour with me and I shall do as is required of him."

The Peenjullie went and delivered the favourable reply to the Wondangar, who seemed so pleased that they hastened away and took up their abode among the sand-hills and upon the white sand beaches. They would delight to go surfing and lying upon the dry white sand, basking in the sunshine. They repeated this day after day, until they developed lazy habits. They would not even hunt for food, but would lay in the shallow water and put their tongues out and wag and wag them until some of the fish would become curious and swim round and round, thinking what a funny sight. Some would become more bold than the others and would venture right into the open mouths of the Wondangar, and they would suck them right into their stomachs, and the silly and inquisitive little fishes would become a meal for the Wondangar. And the other fish that were looking on became more curious than the first, because they could not understand the mystery of the thing. It seemed a cave, and they too would like to explore and find out all about it, and their friends, thinking they had entered some wonderful place, with all kinds of beautiful and pleasant things. "Come," said one, "let us enter," and they timidly approached, and, suddenly, without warning, they were sucked into the mouths and carried farther on, and they helped to supply the hunger of the lazy Wondangar. When they found that food was so easily obtained, they became more lazy, and would lie in this way for hours until they had gorged themselves with more food than was good for them. Then they would rise from the water, walk up among the hot sand, and sleep and sleep until they became hungry. This was the everyday life of the Wondangar. They were not like the Kangaroo, who would take spear and nulla nulla and hunt for food. All the other beings hunted for food, but the Wondangar in their laziness procured their food in this unique way.

Now the Wondangar thought themselves very clever folks because they captured their food in this fashion. But it had a very bad result, for lying like they did for hours and hours like some lifeless object, the little periwinkles thought to themselves, what a nice thing to cling to. And they came and fastened their homes to the bodies of the Wondangar, and other shell-life came, and they to clung to them and some of the tiny weeds, wandering along the coast looking for a home, decided that they too would join in clinging to this object. The Wondangar after a while had accumulated upon their bodies other parasites, lives that were seeking shelter and a home.

Now there is another outstanding feature about the Wondangar. They were beings with a large head and body but small legs and arms, and they did look such queer people. You would expect that being possessed with big heads they would be great thinkers, but not so. This was one of the greatest defects of these queer beings, unable to reason. It was fortunate for them that there lived not far away the Goon Na Ghun, who volunteered to become the friends of the silly lazy Wondangar. These beings came in a large canoe that kept in touch with the canoes of the Wondangar, and during their voyage their canoes would in a calm sea tie together and travel in this way, and in rough weather untie, and sail separately, so that they would be in no danger of bumping. And it was in this way that they developed a friendship, or, let us say, that the Goon Na Ghun got to pity and sympathise with the thoughtless and lazy Wondangar.

And now when they arrived in another country, the Goon Na Ghun took upon themselves to be their friends, to help and advise them in anything that they wanted or liked to know. But, sorry to say, the Wondangar were so dense that they did not know what was their want. Now the Goon Na Ghun were smart beings. They were rotund in shape, with always a smiling face, and always on the alert to do some good act, trusted every other being, thought no evil of anyone. They lived a perfect life, no one was able to accuse them of any wrong. Being perfect themselves, they thought others perfect. Thus they looked upon the Wondangar as good in spite of their laziness.

The Goon Na Ghun, with the permission of the Koala, occupied all bays and coves along the coast, or bays where the water was calm and clear, with white sandy bottom free of rock and weed, quite an ideal spot for such good and perfect beings. Now they were very industrious beings, and built their homes in the rock and made beautiful terraces, canals, made in such a way that the fish swimming into them would be trapped, then they would take trips in the adjoining scrubs or forest and procure berries and grubs, and fill their storehouse with supplies prepared for the coming winter months. How different from their neighbours, the Wondangar.

When a straying Possum, turned out from his tribe for breaking some of their laws, became a fugitive, he would often seek the protection and hospitality of the Goon Na Ghun. Sometimes the Thooyoungie would take advantage of these good beings, and would come with a pitiful story of how he had helped to support the Kookaburra in a time of illness, relating a story how every day he would capture food and carry it to their home in the hollow of a large tree; many were the times he would climb the tree with a large bundle of food, sometimes the load was so great that he would be overcome with exhaustion and fall to the ground from a distance which would have killed a Possum or a Koala. And it was a wonder that he was able to be there telling the story: "I have given my last meal to them, and now I feel too weak to hunt." "Come, my friend," said the Goon Na Ghun, "stay with us awhile until you have rested and ate sufficient to gain your former strength." But in this case the Thooyoungie would be telling a lie. He would take advantage of the trustfulness and kindness of the Goon Na Ghun. When their eyes were turned he would steal from the larder and run away, feeling satisfied with himself that he was smart in tricking the Goon Na Ghun. "Ha, Ha," laughed the Goanna in his way, "how foolish they were to believe such a story. What a clever chap I must be. Now won't I have a picnic all to myself. What nice berries and what an appetising smell their preserved fish have."

Now as the Thooyoungie was flattering himself upon his

cleverness in stealing the food from the Goon Na Ghun, he sat down beneath a large tree that towered above all other trees, and which sent out its branches, making a welcome shade for bird, beast, and reptile. Presently a voice from among the boughs accosted him. "Hello, Thooyoungie, where did you spring from with such nice and tasty food? I am sure that it's not your own gathering, it must belong to some other unfortunate being who will be looking for his food." "What do you take me for, a thief?" said the Thooyoungie. "You have said rightly," replied the voice, "you could not be otherwise. You have always been a thief, and will continue so till time shall be no more."

Then the Thooyoungie became angry. "Who are you, and what are you, with such impudence. Come down and I'll teach you a lesson not to be so insulting with honest people." "Ha, Ha, Ho, Ho, Hee, Hee," mockingly laughed the unseen being, "I would not like to quarrel with you, Mr Thooyoungie, oh you silly and weak as a child person. It would be a one-sided battle." Just then the Koo Ka Kee came and sat on a limb not far away, and heard the conversation that was taking place, and heard the mocking remark made by someone hidden behind the boughs, and he began laughing too, "Koo, Koo, Koo, Ka, Kee." The Goanna said, "And now what are you laughing at." "I am just laughing at a thought that struck me that a thief is sometimes a coward, or a coward a thief." "Do you think," said the Goanna, "that I am afraid to do battle with one who calls me a thief?" "Certainly," said the Koo Ka Kee, "I would not allow anyone who insulted me to go free, but would offer him a challenge to fight with spear and nulla nulla. Go," said the Koo Ka Kee, "and bring your weapon and teach that impudent rascal a lesson." "All right", said the Goanna, "take charge of my food until I return." So the Koo Ka Kee took charge, and the Goanna went for his weapon.

Now the being who spoke from within the bough was the Crow. He came down from his hiding place and said to the Koo Ka Kee, "The food you are in charge of is stolen. The owner will be here before Goanna returns and you will be blamed." "Well, if that is so, I do not wish to be found with stolen property. Can I entrust it to you?" "Certainly," said the Crow. The Koo Ka Kee flew away as fast as his wings could carry him. When the Goanna returned he saw that the Crow was in charge of the stolen food. He knew that he was tricked. "Now," said the Crow, "I heard you laugh of your cunning, and heard you say how clever you were. You forget that there are other beings with minds better than yours. It was I who called you a coward, a thief, and challenged you to battle. Have I not won? See, I have your spoil. It shall not be Thooyoungie that shall eat of the berries and fish, but I, your superior." The Goanna bowed his head in shame at this simple defeat of the wily old Crow.

Now the Goanna was so very hungry that he became weak and unable to hunt for food. The Wild Pigeon, on his way home, saw the poor Goanna looking despondent and inquired what was the matter, and he said "I am very hungry, I have had nothing to eat all day and am feeling weak with hunger." The Pigeon hastened on and told the Goon Na Ghun of the plight of the Goanna. So they hastened along, taking with them food and herbs and berries and fish. They wended their way through the scrub until they reached the Goanna. When he saw them he felt greatly ashamed of himself, because here were the beings who gave him hospitality, and what was more, instead of thanking them for their kindness, he had stolen their food. They knew all about the theft, and yet, when the Thooyoungie was hungry they came to his assistance and offered him food. Then he said with sign and gesture, "Why do you come with food and with kindly smiles upon your faces? Are you not aware that I stole your food?" "Yes," replied the Goon Na Ghun, "we saw, and pitied you, and said to each other, and let this impress upon your mind, 'That he that steals, from he also shall be taken that which he stole.' Never in future, oh Thooyoungie, think thyself too clever for others. Remember they too have minds thinking the same. If thou art clever, let others speak of it. But thou must strive to become better every day, and with a humble mind and spirit endeavour to improve thyself." The Thooyoungie sat with bowed head, listening to the kindly words of advice of the Goon Na Ghun, who, placing the food before the conscious-stricken Thooyoungie, instructed him to eat. "But," he said, "have you forgiven me?" "Certainly, we forgave before we came to you. Good-bye." And the Goon Na Ghun returned to their homes beside the seashore, where they lived happily with their wives and children. Now they were noted for their sympathy and kindness, always seeking to do good and relieve the distressed. Many and many kind deeds were shown to the Koala,

Whygammie, Peenjullie, Peewingie, Prolgie, and many others of the various tribes. And for this they were honoured and respected. None dared to molest them, lest they would bring the wrath of the many upon their or his head.

Now as the beings were thus living together for a short period before going away to various parts of the country, the younger folk were vying with each other in their own kind. Some of the youths would dress themselves in some of the beautiful colours of the rainbow; some would spend quiet moments away from their relations and companions, developing their voice, and when they think or are satisfied with themselves, guided by instinct, would sing love songs. Others would choose to be with their better sex during the midday sun in the shade of the large tree. Some would go in the little stream that flowed through the steep mountain-side just by the waterfall. Some felt that they could pour out their soul to the girl they loved, or sought to win, by serenading her at twilight. Some whose hearts were overflowing continued to sing at twilight right on through the still hours of the night under the soft silvery moon beams, until the deepest night, and the soft moon waned before the sunlight.

Among the bird tribe the songs are beautiful, each note sounds perfect, conveying to her ladyship the heart-beat of the songster. The young beings of Wondangar and Goon Na Ghun were each in their own kind singing love songs, each heard by their kind. Thus the young Wondangar day by day on the beach amidst the noise of the breaking wave, with voice not heard by the keen ear of Kookaburra or Muldarie, they heard not the sweet note of love that awoke in the bosom of the lady Wondangar a similar note. And yet with the unheard song the youth Wondangar wooed his love, and decided that they would in a few days hence go on their honeymoon.

Now when all the youths and maidens of the animal, bird and reptile tribes were love-making, the parents were anxious that the girls should marry someone who would love her and provide a nice home. Now the Wondangar had been lying so much in the sea that there were other curious beings, but they were not filled with the curiosity of the silly little fish that made many a good meal for them. But these strange beings were on the look-out for some object that would make a solid foundation on which to build a home. These strange lives, the Periwinkle, Barnacle, and still stranger being, Weed, were all funny beings and made a home on the Wondangar body. And they would roll and roll to try to get rid of them. But they refused to be dislodged, and clung the more. "Oh, what shall we do?" Just at that moment the Goon Na Ghun were approaching their mia mia and heard them making the remark, "Oh, what shall we do?" and they could see that they were in distress, so they said they would consider it a pleasure to relieve them of the parasites that clung to their bodies. And the Wondangar lay themselves down upon the white sand whilst the Goon Na Ghun got busy. And oh, it was a task. The barnacles clung so fast that the Goon Na Ghun had some difficulty in removing them. So the Barnacle and weed refused to be moved alive. The Goon Na Ghun would take a firestick and burn them before they would let go their hold; at other times they would take a nulla nulla and beat them so hard that they would break the shell and destroy the parasite. Oh, the Wondangar had a very bad time of it. They would often say, "Oh Goon Na Ghun let me rise, I cannot endure the pain much longer." "Oh, you must allow us to do just what we think, although it may cause you pain. But it will be only a short time. Better to suffer pain in this way than allow them to eat your body and give you a slow and painful death." And in this way the Goon Na Ghun continued day by day.

Now the young Wondangar thought that whilst the father Wondangar were treated and occupied in this manner, it would be an opportunity to elope with their sweethearts. So they met among the sand-hills and discussed the matter. "Have we not asked the Wondangar for the hand of their daughters, and they refused. We shall no longer plead to these lazy and silly beings. But let us at sunrise tomorrow prepare our canoes and take our sweethearts to some other country farther south." "Yes," said the other youth Wondangar, "come let us prepare and speak to our sweet ones to-night." So that afternoon was spent in preparation for the morrow. They patched up the leaky canoes, placed gum into the cracks, made strong as well as light paddles, and went into the bays and creek to procure fish so that they would not be wanting food. Now all was ready.

At evening, when the moon was shining brightly upon the ocean and sandy beach, the girl Wondangar stood upon the beach awaiting their lovers. Presently they came hurriedly towards them, full of excitement, and they wondered why they were so agitated. And they enquired each of their lovers, "Oh, dear, why you are trembling, your heart seems to beat fast. What is the matter? Has someone annoyed you, or did someone die of your relations. speak." Then the youth Wondangar told her of his intention. "Your father will not give his consent, and we intend to take you away to-morrow morning whilst the Goon Na Ghun are busy cleaning their bodies." And the Wondangar maiden said, "First let me speak to father, and if he consents there will be no need to run away, but if he becomes angry and refuses to give his consent, then we are willing to go with you, even to the uttermost parts of the earth." "Well done, girls, you have spoken wisely, so be it as you say," so pleased were the youths at the intelligence of their lady loves. Off ran the maidens without hesitation. "Father, a being has asked me to become his wife and to go with him to his people and country and to become one belonging to his tribe. Father, I love him, will you kindly give your consent." "No, no, my child, I am not going to give my consent, and what is more, as soon as the Goon Na Ghun finish cleaning my body I shall not allow them to come around our home seeking company. Do you hear that? You shall no longer see him. I shall be about to prevent him speaking to you. Now run away and enjoy yourself, for the day after to-morrow I shall take away your liberty of speaking to him."

The maiden Wondangar returned to their lovers, looking very sad, their eyes filled with tears, because they dearly loved their unreasonable father. But they felt, too, that they loved their sweethearts more. So they told their lovers of their interview with their father, and their refusal. "But," said the girls, "we have decided that we shall become your wives." The youth Wondangar were glad at the decision of their sweethearts, but they felt sad that they would have to take the only course open to them of eloping with them. They sat on the beach a while, watching the moonbeams reflecting upon the sea, and as the rolling waves rose and fell, would reflect the moon's ray like a mirror. Then they listened to the love-song of the swans as they were riding on the smooth still water of the near-by river and fresh-water lake. Then from the tree not far on the hill they heard the Muldarie singing his love-song serenading his lady-love. The love-song of the bird tribe intensified the love within the bosom of the Wondangar being. "Now," said the youth, "we must part to our homes, for to-morrow will open up to us new prospects with new experiences. Good night." So the young Wondangar departed to their respective homes.

Just before sunrise the Goon Na Ghun were up and astir, breaking their fast, whilst the Mrs Goon Na Ghun were placing food into the dilly-bags for their lunch. And they advised their husbands not to be giving too much time to those ungrateful beings, because they were so quarrelsome and treacherous that they would at any moment without warning attack any one. "Now this must be your last visit to the Wondangar." So the Goon Na Ghun departed upon their mission of love. Little did they know that their soul or me wee would accompany the sun to the mysterious west. They arrived at the Wail lar roo mundi, that is the camping ground of the Wondangar, and the sun was shining brightly with a promise of a perfect day. They roused the Wondangar from their slumber, and told them to hurry with their breakfast as they were anxious to complete their work and return home at an earlier hour. And they soon had their breakfast and laid themselves down upon the sands, the maidens clinging to their mothers, fondly caressing them, with the thought that in a few hours they would be far from them, and perhaps would never see them any more—these loving souls who had spent many weary hours during the weeks and months and years in feeding them in babyhood and girlhood, up to the present moment, still loving, still caring.

They bade their mothers good-bye as if in fun. The mothers treated it as a joke. "Good-bye, girls," and they ran off toward the beach and walked along until they came to a bay. And there were their lovers waiting patiently. The maiden Wondangar took their seats in the canoes, and away they sped, into the Kol Ka Nia sea. Just after midday the elder Wondangar enquired of their wives, "Where are the Yartooka (girls). It seems strange that they have not been home to supply us with water to drink. What is the matter with them? Of all the days since we have landed upon these shores, this is the first time they have neglected their duty. Up and begone, find those silly girls, and I shall flog them severely." The mother Wondangar began to think of what the girls said to them. Could it be true? These words were said jokingly, "Good-bye mother." The vision of those girls flashed vividly before the mental eye. It must be true, they were gone. So the mother Wondangar began their search for their girls. They followed their footprints all along the beach to the bay, and saw other footprints leading to the water's edge. And it dawned upon them that their daughters had fled with their lovers. And with a heavy heart they returned to their husbands with the unpleasant news that their daughters had gone away with their lovers, perhaps never to return.

As soon as the Wondangar heard that their daughters had eloped with the youths they became very angry indeed, and blamed their wives for not paying more attention to them, allowing them too much liberty. The mothers made no reply, but sat down and wept bitterly. The Wondangar became so angry that they rushed into the mia mia and brought out the spears and nulla nullas and boomerangs and threatened to beat their wives. But the Goon Na Ghun got in between them, acting as mediator. The Wondangar turned to the Goon Na Ghun, and began to accuse them for being a party to the plot. "No, we came here with one object only, and that was to take the Barnacles from your bodies." "Yes, that was only a blind," said the Wondangar, "that was only to keep us in a state so that we would not see what was going on between our daughters and the youths." Then their anger became uncontrollable. They turned upon their wives and began to beat them, the Goon Na Ghun rushing into the fray to defend the wives. Then the Wondangar attacked the Goon Na Ghun furiously striking them with the nulla nulla, causing great flesh wounds. Oh, the poor Goon Na Ghun were covered with blood. The Wondangar were twice the size of the Goon Na Ghun, and the odds were against the smaller beings.

Now the Pelican has a custom after fishing in the early hours of the morning to seek a place upon the beach or sandspit when the tide goes out, where he can rest awhile. Then, when they have done resting they take to their wings and fly into the blue sky, circling as they go. Well it was just then that they looked down upon the lakes rivers, sea and land, that they saw what appeared to be a battle raging, and from their height they could distinguish the Wondangar mercilessly beating the Goon Na Ghun, who were fast weakening with the loss of blood. One of their number, a youth, half folding his wings, turned earthwards towards the home of the Koala away on the hill-side among the tall towering trees, etc. He came with increasing velocity, rending the air as he came, causing a great noise like that of a mighty wind. All beings within that locality looked up and saw the Pelican. "Hello," they said, "it is not often we see the easygoing Pelican travelling with such speed, there must be something very important causing such haste." "Prepare yourself, let us arm ourselves," said the Whingammie, Peenjullie, Thooyoungie, and Muldarie; so they equipped themselves with the Nulla Nulla, Ky Kee, Rankagee, and stood at ease, waiting for further developments. The Koala, hearing the noise, came out of the hollow of the tree and from among the thick boughs and out of the rock ledges. The Pelican came right to the door of the home of the chief of Koalas, and told him what he had seen. "Oh and the Wondangar are flogging the life out of the poor Goon Na Ghun. Come quickly, before they are beaten to death." When the Koala heard this he rushed into his home, siezed a spear and boomerang, and coming out, he leaped from the doorway on to the ground, gave one shrill war note, and with the speed of an express train ran towards the home of the Wondangar, with the other Koalas running from all directions following their leader and shouting as they ran. Then the Whingammie, Peenjullie, Peewingie, Thooyoungie, all joined in flourishing their weapons as they went down the hill-side, leaping across the stream up the hill-top and down, swimming the rivers, on to the sand-hill, whallaroomundi, the home of the Wondangar, on they ran across the sand-hill. They stirred up the dust as if a hurricane blew, still shouting the war-cry. When they arrived at the seat of the disturbance all was still, but upon the ground were the wounded and bleeding bodies of the Goon Na Ghun. The Koala, Whingammie, Peenjullie, Peewingie, Thooyoungie knelt down beside them, bathing their wounded bodies with the salt water, and placing the shell vessel to their lips to slake their thirst. After ministering to their wants they carried them to their homes, and when their wives saw the great company coming, they felt a something within themselves that something serious had happened, and when at last they placed their husbands down before them they began to wail, "Narpinunda (husband of mine, food winner, protector, and friend) Mee willim Manpong, Oh it was thy kindness, thy bowel of mercy, thy sympathy, ever seeking to do good to friend and enemies alike. And now this reward, Thock Kal limdoom Ploombie, Thou wouldst not listen to the warning given you of the treacherous Wondangar, but continued to minister their wants. Tharn and Thungara, Thou wouldst not even listen to me, thy wife and helpmeet. Yan up el lun, Oh, what shall become of me and thy children." They would repeat over again and again all through the evening into the midnight hour, and then they retired to rest, with a broken heart.

The Koala with the rest of his tribe, the animal tribe, the bird tribe, reptile tribe, came very early in the morning before the sun rose to pay their last respects to the dying Goon Na Ghun. When they arrived all was still, for during the night the burden of sorrow was so great on the wives of the Goon Na Ghun that they passed on first to the mysterious west, awaiting the coming of their husbands. And the various tribes gathered about and around them, anxious to do some last act to those whose lives were spent in doing kindly acts, by helping to feed the aged and infirmed and the sick. They felt greatly the passing out of a whole race or tribe so good, and they asked the dying Goon Na Ghun where they would like to be laid to rest, and they whispered back a reply, "In the bottom of the clear sea water in the quiet bays and coves where the white sand is free from weed. Place us gently down into the water and let us lie peacefully, do not allow anyone to disturb us, whilst our spirit goes to Wyerriwarr" (to the skies). So when their spirit took its departure from the torn bodies of the Goon Na Ghun, the animals, birds, and reptiles wept bitterly, and that night they committed their bodies to the water. And the moon rose and looked upon this great and solemn gathering, and it shone so brightly, lighting up the hill-side, shedding its beam upon the water of the bay. Everything looked so pleasing that the animals, birds, and reptiles, expressed the parting wish to gaze one long last look upon the Goon Na Ghun. They looked and looked with eyes dimmed, with tears of sorrow welling up into their eyes, as if the fountain of grief broke loose. But they looked more eagerly to impress upon the mind the memory of a good people.

Presently a transformation took place. Was it that their eyes were deceiving them, for behold, beneath the clear water of the bay they saw the star shining Neppellie Nabellie Wyyoungarrie Geerillang

Mungungie. They looked with wonderment and amazement. They wiped the tears from their eyes to get a clearer vision and they saw the stars shining upon the white sand bottom, reflecting the moonrays back up through the clear water. The Crow whispered, "They are not dead, but live, fulfilling the great plan for which they were intended."

Before parting, the Koala asked that everyone present should come along to-morrow to hold a meeting in the valley, "to discuss what we shall do with the Wondangar, because they have committed a grave crime, which must not be overlooked, in causing the death of one of the most goodly beings, and the other matter of considering whether we shall adopt one common language. All previous intercourse we did by sign and gesture, and now we must come to some understanding so that we can converse one with the other." They all shouted "Kay Hey," and departed to the various homes, some among the great forest in the valley, others on the hill-side, each to their fanciful homes. Now, when they arrived at their mia mia, they sat down, thinking of what they would say and what questions would be asked, some keeping later hours than others. But after a while they were snugly asleep in their warm bed, dreaming of hunting and fishing, etc.

Now, when the sun rose with promise of a bright and beautiful day, all life was astir, hastily partaking of the morning meal, all eager to be present at the conference. After everyone had enjoyed his meal, each made his way towards the appointed place in the valley. Every member of the various tribes and families was represented. The Whygammie and Peenjullie took it upon themselves to place everyone in order. They had them arranged, sitting tier above tier on one side of the valley. In the centre of the valley was a stump of what was at one time a large tree. The stump stood about ten to fifteen feet high. "That," said the Whingammie, "will make a splendid pulpit from which the Koala will be able to see every being, and all beings will see him, and from such a position as that he will be able to deliver his address." So it was decided that it should be so.

Now they were all seated, and waiting patiently for the Koala. Presently, with his bodyguard, he arrived. The Whingammie and Peenjullie went forward to meet him and escorted him to the stump, and with sign and gesture explained that they would consider it an honour for him to mount the stump and address them from it, as he would have a better view and command of the audience. So he expressed himself that it was very considerate of them to provide such an admirable position. So he mounted the stump, followed by his chief bodyguard, who had their Spear and woomera and nulla nulla. They stood on either side of him, and the rest of the bodyguard were arranged in order around the base of the stump. Now this old Koala was Moochombulli, a philosopher and a linguist. He had during his voyages studied the various languages, customs, and traditions, and during their short sojourn in Australia he became proficient, and that is why he was bold enough to summon them all to a conference in which he dared to address each tribe in its own language. Not many of the tribes knew this, and they were wondering how he was going to make himself clearly understood. But he first spoke the bird language, and told them of his wish that their language was much better than the others and would they object to the others acquiring it. "Oh, not at all," answered the Lyre Bird and Cockatoo, who were the chief speakers selected by the Peewingie and Peenjullie. The Lyre Bird said that it would be a splendid idea if they would come and be taught by the Cockatoo. Continuing, he said, "I propose that he shall be selected as a schoolmaster." "Yes," said the Crow, "I support the proposition made by the Lyre Bird," and it was carried by all the birds exclaiming "Hick Ka, Yes be it so as you wish."

Then the Koala turned and addressed the reptiles and lizards in their own tongue, and oh, you should have seen the astonishment on the face of the Thooyoungie, Goanna. He turned around, and, addressing the Frilled Lizard, said, "Am I awake, is this all a dream?" Turning his head to the right and then to the left he said, "I was about to ask you the same question. Something has come over us, or we are affected by yesterday and last night," referring to the Goon Na Ghun. "Perhaps that may be so, but why is it that everything looks so real, nothing fanciful about the visions that are about us? The voice of the Koala is so distinct that there is no doubting the sound of his voice, and I feel sensitive of all my surroundings. And the sun is well, right reaching the home of Nabeloe. I cannot be dreaming."

The Blue-tongued or Sleepy Lizard was sitting quietly enthralled at the wonderful style and delivery the Koala had of their language, and when the Thooyoungie and Frilled Lizard were whispering to each other and shifting from side to side, they would annoy the Monarrie, for that is the name of the Blue-tongued Lizard. He became so angry that he took hold of his nulla nulla and struck the Thooyoungie and Frilled Lizard such a blow upon their heads, so suddenly, that they leaped to their feet and, staggering, they saw stars, and it looked as if the earth was rolling over and over and the trees and other objects being whirled round and round so quickly that it was difficult to distinguish what they were. When the Kookaburras saw what had taken place, and saw the Thooyoungie and Frilled Lizard reeling like drunken men, they burst into a fit of laughter, "Ha Ha Ho Ho Hee." The Cockatoo could not remain solemn much longer, and joined in the laughter, and all the other birds, the Muldarie, Magpie, and Tharrangarie (Crow) would have joined in had it not been for the Peenjullie rising to his feet and calling "Tou, a, tou, order, order." They instantly ceased laughing. "Remember we are not here to entertain Runballarumb, but to consider more matters than one of a serious nature relating to the tragic event of yesterday. Now who is the culprit who has dared to disturb this assembly?" Then, turning to the Koala, the Peenjullie said, "Will you pardon me, as next in command to the majority of this great gathering, that someone of my race has caused this disturbance? Will you kindly be seated until I shall endeavour to quell their feeling." "Thanks," said the Koala, "I shall be seated."

"Now," said the Peenjullie, "let the person or persons, the beginners of the interruption, come forward and explain yourself or yourselves." The Monarrie rose to his feet and strode forward towards the platform, and, facing the audience, said, "Well friends, I was so fascinated by the flow of language, which was so perfect and delightful, coming from one who is a foreigner to my kind and race, that when the Thooyoungie and the Frilled Lizard who were as others no doubt filled with wonderment, could not believe their vision nor the sense of hearing, began to express themselves in loud tones which disturbed and annoyed me, I struck them on the head with my nulla nulla, and now the rest you know." Then, turning to the Koala, "You will pardon me, won't you. Your command of my language overwhelmed me, and I did not know what I was doing at the moment." The Koala rose and said that he forgave him, and returned to his seat, and the Thooyoungie and Frilled Lizard came forward, and each was given time to make an explanation, which both expressed in the same words. "First, we were so astounded at your selection of the vocabulary of our language, that we thought all we heard was a dream, and instead of continuing to that, we both gave vent to our feelings, and turned first one ear and then the other to be sure what we heard was real. And what is more, we spoke out so loud that we caused a disorder and annoyed the Monarrie, and he struck us a blow on the head and almost stunned us." "Will you forgive the Monarrie?" "Yes, I forgive him," and they returned to their seat beside the Monarrie and sat throughout the meeting, satisfied that all they heard and saw was real. "And now with your permission, shall we be seated?" The Koala replied, "Will you be seated," and the Thooyoungie and Frilled Lizard took their seats beside the Monarrie, and they listened more attentively with the full assurance that what was taking place was a reality and not a dream. They all agreed to what the Koala advocated—the necessity of one common language.

At this juncture the Koala announced that they should adjourn for lunch and a few moments' rest, and each respective tribe retired to the shade under the larger trees, others sitting upon the green grass by a little stream near-by wending its way to the mighty ocean, with little fishes sporting in the limpid water. Some of the feathered tribe sat on the bank and caught fishes for lunch, and some, who were in such a hurry that they forgot to bring their lunch, hunted among the wattle and honeysuckle trees for grubs to supply themselves with food. When lunch was over, they sat in the assembly, and again the Koala mounted his platform with his bodyguard beside him and upon the ground surrounding the platform. He began his address, calling their attention to another aspect which was of a more serious nature than the former, that is, the cruel assault of the Wondangar upon the good-natured and sympathetic Goon Na Ghun. "We shall always remember the untiring labours of these good beings. There is not one family among this great gathering but what has been helped and relieved of their tiresome burden of domestic life and things in general, not only so when the heart was bowed in sorrow at the loss of loved ones and friends. There was always one who, with kind words, poured the oil of comfort into the wounded heart and pierced soul. What makes it so sad is that there is not one of them left, and unlike the others of the great and good beings, they have not ascended into Wyerriwarr, but expressed their dying wish to be committed to the water. That wish we have fulfilled. Now what shall be done to the Wondangar. Are we to allow them to go free? They have become a menace to the safety of all tribes. I and my family would have dealt with them more severely some time back, but for the Goon Na Ghun's sake we did not like to do so. No doubt you have, each respective tribe, had the same thought. And now we must take steps—What shall the punishment be?" They replied, shouting, "Chastise them with nulla nulla or one stroke from Marpungie, a weapon like a boomerang, with one and eighteen inches or two feet longer, which forms the handle, and this is used to cause a very bad wound, sometimes with fatal results, fracturing the skull." And the assembly moved that they would suggest that a select number of the Koala family should be entrusted to deal with the Wondangar at sunrise to-morrow, and that all tribes should be present. The chief of the Koala accepted, on behalf of his family, the duty of carrying out the punishment. So the meeting closed, and each one returned, some to their homes, others to hunt food, and the reptile went along the rocks and sheltered spots and lay basking in the sunshine.

At sunrise on the following morning all tribes were gathered upon the sandbeach, the home of the Wondangar, waiting the arrival of the Koala. Out of the shrubs that grew by the sea shore came the Koala, marching in order four abreast with their leader walking in front. They bore upon their faces the seriousness of the position. The other tribes formed a semicircle around the Wondangar, with the opening part leading into the sea. Now the forming of this semicircle was for a purpose, as you will see later on. The Wondangar were within this enclosure. They were looking half-sleepy and stupid, wondering about this visit.

Then the chief of Koala called the attention of the Wondangar, and spoke, addressing them in their own language, saying, "Oh Wondangar, through your hasty temper with no justification whatever, you have beaten with your club unmercifully the Goon Na Ghun beings, from whom you have derived greater assistance than any of the other beings of the various tribes. And it was whilst in the execution of one of these kindly acts that you attacked with nulla nulla and spear. And now we, the animal, bird, and reptile tribes, have decided to mete out to you the punishment you so justly deserve. And it will be one severe blow delivered by a select member of my tribe with a Marpungie. Come, rise and receive your punishment."

But the Wondangar said, "We are going to fight you. There is no hope of you carrying out your threats. Come Whingammie, Peenjullie, Thooyoungie, take and bind the Wondangar securely with ropes." These three beings whose names were called stepped forward and bound the Wondangar, and each select Koala moved forward, and raising their Marpungie, delivered such a mighty stroke that it sent the weapon deep into the hard and brainless skull of the victim, burying the point of the Marpungie right up to the handle. And the shock was so severe that it stunned the Wondangar, and the Koala withdrew the weapon, covered in blood, and the Wondangar lay so still that the assemblage thought that they were dead. But presently, each Wondangar took in a supply of fresh air, and the breathing caused the blood to squirt up through the fractured skull, and when they awoke out of their stupor, and came back to their senses, they were aware of a severe pain in the region of the head, and, feeling the warm blood trickling down their cheeks, they rushed into the sea to bathe themselves, diving into the water and rising to breathe, continuing as they went farther and farther out to sea. And this is what they have been doing since that eventful day witnessed by the animal, bird, and reptile tribe, right up to the present day from time immemorial, in the form of a whale.

And as for the good-hearted Goon Na Ghun, you will see them lying in the bottom of the sea, although victims of the cruel Wondangar. But for their good work in doing for others what they would others to do for them, but going further into works, they did more by doing for them kindly acts and speaking words of comfort. And although beaten, and arms and legs severed from their bodies, their good spirit after their death gave them the form and shape of stars, and their bodies, lying in the deep blue sea, are reflected in the stars above us.

Testimony to Gawler

This "testimony" to Governor Colin George Gawler (South Australia), dated 15 May 1841, is in the Kaurna dialect (Adelaide tribe). The handwriting is occasionally ambiguous (eg "t" looks like "l"), but is neat, well-formed copperplate. The translation may be in the same hand. There are nine signatures, four Aboriginal girls and four boys. The girls' signatures look as if they are in the same handwriting as the testimony. The boys' signatures, again perhaps by one child, are less well-formed. The testimony is enclosed in a larger testimony to Gawler's care of the Blacks signed by two missionaries and the Protector. As the colony was only founded in 1836, someone must have got busy teaching these children to write.

The natives have felt the influence of your Excellency's Kindness and when we informed them of your departure they expressed themselves in the following words, inscribed by a Native Girl and signed by several children:

Ngadlu kundo punggorendi parnu kurlangga,
us   the chest   beats   at his   absence

ngadlku yerlteriburka pa tikketti,
our   commander   he   did sit

parnu kurlangga ngadlu tikketti, ngudluko
on his   side   we   did sit   for us

birra pa turlalaetti, padlo ngadlu tirraappetti
he   did contend   he   us   did hide

perkanna meyuunungko tauaninnanna
from the white men   who insulted

Murkandi   ngadlu   parnu   kurlangga,
Lament   we   at his   absence,

padlo   ngadlu   numa   nakketti
he   at us   well   did look,

ngadluko   yerlita   ba   tikketti
our   father   he   did sit

maüngga   parrungga   mul   yertilla,   maü   mutyerla
regarding food   meat   clothing   food   clothing

padlo   ngadlu   yungketti   maüyerta
he   us   did give   land for food

ngadluko   padlo   nungko   kudlaityappi,   pepa
us   he   back   gave   school

worli   padlo   ngartuila   ngadluko   taü
house   he   for the children   of us   did build

warra   naingkurntitya,   parkanna   wakwakurli
words   to learn   as white   children

waietitya   pulyunna   wakwakunna
do thus   black   children

Letter from Nepabunna

Nepabunna,
Via Copley,
17.11.[19]66

Dear Sir,
This is a request from the undersigned people of Nepabunna for the Government of South Australia to take over this establishment.

The land on which the Nepabunna Mission stands was given to the Elders of our people by the late Mr Thomas who at that stage owned Balcanoona Station. At no stage was this land given to UAM [United Aborigines Mission]. This is our land and we want the Government to come in and take over control of it from the present authorities. We would like a church authority left here to act purely as spiritual leaders, but we want the rest of our land to be run by the Government.

Over the years there has been a severe lack of water at Nepabunna, there is also a shortage of rainwater tanks on the houses. The only time that water is really pumped is when someone is coming to visit and "when the people go back the water goes back". The bores as such are not deep enough to cater for the needs of our people, our supply at present is insufficient and inadequate.

There have been no housing improvements carried out over the years, and our abodes are totally inadequate for the conditions of extreme heat and cold which are experienced [spelling corrected in ink] in this area. The houses are, with the exception of four, are [sic] only three rooms and so overcrowding occures [sic] in many instances.

Our houses lack facilities. There are no cupboards or sinks and we wash in tin troughs. The bathroom and laundry are combined and our coppers are situated outside. In many instances we have no guttering and there are no verandahs on any of the houses.

We have no proper fences around our homes and when we have

asked for improvements they have not been carried out as requested by us. We pay rent for our houses but we do not know where the rent goes to or what it is used for.

For many months now the truck has been out of action and so no rubbish has been collected from our yards. It is a hard task for mothers to handle this work when father is away.

When we buy from the store we receive no receipts for our money and the only fresh vegetables that we are able to buy are potatoes and onions. As many of us have growing children we feel that they need such things. Our language has been suppressed while we are at the store.

Our friends are hunted off the mission almost as soon as they arrive and when we come back from Copley we are "smelt" for signs of drink.

Sir, we want a say in the running of our own community, we want our own council. It is time that the authorities stopped treating us like people with no brains or abilities. We were brought up amongst white people long before the missionaries ever arrived and it is time we had our say in the way we want to live. We want to be treated like human beings and not like some wild person. WE WANT THE FREEDOM THAT WE ARE ENTITLED TO BY LAW.

Even tobacco has not been sold at the store since the Hathaways took over, and today it is brought in almost as though it were illegal.

When our people are out of work no effort is made to find them work.

If the Government will not take over then we will be forced to leave Nepabunna, as we will find it impossible to live on as we are at the moment. We haves [sic] stood this state of affairs too long and it is time that something was done. We appeal to you Sir in your capacity to help our cause NOW. We want action immediately, not in the future BUT NOW.

Yours in trust
[35 signatures]

A Good Thrashing

Tilly Bails

Port Noarlunga
July 11 1925

Dear Sir,

    I got a summons tody for
thashing
    a man, Mr Young, with a
whip he told a lie about me
and said that he did not read
a letter I took to him from
Mrs Bosworth when he really
did read it. So I gave him 4
2 months to clear that lie of
me When he came here
after tw four months were up
I thrashed him will you
protect me in law Court at
Morphett Vale on Friday 17 July
    from Tilly

Mrs Bosworth is out of the State [sic]

*(Tilly Bails, an Aboriginal woman, wrote to the Chief Protector to represent
her in this case which became a sensation: "several char-a-bancs and at
least a dozen cars lined the roadway in front of the court building" said the
newspapers of the time, which also ran jocular descriptions of the trial and
a cartoon of the whipping with the "leading citizen" stuck in a barbed wire
fence in an attempt to get away from Tilly. Young took action because he
feared sexual scandal might attach to him if the matter were not aired in
court. Tilly had evidently sided with her employer who had quarreled with
Young, described as a mild man who "wears horn rimmed spectacles". Tilly
was fined 18/- with costs of £5.)*

JILJI KURMALYI   JIMMY PIKE
(sandhills)

Kurkuminti-Murkuminti (hollow surrounded by sandhills).

People used to walk around that area looking for food.

I Went to Perth Once Too

Paddy Roe

I went to Perth once too *(rasping)[1]*-
that's where I-
that's the place I went to, Mt. Lawley (Krim[2]: Mt Lawley College,
mm) mm (Krim: You didn't like Perth, eh? didn't like Perth?)-
that was 'nuff for me one time *(laughter)*-
I went there 'cos I was a*(rasping)*-
this er—
NAC[3]-
first time NAC started-
they didn't have any NAC people in this part of the country—
so that's what I went for, so *(rasping)*—
to go round and get all these people *(rasping stops, tap, tap)*—
oh musta been some NAC people in other countries-
you know but not in this part of the country-

So *(rasping)* that's the first time they started that's what I went for,
you know-
so all the NAC man all over now in Broome, an', Perth, everywhere
(Stephen: Oh yeah)-
(tap, tap, tap) yeah they didn't have-em before *(rasping)* in that
time that's what I went for—

So when I went to Perth-
(rasping stops) that day *(rasping)*—
when I got up from (*tap, tap, rasping)*-
oh I was just laying down I dunno what time I got there, you know
(tap, tap, rasping)-

So *(laugh)* one day, I get up next day *(rasping stops, tap, tap)*-
I got outa my bed-

"Oh Chris'! I musta went to sleep early," I said*(laughter)*-
you know, I got up—
"Oh it's not sundown yet-
oh just about sundown," I said to meself-
just about sundown—

So I *(tap)* went *(tap)* to-
so I went to the shower room had a bath put me pinjamas on an'
everything I was laying down watching book in the, bed you
know—
I was on me own-

So one lady came around-
eer she wanted to take me round, show me the town, you know
(laugh)-
"Hullo! What are you doin?" said-
"Ah, well I just gettin' ready to go to bed," I said *(laughter)*—
(breathy voice) "Whaat?"
"Just ready to go to bed"
"Go to bed?" he said[4]
"Yeah, oh what the time now then?"
"Aah, it'd be about eight o'clock," he said *(laughter)*-
"Eight o'clock, what, in the morning?" I said-
"Yes"
"OOH!" *(laughter)*-
I went in the shower room took all me pinjamas out an' put me
trousers *(laugh)*, hat *(laugh)*, an' everything, coat—
ooh, I got lost *(laughter)* I didn't know what is sundown or sunrise,
can't see (Krim: You can't see the sun, yeah)*(laugh)*—
ah, just like the-
well to ME eer just like the sun was getting up from this way you
know *(laughs)* or somewhere (Stephen: Oh yeah, doesn't get up
very much in Perth, only like this you know)-
yeah?-
(Stephen: Doesn't get right up)-
don't go right up, oh

Notes:

1. Text transcribed by Stephen Muecke from a tape recording. The noise of the rasp being used by Paddy Roe to make a boomerang tends to punctuate the story.

2. Krim Benterrak, co-author of Reading the Country *(Fremantle Arts Centre Press, 1984) with Paddy Roe and Stephen Muecke.*

3. National Aboriginal Council, a now-defunct representative body for Aboriginal communities.

4. This variety of Aboriginal English does not distinguish gender in the pronouns.

"Cuppa Tea" Song

Ngitji Ngitji

Kungka   tjirilalu   kapati   palyanu
Woman   "Porkupine"   tea   made

Wati   kanyalanya   tjirangka   nyinangu
Man   "Euro"   chair   sat on

The Possum Woman

Ngitji Ngitji

This legend is dedicated to my late beloved mother, who passed away 9 December, 1978. For many years, Mother told my sister and I this legend. Our mother was an Antagaringa Elder. — N.N.

Long ago in the Dream Time, a man and his wife lived in a far-away country. These two would sleep by day. Each night, the woman would go hunting possums. She would take up her killing stick. Her husband would hear her singing in the distance:

"I'm going to kill the possums by pulling them out of the hollow of the trees."

The possum woman was very tall with beautiful long hair which hung to the ground. When she caught the possums she would tie them up on top of her head with her hair and a string made of animal hair. When she returned home in the morning she would undo her hair. All of the possums fell out. Her husband then cleaned the possums, cooked meat and later on, when ready, put the meat in a bark shelter to eat.

One night the husband felt uneasy when his wife was ready to go hunting. His nose made a cracking noise, which means bad luck. Even today Aboriginals believe this. He told her to take care. That night she set off singing until she was near the hills.

Suddenly her husband heard an echo of her song, then silence. He waited all night for her return. At daybreak he followed her footprints to the rocks near a hill. There were drops of blood but no strange footprints.

He climbed the rocks. As he looked over the rocks, to his amazement he saw a great giant asleep near the fire. The bones of his wife lay nearby, pieces of her beautiful hair everywhere, her blood spilled on the ground.

The angry husband speared the giant through the heart. He was a very clever man. He said, "I'll bring her back to life".

So he gathered up all the scattered bones, hair, blood, then brought her back to life as she was before. He told her, "I told you long ago not to sing while hunting. A devil or something worse can hurt you."

Later they went to live in another place. The possum woman never sang again as she hunted.

Goanna Hibernating

Robert Churnside (Ngarluma)

Mudunga kurrumurnsu
in the winter Dead-ant Goanna

tarda
covered over

ngarregu mulinga
must lie in a hole

Tarda—tilgu taiai
It must cover the mouth of its hole

ngarregu turnunga tardaba
must lie inside and under its cover

Ngarregu nguntal
It must lie, that one,

ngarregu parruraba
must lie a long time

Minawarra jurngu mirlbagu
When the rains come

karnadi tarlgugu
lightning strikes

mindilminilmagu
making the thunder roll

Pirrikalara
having claws

murgai kalbagu
it must arise from its burrow

A Story of Wongawol Station

Snowy Hill

This is a true story which took place on Wongawol station as told by Snowy Hill one night over the campfire. Snowy's brother-in-law Jimmy told him the story. This and many other stories about relations between white settlers and Aborigines in the Western Desert of Western Australia are still remembered and told over campfires at night, but they have rarely been recorded.

Well this is Tommy Mellon he told Jimmy, he said, "You come with me. We go out bush. You get your missus and you. We three go out." Alright, my brother-in-law, that's Jimmy. They get the gun each and they went out bush. Tommy said, "When you get to camp ... Jimmy. You cart the wood for the camp." Righto, he start. Cart 'em, cart 'em every time he going up and down, you know carrying wood. Cut 'em, cut 'em, cut plenty wood. He chuck plenty wood. He cart 'em, cart 'em, cart 'em, cart 'em, cart 'em and he's more wood gettin' higher and higher.

"That's right boss? Plenty wood for you?"

Well he said, "No."

"Alright, boss." And he keep going saying, "Alright I'll go cut some more." And he cut plenty and he cart 'em with his foot all the time. Carry 'em on his shoulder. Chuck a heap there. Keep on filling him. Soon as high as these trees, get that much. Plenty. Plenty wood stacked up like that.

"That's right boss?"

"No," he said. "Go and get some more."

Alright. He start work. Work, work, work right up to sundown. No pay nothing. Before it gets dark Jimmy cart some plenty wood again. He cart 'em cart 'em, cart 'em, cart 'em, right up.

"That's right boss?"

"No, more Jimmy."

"Look, this is enough wood here to cook a bullock," said Jimmy.

Old Tommy Mellon get upset. "Don't say that to me," and hit him. Alright, he drop him. "Look no cheek. Come on," and he starts to hit him again, trying to hit Jimmy. Jimmy was strong, he was pretty good too. He belt the boss. Bang, bang—one, two, three, four, five. Hit him alright. Tommy picks up the rifle ... going to shoot. He had a 22 rifle, early day one.

Jimmy's missus was not far away. She said, "Look, you been enough shoot native people, Wangkai people. Now you going to shoot Jimmy and what about you? Your time is coming. Look this way, Tommy. I'm going to drop you with this gun if you shoot my husband. You have been shoot black fella. You're not going to do it my husband." His woman bail him out. Tommy said, "Alright. Leave it." He never say nothing else. He went back to see that heap of wood and came back to her and said, "Oh, we shift away from here. Leave that wood for when we come mustering cattle, for the cook."

They went on to another windmill, going windmill to windmill. Have a look around to see if the cattle was going right, or getting enough water in the trough. They track up every tank and windmill. Then, they go back to the station, and camp there. And Jimmy's missus, said to him, "You got to be careful now. You know he was going to shoot you out in the bush only for me. You want to watch your step. Don't be rough with him. Take notice what he tell you. And they might put you and another bloke, see?"

"Oh, I'll be alright" Jimmy said, "I'll be right, missus."

Later Tommy Mellon tells Jimmy. "I'm going to send you with another bloke." Saddled up and everything, get the blankets ... with this other bloke. Oh he very bad bloke too. He had a revolver and cartridge bullets around the belt. He think he was a cowboy, see. Jimmy said, "Boss, what about my rifle?" Tommy said, "Oh the other bloke, this bloke, he'll shoot some meat for you. Leave your rifle."

So he went out with this half-caste bloke, Dick Talfort.

It was spring time, quondong ripe time. Jimmy rode ahead and this bloke coming behind. Where Jimmy see this quondong tree there, he goes up to it. He gets all the quondong in the bag and go along behind and eat them all. Talfort is going along in front now, he just looks around and he sees alright. "I don't know how many times you're going to do that," he's thinking in his head, he must be going to do it again. Jimmy see another tree and pulls up his horse. He grabs all them quondongs and puts them in his bags. They go along. He sees another tree and gets another lot more quondongs.

Then, when it gets to be about five o'clock Talfort says, "Jimmy, we're going to make camp here." They make camp and hobble the horses out. They had dinner and sitting down talking. Talfort never says anything about chasing quondongs. Next morning comes. In the morning Jimmy goes to get the horses and comes back. They start going back towards the station. They camp two more nights on the way at windmills. They had dinner and put a coat on each. Jimmy lights a fire for himself and the half-caste lights a fire for himself. They sleep by the fires. Next day they go along riding through another two windmills. Jimmy sees another quondong tree and gallops the horse and fills the saddle bags. Talfort's throat was dry and he felt like arguing. "Never mind," he says to himself. "I'll leave it to the boss when I get to the station. I'll fix that fellow, Jimmy."

Next night they get to the windmill. This half-caste bloke had the rifle. He's supposed to shoot the kangaroo and give it to Jimmy to have a feed. Well he doesn't shoot anything. He's saving bullets. Jimmy gets up early to get the horses and saddles them. They go a long way back to the station. They get back and let the horses go in the paddock and feed them. Talfort tells the story about Jimmy to Tommy Mellon.

"You know Jimmy been galloping, nearly kill the horse."

"Yeah?" Tommy Mellon says, "What he been chasing?"

"Chasing go every day tree to tree for quondongs. He fill the saddle bag and fill his coat pockets."

"Yeah? Alright I'll fix that fellow. I'll send him with this white bloke next time."

Two days later Tommy says, "Jimmy you're going out with this fella now." Jimmy said "What about my rifle? Other time I went without no rifle." Tommy said "The white bloke can get you meat." Jimmy's missus tells him "See that now? He's trying you out with every bloke. You got to watch yourself now and no cheek. When they tell, don't say nothing, don't give them answer. Just say, 'Yes boss, you good man,' alright?"

They start away. Riding along, riding along, riding along, riding ... and they had dinner half way. The white bloke said, "Right, Jimmy, no time to sleep. You know, we got a long way to go." Righto, they start away. This white bloke was a big bloke, broad and fat and he had a big chest. He had a 44 colt revolver, a 33 rifle in the pouch and bullets right around. They keep going riding along, riding along, riding along ... When they get to camp the white bloke said, "Well Jim, I'm a bit tired. We'll have to camp here." It was a good camp by a big creek. He starts cooking tucker for supper and he lay down to have a rest. Jimmy walks around a bit and finds a big bangara, a yellow bangara. He kills this one and comes back.

"Look boss, I kill a bangara."

"Oh, bring him up here. I want to have a look. What do you want to kill him for man? Aren't I not feeding you? What, are you starving?"

"No, I not starving. You feeding me."

"Then what do you want to kill that one for?" Alright he grabs the hobble chain and gives Jimmy a good hiding. Oh, hit him everywhere, this way, this way, in the back, everywhere. Hit him there and cripple him. He couldn't hardly get up, blood shooting out of his mouth nose head. Everything shooting blood. Jimmy was very sore. He lay down by the fire. He gets bushes and smokes himself. He smokes himself all night and all that pain goes away. He lay down in the hot leaves. First he cleans the coals away and puts the leaves, bushes there. Then he sleeps. Feels a bit better, you know.

Next morning the white bloke said, "Jimmy you go get the horses and saddle them up," Jimmy goes for the horses, never mind sick, and saddle them up. Have breakfast and start to leave. Jimmy couldn't get up on the horse. The white bloke put him in the saddle. When they got halfway to the other windmill he said "Jimmy, look, I'll learn you for killing that bangara."

"That's right, boss." Jimmy said. "You'll learn me. You'll win."

"I learn you for killing that bangara, poor bangara. I never starve you. I give you plenty of tucker."

They keep going long way, windmill, to windmill. Jimmy is getting better. He feels the pain going away. It's a long ride and he getting better, feeling good and strong now. He is going to train himself now in the bush."Now I think I can manage that fellow," he thinks, "I'll learn that white bloke."

Every day the white bloke reminds him. "I'll learn you for killing that bangara. I'll learn you Jimmy."

"That's right boss. You feed me. No more I won't do that. You good man."

When they get to the halfway station the white bloke forgets about it. He says, "Jimmy, pour water on my head so I can have a wash." He want his shoes off too. He said, "Oh, my boots are hurting a little bit. Take them off and leave them. Wash my feet too. Pour water on my head and where's the soap?" Jimmy gets the water and he pours it. He pours plenty of water and the white bloke is covered with soap.

"More, Jimmy. I want plenty more. I want to wash plenty." He keeps rubbing soap in his head. "Oh, that's lovely."

The next minute Jimmy pulls the revolver out of the pack. The white bloke is watching, he can see his revolver going away. He hits Jimmy, knocks him back. Jimmy fell back on the granite. The white bloke hits him in the heart. Jimmy finds his feet again. Jimmy hits the white bloke as soon as he comes back up. When the white bloke comes near the revolver Jimmy tries to kick it away. The white bloke knocks Jimmy down and kicks him in the heart. When Jimmy comes back up he grabs the chain and keeps on kicking the revolver away from the white man. He says, "You want that revolver you got to fight me." Jimmy knocks him out. "My turn now," he says and grabs the revolver too. He said, "What you been done to me over there, what you belt me with the chain. You got to get big log on you now and a chain on top of it." He gets a big stick and gives him a good hiding. He puts the boots on and kicks him.

"You lay there until the dogs eat you," Jimmy said. He got the revolver and went to Wiluna. He took the rifle and all the bullets and left the white bloke with nothing. The white bloke lay there for a long time, right up to day light. He wakes up and moves around. He thinks, "Where am I? Where is my horse? My rifle is gone, my bullets are gone." He calls to his horse ... he managed to get on the horse and go home. The boss sees him coming. Jimmy's wife sees him and thinks, "Oh no, my husband got shot." They see he has no revolver, and he's cut everywhere, covered with blood.

Jimmy went on to Wiluna with the rifle, revolver, everything. When he comes to this shepherd and sheep he sneaks up to their camp and steals the tobacco, flour and everything. He lifts the lid of the kettle in the fire cooking damper and grabs the damper. He puts the lid back and put the ashes back good, you know, so nobody could see, but he never covered his track. He's walking about forty chains away and he can hear: "Oh I put the damper in the kettle and look it's empty. Oh come and have a look, big nigger take 'em. That's a foot there, big Wangkai take 'em."

When Jimmy got to Wiluna he went to the police station and passed the guns to the police sergeant.

"What happened?"

"Oh this Tommy Mellon, they chain and try to shoot me."

"Yeah?"

"He try to shoot me. He nearly kill me out in the bush."

"Oh yeah, Jimmy, I'll tell that to the government in Perth. We'll send one policeman out to Wongawol like he was prospecting. We'll keep the guns and you keep going out to Pig Hill. You stop there, nobody will touch you. We'll fix that Wongawol mob."

The policeman went out to Wongawol prospecting. He wore raggedy old trousers, a patch here, a patch there, everywhere. He looks for gold, knocking rocks, taking samples, "I see everything now. I'll get that Perth mob to come out to Wiluna," he says to himself. He stays there dollying his rock. He sees everything. He sees who sleeps with all the white men. He comes in to the station to get the story and goes out for samples again. He writes it all down in his book. Then he tells the station people, "Oh I'm going away now ... Yalma way."

He meets the police truck down the road. They sent a big military bus and all the policeman. Many trucks came to Wongawol. Plenty. This bloke chuck all the patches clothes away and puts the uniform on. He suits up in his police clothes. When they get to the station Tommy Mellon said, "If I knew that you were a policeman I would have shot you right here." They rounded him up and put Tommy Mellon in the chaff bag and tie him up. They leave him hanging in the killing pen while they get all the women and kids and go mustering. They let all the horses, camels and bullocks go in the paddock. They left two men there and sent all the women and children to Mugumber. His wife went away too. They sent all the kids, half caste and full caste to Mugumber. That was a long time ago before the war. There was the Depression on then.

They are all gone, those people. All in the southwest—Bunbury, Bridgetown, some in Albany, some in Perth. We never see them, they are still away now. They all got married and stopped back there. There were so many kids, Tommy Mellon's and the other white blokes half caste kids. Tommy had a trial in Wiluna, but they sent him to Perth. He lost his station and everything. He came back after a long time and then he was the owner of the butcher shop in Leonora. The Native Protection wouldn't let him go back to the station.

That's finished now. No more.

(Transcribed by Anne Parker)

PURNARRA JIMMY PIKE

Purnarra — this marking is like a number, a brand. It is used by all the Aboriginal people over a big area. It shows that anything with this marking comes from the bush-desert south of Kimberleys.

When people see this purnarra carving, they know what number that country has. "Ah, that come from my country". Many tribes use the same number, same meaning, cut different way.

It is part of the law. Aborigines believe in this number. Carving on nulla nulla, spear, woomera, shield, coolamon (water holder), Marrillaly (shovel for cooking), wangkuli (sieve for wheat), tarta (cup).

The Letter

Sally Morgan

The bus swayed back and forth making my tired old head hurt even more.

Really, I wanted to cry, but no-one cried on a bus. I glanced down sadly at the old biscuit tin sitting on my lap. Scotch Shortbreads, they weren't even her favourites, but she'd liked the colour of the tin so I'd given them to her.

I sighed and wiped away the tear that was beginning to creep down my cheek. She was gone, and I felt old and lonely and very disappointed.

My fingers traced around the lid of the tin and slowly loosened it.

Inside was all she'd had to leave. A thin silvery necklace, some baby photos, her citizenship Certificate, and the letter. I smiled when I remembered how it had taken her so long to write. She'd gone over and over every word. It was so important to her. We'd even joked about the day I would have to take it to Elaine. That day had come sooner than we both expected.

I've failed, I told myself as I lifted out the necklace. It'd been bought for Elaine's tenth birthday, but we hadn't known where to send it. Now we knew where Elaine lived but she didn't want the tin or anything in it.

I placed it back gently on top of the photo.

Elaine had said the baby in the photo wasn't her. She'd said it was all a silly mistake and she wished I'd stop pestering her.

It was the third time I'd been to see her and it looked like it would be the last. I picked up the letter. It was faded and worn. I opened it out carefully and read it again.

To my daughter Elaine,
I am writing in the hope that one day you will read this and understand. I suppose you don't want to know me because you think

I deserted you. It wasn't like that. I want to tell you what it was like.

I was only seventeen when you were born at the Settlement. They all wanted to know who your father was, but I wouldn't tell. Of course he was a white man, you were so fair, but there was no love in his heart for you or me. I promised myself I would protect you. I wanted you to have a better life than me.

They took you away when I was twenty. Mr Neville from the Aborigines Protection Board said it was the best thing. He said that black mothers like me weren't allowed to keep babies like you. He didn't want you brought up as one of our people. I didn't want to let you go but I didn't have any choice. That was the law.

I started looking for you when I was thirty. No-one would tell me where you'd gone. It was all a big secret. I heard they'd changed your last name, but I didn't know what your new name was. I went and saw Mr Neville and told him I wanted to visit you. That was when I found out that you'd been adopted by a white family. You thought you were white. Mr Neville said I'd only hurt you by trying to find you.

For a long time I tried to forget you, but how could I forget my own daughter? Sometimes I'd take out your baby photo and look at it and kiss your little face. I prayed that somehow you'd know you had a mother who loved you.

By the time I found you, you were grown up with a family of your own. I started sending you letters trying to reach you. I wanted to see you and my grandchildren, but you know all about that because you've sent all my letters back. I don't blame you and I don't hold any grudges, I understand. When you get this letter I will be gone, but you will have the special things in my tin. I hope that one day you will wonder who you really are and that you will make friends with our people because that's where you belong. Please be kind to the lady who gives you my tin, she's your own aunty.

From your loving Mother.

My hands were shaking as I folded the letter and placed it back in the tin. It was no use, I'd tried, but it was no use. Nellie had always been the strong one in our family, she'd never given up on anything. She'd always believed that one day Elaine would come home.

I pressed the lid down firmly and looked out the window at the passing road. It was good Nellie wasn't here now. I was glad she didn't know how things had turned out. Suddenly her voice seemed to whisper crossly in my ear. "You always give up too easy!"

"Do not," I said quietly. I didn't know what to do then. Nellie was right, that girl was our own flesh and blood, I couldn't let her go so easily. I looked down at the tin again and felt strangely better, almost happy. I'll make one last try, I thought to myself. I'll get a new envelope and mail it to her. She might just read it!

I was out in the yard when I heard the phone ring. I felt sure that by the time I got inside it would stop. It takes me a long while to get up the back steps these days. "Hello," I panted as I lifted the receiver. "Aunty Bessie?" "Who's this?," I asked in surprise. "It's Elaine." Elaine? I couldn't believe it! It'd been two months since I'd mailed the letter. "Is it really you Elaine?," I asked. "Yes, it's me. I want to talk to you. Can I come and see you?" "Ooh yes, anytime."

"I'll be there tomorrow and Aunty ... take care of yourself."

My hands shook as I placed the phone back on the hook.

Had I heard right? Had she really said, take care of yourself Aunty? I sat down quickly in the nearest chair and wiped my eyes.

"Well, why shouldn't I cry?," I said out loud to the empty room, "I'm not on the bus now!" Nellie felt very close to me just then. "Aah sister," I sighed, "Did you hear all that? Elaine will be here tomorrow?

"Did you hear that sister? Elaine's coming home."

Unwritten Policy

Gloria Brennan

She was only sixteen, just out of school and working in a white world where it was absolutely necessary to prove her worth to others at all times, particularly to whites. Then she met someone who really mattered. He was white. This difference was only recognised after it was all over, and she still asks, "Did it really matter that much?" At sixteen it was not only decorative but functional to have a guy who owned a sports car, who was shy, intelligent, a humanitarian concerned about the welfare of the Aborigines. He was a Community Welfare Officer, the only eligible bloke in a small pastoral outback town. Yet he was a person she did not have to act for. What was important, vital, was that she could talk to him about anything. Anything you cared to mention.

Then one day she felt very strange, something funny had happened or was about to happen; she could feel it. It was the feeling that most Wongais feel when something unbearable is about to happen. This premonition has a function too. It softens the blow when it comes eventually, and somehow continues to control the gradual unfolding of a sad event so that you can cope with whatever it is—alone.

It was the day the Superintendent for Community Welfare hit town. Yes, he came to the dusty little town, feeling self-righteous and important in his double-breasted navy blue suit and tie, head held high, held towering above his dusty polished shoes. He could have been mistaken for a hollow nodding statue, walking mechanically with Don the Community Welfare Officer.

Don looked pensive, grave and silent from where she could see him, as she stood, stooping to peer under the awnings outside Elders-GM.

"I'm not to take you out any more—orders from high up—no reasons given."

She, her body, her mind, went blank, then one teletyped word appeared "WHY?": demanding a sane, logical, reasonable, enlightening answer.

But she knew the answers. The non-reasons were always swept under a carpet in some distant region of her mind.

The Boss spoke, rather confidently, the carpet lifted revealing ... "Don is a Community Welfare Officer, one of my boys. It is unwritten policy, law, rule, call it what you like; I can't do much about it I'm afraid. Yes, okay I admit, I had to find a reason after I jumped on you ... but, after all you are a native, and er the act states you are still a minor ... it's not good for the image to see a dark girl going around with a Welfare Officer. I'm not saying I agree with them. I can't disclose what I said to Don, you are a minor and you keep that in mind. Yes, I checked all this with the act. You will thank me later I bet, thank me for stopping all this before anything silly happened. You understand what I mean. Anyhow, you'll get over it, Don has my orders and it is now none of my business. So the matter is closed."

Some planning of a strategy to win any verbal battle with logic was contemplated before that meeting. It was futile to pursue all of them, she thought as she watched the lips, the mouth the teeth form words, non-words, between breaths, that heaved endlessly from the hollow cavity that was his mouth. She wondered if Don had tried, and had felt as alone as she did.

She had a name, yet the superintendent never used that name once in that agonising half hour as he sat fidgeting, with every little knob, in the grey government Holden, parked in a deserted car park that Sunday afternoon. She had a pair of eyes too, but the Boss never saw them.

Not until December last year. Those eyes saw the one-time Superintendent for Community Welfare, now with eyes greedy with power. A new party had just won the elections, he was now a prominent politician celebrating his party's victory and slightly drunk when he spotted her. He asked her friend, "Who is that dark girl over there—I've seen her somewhere before, is she a native? Oh! Of course! Ginn and I are very good friends." She saw him floating towards her, a minor not good for the image ... checked with the act ... You'll get over it ... dark girl ... had to find a reason. Unwritten policy.

Waterdogs

Jimmy Everett

We had moved to a farmhouse just on the outskirts of Morwell. We rented the house from an old lady, Mrs Bayliss, who lived nearby in the main farmhouse. Mrs Bayliss was short and wrinkled with a kindly face and she had guinea pigs and goats, the guinea pigs were in a pen in the backyard and the goats ran loose, they were forever chasing Barbara and me.

Not long after moving Mum enrolled me at the Morwell State School, and on my first day I remember swaggering proudly around the school's playground, and everyone seemed to be looking at me. One kid called me "Blacky" so I whopped him good, and the bigger kids all patted me on the back and called me mate, this made me swagger even more. My brother Eric, being six years older than me, had his own mates but it was easy for me to have some mates as long as I could fight and win.

School seemed to be another world which had no part in my real world at home with my family. At home everything was clear for me to understand, Mum would firmly detail our chores and duties, and reinforce the need for us to be clean and wear our boots. At night around the open fire Dad told us about all sorts of things he had seen that day, and eventually he and Mum would talk of the "islands".

Just listening to their talk made me see the wonderful things our island had, like tons of fish, all kinds, swan eggs, goose eggs, periwinkles, wild turkeys, muttonbirds?! Oh, well, Mum and Dad reckoned they were okay, so they must be.

Going to school eventually became an unhappy chore for me, somehow it seemed that I was different than the other kids. They were always saying I was dirty, but I knew that wasn't true. Anyway, such talk always led to me fighting some kid and it sort of made me feel better, especially as I seemed to win most times.

I don't remember having many mates at this school. Barbara was my mate at home, and I made believe I had a mate called Tommy. Tommy had "waterdogs".

Of course when Tommy was to be about, then I had to pretend I was him, mainly I tried to let only Mum and Dad know about Tommy, but Barbara knew too.

Tommy's waterdogs could do anything, they could fly, walk through fire and were strong as could be. Of course no-one even saw the waterdogs, excepting me; well Tommy, depending who I was. Dad used to make up all sorts of tall stories to put up obstacles for Tommy's waterdogs. We would spend hours trying to beat each other with stories of what could be done by the waterdogs and Dad's stories of what they couldn't do.

Sometimes I would be going to "work" with Barbara along the fence line when I would run back to our house and knock on the door, and when Mum would answer I would pretend to be Tommy and call Mum Mrs Everett.

Mum would know then that I was Tommy and we would talk about Jimmy and where he had gone. I would say good-bye and say I was going looking for Jimmy. Then I would run around the house and into the kitchen and be Jimmy again, looking for Tommy. Mum would tell me he had gone to look for me and I would go after Tommy.

It was sure funny.

Once "Tommy" told Dad that the waterdogs were going to go the bottom of the sea and find a big treasure for him so he could buy a new house and his own truck. Dad was sort of quiet for a minute then he said he reckoned the dogs would probably get eaten by a whale.

"Tommy" just laughed and said that his waterdogs could pick up any whale about and put it on the land where it couldn't do anything. Dad said that he knew of a whale so big nothing could lift it, and it loved to eat dogs, especially waterdogs.

Tommy insisted that there was nothing his waterdogs couldn't lift and they were far too fast for an old whale. And so the storytelling went on and on.

One day Barbara and I were "working" on the fence line when we saw a cow lying on its side. When we went close we could see that she was sick and couldn't get up.

We pulled grass out of the paddock and put it close for her to eat, but she didn't touch it, she was far too ill.

We didn't stay there very long, but went further along the fence line to get some blackberries. On the way back we came close to the cow and there were two men with her. One had a gun and we knew that they were going to shoot her. We quickly rounded up as many stones as we could and began to pelt the men, calling them names like "killers" and "devils".

One man chased after us and we ran home crying to Mum.

Mum sat with us next to our big water tank out back of the house and said that sometimes it was the best thing to do for sick animals. But Barbara and I were sure that the cow could be made well if only someone would try.

Then we heard the gunshot.

Later in the afternoon we went to look and saw that the man had piled a lot of brushwood onto the cow's body and set fire to it.

Barbara and I sat down together and cried and cried. After a while we got up and walked home feeling very sad about the day gone by.

Some time after this incident, Dad bought a truck to cart his pulp wood with and we all went for a ride, just to go riding in our own truck, a green cabin and bare frames with pins up the back to keep the wood on.

Well one day Dad drove into our yard after work and the yard had puddles of water everywhere because it had rained earlier. In came the truck and ran right over my toy truck I had left in the yard

Well! I was so wild about it that I took one long look at Dad and ran at a big puddle of water. Without hesitation I jumped in the air and came down flat on my back in the middle of the puddle, what a mess.

I looked at Dad as if to say "There, what about that then?" Dad just laughed but Mum put a switch across my backside and sent me to the laundry to undress and wash up. I was sent to bed early that night.

Another day, when it was nice and sunny, Dad has the truck parked in the backyard and I was out playing. Mrs Bayliss had a barn between our house and hers, and I would play there sometimes. This day I was half way to the barn when around the corner came Mrs Bayliss' goats, three of them. As soon as they spotted me they started to run at me, and I took off quick smart. Well Dad's truck was the nearest thing to run for, and I got there just before the goats and climbed onto the roof. One goat got right up onto the bonnet of the truck and could almost touch me. I was yelling and screaming for help and Dad came and chased the goats away with a broom.

I couldn't see what he had to laugh about though, I suppose it was funny to him but I didn't think so.

I was sure to keep an eye out for the goats after that I can tell you.

Laddie, in the meantime, was a little left out of things and one day a stray dog happened to settle on our place to live, probably because Laddie made a good mate. It was a black dog and really friendly, always wagging his tail and mooching around for pats on the back. We called him Blackie.

Well Blackie soon settled in and we made him welcome but one day he chased Dad's fowls, just to play I reckon. But he killed a couple of fowls and Dad was furious. After that he was kept on a chain most of the time, especially when the fowls were out to feed.

It happened that one day I had Laddie and Blackie with me; I was Tommy then and they were my watch-dogs. Well Blackie took after the fowls again when I wasn't looking and killed five of them. I was fair frightened of what Dad would say.

When he got home that night he didn't say much and I heard him talking to Mum in their bedroom in low voices.

When Dad came out he told me to take Blackie up the paddock and tie him to an old stump there. He said he would have to shoot Blackie.

Barbara and I both began to cry and pleaded with Dad not to, but he insisted. Dad said that Blackie could not be let free to run wild, not even on someone else's property and that it wouldn't be fair to Blackie to just dump him or keep him with us on a chain for all time. He said that it was the human thing to do.

That night we heard the shot and cried ourselves to sleep. Next morning we noticed Blackie's grave near the stump, Dad had put a wooden cross on it. Dad came and looked too and I could see the tears in his eyes and knew that Dad did some things even if he didn't like it. I forgave him in my thoughts right at that moment.

Some really good times on the farm were had like when we could help Mum cook scones and damper and eat them hot with heaps of butter and honey. Mum would say that "honey made you money" and we'd eat loads, then after eating we would look under our plates and there would always be a penny there for each of us.

At evening just on dark we usually had a bath or a good wash and got into our pyjamas before eating. Afterwards we would, as usually, sit in front of the big open fire and talk, and listen to Mum and Dad talk. And as usual talk would lead to the islands and we kids would ask lots of questions about things there. Our questions would be endless as our minds would be racing in a big fantasy and there was so much to know.

One night Barbara and I were playing out in the paddock when we heard Mum calling us for bath time. We were playing in the long grass and didn't want to go in just then.

Eventually Dad came out and began to call us, but we were hiding in the long grass and as the sun was very low he couldn't see us. A bit later Mum joined Dad and they were both calling out for us.

By this time both Barbara and I had realised that our hiding had gone beyond being a joke and we were now in a bit of trouble.

Mum and Dad were walking into the long grass, still calling us, and came quite close to me. As they got past me I jumped and said "BOO"!

Mum got a real fright and Dad laughed at the sight.

Mum didn't see the funny side of it and took Barbara and me by the ear and walked us to the house and put us in the bath.

Somehow I believe that Mum was sort of amused at our "trick" and that's why we didn't get a hiding, anyway, she was smiling at the tea table.

"Tommy and the Waterdogs" would sometimes go with Dad to get firewood for the house and of course talk was always on what the dogs could do.

During one of these trips Dad pointed to a big quarry just off the road and told "Tommy" that it would not be wise for him to take his "waterdogs" near there.

"That quarry's full of water Tommy," said Dad, "and there's a giant electric eel in there big enough to eat your waterdogs."

"Yeah"! said "Tommy", all awed and not having a quick answer to that one.

Later that day, after the wood was unloaded at the house, Tommy ran into the kitchen saying "G'day Mr Everett, where's Jimmy".

On being told that he had just gone looking for Tommy and the waterdogs, Tommy said, "Righto Mr Everett, I'll go see if I can find him", and headed out the door. Just before getting out of the door he quickly turned and said, "My waterdogs can beat that big electric eel anytime!" and he bolted real quick before Dad could answer him.

About that time I was prone to have a go at Dad's tobacco and one day Dad noticed that a whole packet of tobacco was missing from the truck cabin. Naturally he questioned me about it and I think I must have looked a bit guilty at the time.

So, my quick solution was to blame Tommy and the waterdogs. Dad didn't seem to believe that one but I told him that "Those damn dogs love a smoke and were always getting in the truck for a nap".

Some days later when "Tommy" happened to wander into the house to ask for me Dad quickly seized on the chance to ask about the tobacco.

"Tommy" said he knew nothing of it and if the waterdogs had done it he didn't know about it.

Dad told "Tommy" that if he caught "those damn waterdogs" he'd cut their tails off. Well Tommy ran out of the house quick smart, and you know, we never saw Tommy or those damn waterdogs ever again.

Old Cobraboor

Ellen Draper

By the early 1880s, Australia was getting to know the determination and the ruthlessness of the pioneering people. Through fire, drought and flood they fought to keep a hold on what little they had. A lot of the strong-hearted ones built and rebuilt and prospered. Some lost heart, packed up and went further out to find new heart and build again. Somewhere along the way, greed and callousness joined in. A handful of gold can turn the heart to cast all else aside. This story is based on such an instance. The true story was never written before because the shame of it prevented it from ever being disclosed.

The old black man sat very still on the fallen log. A tall, shady gum tree kept the sunlight from him. That suited his purpose. He had an old brown hat pulled down over his eyes and the clothes hung shabby on his thin black body. His trousers were held up with a string doubled round twice. His eyes were furtive, scanning the surrounding bushland for the slightest movement.

At last satisfied that no-one was near, he leaned over and started to dig at the root of a large gum tree. After a few moments he uncovered one of the largest gold nuggets this country will ever see. He chipped some smaller nuggets from it and put these into a small leather bag which he shoved into his pocket. Quickly he buried the nugget and smoothed over the ground. Old Cobraboor was short of tobacco and tucker so he went into town to get more supplies.

For six weeks or more this old black man had been using the gold nugget to keep himself in money between rations. He had hidden it at the foot of this big gum tree and only he knew where it was hidden. The tree was marked by a small tomahawk embedded at the top of the first branch. He only had to go to the tree which held the tomahawk and he had the right one. The bushland around him was very shrubby, thick grass and vines grew well over knee-high, taller in some places.

Three miles away, down along the creek, was an Aboriginal camp. About one or two hundred people lived in it, counting the ones living nearer town as well. Where they came from no-one knew. Old Cobraboor knew very little about them and they knew even less of him, yet he lived with them and shared his tobacco with them. He always gave them flour and such-like whenever they needed it, especially before rations day.

On this particular day, old Cobraboor was heading for the town of Talcum, walking like always. Talcum wasn't such a big town: a one-horse town, in fact (although horses were the main transport of the day!). It consisted of one post office, the pub and police station and courthouse combined. The main road ran right through it, mostly used by Cobb and Co. coaches.

The blacks' camp was about five or six miles up the creek and well in the bush. At various times the women and girls would do some housework for the station further out, walking to and from work. A handful of blacks could be found most times lounging under the hotel's striped awnings. Some would be asleep. Others would be just sitting and staring at nothing yet seeing everything. It was to this hotel old Cobraboor sold his gold pieces.

The Assayer's office was combined inside by the owner who, between serving drinks, bought and sold gold and tin, sometimes hides as well. About half-past two on this Tuesday in April, 1885, old Cobraboor walked into town, his sugarbag rolled up under his arm, pulled up at the pub's door and shook the dust from his clothes with his old brown hat. Then he breasted the bar where the mining office was set up, partitioned off from the main bar by glass. The owner knew old Cobraboor and knew that he always brought good stuff when he came in to sell.

There were seven men sitting at a table in the corner of the pub pretty near the doorway. They all had very gloomy expressions on their faces. Apparently things weren't going right for them. They had met for a drink and to discuss each others' problems. All wore the same type of working clothes: dungarees, flannel shirts and high-heeled leather boots. They all sported beards except for big Cec Beal and George Crearly who were both clean-shaven and very tanned from working in the open.

"Well, I'm packing it in this time for good," said Les Somers, tilting his chair back. "I'm busted, flat broke, just can't seem to make a go of it with my place somehow."

"Same here," said Edmund Connors. "My plough broke yesterday and I've only just started ploughing too. Can't get another loan, haven't paid off the old one yet. Besides it'll be too late to start by the time a new one gets here. I'm buggered for money too."

"Us too," said George Crearly. "Me and old Jim here are thinking of chucking everything up and shooting through to the goldfields down south. Might strike it rich there. Who knows?"
Jim Collinswood nodded in agreement.

"Yeah," he said.

"Yeah, I think I'll chuck it in too," said Fitzwilliams. "Nothing much around without dough."

Frank Mackay got up and gathered the glasses for another round of drinks. He walked over to the bar just as an old black man walked through the hotel's door. As Mackay stood at the counter, the black man was next to him, on the other side of the glass, also waiting to be served.

"Hiya Cobra," said the bartender as he came into the room and spotted the old man at the counter. Ruben Georges was a big friendly man with a black beard and a paunch. He wore a striped long-sleeved shirt, brown corduroy breeches and black boots. A big white apron completed the picture.

"What have we there eh?' Georges asked Cobraboor.

"More tobacco, some flour and some matches too," replied old Cobraboor. "Some other tucker too."

"Righto then, me lad. Let's have a look at what you have today," said Ruben Georges, taking the small bag old Cobraboor passed over to him. The gold nuggets fell into the scales, catching Frank Mackay's eyes. All thought of drink left his mind.

"Top weight mate," said Ruben Georges "You've got some good stuff wherever this came from."

The old man just nodded his head and waited patiently to get paid. Mackay's eyes slanted as he watched the gold being weighed and locked away. He saw Georges hand over some money and speak to old Cobra.

"Sit down here, Cobra, and I'll soon have your order done for you. Same as usual I suppose eh?"

"Some more flour and a pot of black paint and some roofing nails."

"Hey Peter," shouted Ruben to someone in the back room. "Do an order for old Cobraboor will you and add some roofing nails, and a tin of black paint. See that he gets plenty of tobacco as well."

Only then did Ruben Georges set to do Frank Mackay's order for drinks.

It was a very quiet and thoughtful Frank Mackay who sat back down at the table and handed the glasses to the men. The men noticed their mate's frowning face.

"What's up, Frank?" asked Les Beal. "Looks like you lost a tenner and found sixpence."

Everyone laughed.

"I'll tell you in a minute, just keep on talking," said Mackay under his breath, all the while watching the old black man awaiting his order. The men noticed his interest, but didn't say anything, just kept on drinking and talking. Goodness knows they had seen him often enough over the past weeks or so. Old Cobraboor, someone said his name was.

Ruben Georges brought the sugar bag out chocka-block and gave it to old Cobra, who gave a small nod and walked out, heading home.

Frank Mackay turned to his mates and spoke.

"Saunter out front casually and I'll let you in on something."

With this he slowly got up and walked outside. The others drifted out and leaned against the hotel's rails.

"See that old coot there walking?" Mackay asked. The others nodded.

"Well what he just put over that counter in there was the prettiest little sight I've ever seen. What he had was gold nuggets and top weight at that too."

Jim Collinswood whistled. "Gold eh? What'll I give for a strike now?"

"Why not find out his strike instead?" Mackay said.

The men stared at him. Big Ed Connors spoke up as he lit a cigarette.

"Well for a start, that gold could do a heap for me, If I had it that is."

"Yeah," said Somers, "I could do up my place real good and restock it too. Why should we stand back with nothing when these blacks have what we want, I ask you?"

Old Cobraboor was out of sight of the town now which is what Mackay was waiting for.

"Let's take a ride, boys and see where he heads to," Mackay told them as he made for his horse.

"Could be he might be persuaded to show us his gold mine."

They all sauntered over to where their horses were tethered and mounted up. With a nod from Mackay they rode off up the road following the old black man.

Cobraboor, on getting out of sight of the town, quickly took to the bush and once enfolded in its changing shadows he moved as quickly as possible carrying his load. It was well that he did. Hoof beats were coming his way along the road. He froze and looked back.

"Those men at the pub," Cobraboor said to himself, "I seen one of them watching me at the counter. Now he's told his mates of my gold and maybe looking for me. They might do me harm so I must hide."

He quickly threw his bag under some sticks and bushes and hid himself out of sight.

The horsemen went by making straight for the camp. They were looking for him but couldn't seem to find him at all. They must have passed two or three times before finally going on to the blacks' camp up along the creek.

"Probably seen us coming and hid," said Williams.

Crearly spoke out. "Wonder where that old coot got to."

"Anyway let's go to the camp. They'll know something or should," said Mackay.

"Yeah, come on," said Williams and they spurred their horses a bit faster.

The camp was made up of tin shacks, old humpies and lean-tos with bits of bags and old blankets hung at the doorways. Some had bark walls and roofs. It was a pretty big camp with a handful of mongrel dogs here and there. It was very quiet. Probably everyone was asleep or cooking and suchlike. Across the creek was a large cattle pen, high and built with roughly hewn boards. It had only one entrance and some trees still stood in the yard. The creek itself was very low and just barely running. There hadn't been any rain now for months. There was a drought on.

The mongrel dogs spotted the horsemen as they rode into camp and didn't they go mad! People came out of doorways to see what was happening. The horsemen pulled up in the middle of camp. Curious eyes watched them as they gave the camp a good looking over before dismounting.

"Gooday to you there," said Mackay as everyone crowded together. Kids hung onto their mothers' skirts.

"Gooday, gooday," some answered. Others just nodded their heads.

"What do you want here?" asked an old man who stepped in front of the crowd.

"Well that could depend on what you got here," replied Mackay. Crearly leaned over, put his face right in front of the old man's.

"Yeah," he said, "got any more of that shiny stuff around?"

"Shiny stuff?" the old man said.

"Gold man, gold," explained Crearly.

"No gold here," the old man said. "Nothin' much here at all, let alone gold."

"Where does that old bird get his gold from to come into town?" Mackay said.

"Old man?" they asked. "No-one's got any gold here. "

"Don't tell me that," bounced Mackay. "I was right in the pub today when he walked in with a fist full of gold nuggets. Old Cobraboor you call him."

The old man nodded and said, "Must have been Cobraboor you seen. He always go to town more times than us. He stays with us. We don't mind him. He always gives us tobacco when we get short before ration day."

"Which is his camp?" asked Jim Collinswood, "I'll take a look-see. Might be somethin' in it there."

"Over there," the old man replied, pointing to a bagged shack, slightly away from all the other shacks.

Collinswood and Crearly walked over to the shack and tore the blanket from the doorway. Then they started searching through his belongings. Pots and pans were thrown out, blankets and bedding was ripped about. The place was a pure shambles but they did not come across anything indicating gold in the place.

"Nothing here," they shouted.

Mackay looked back to his men then he looked at the group of blacks all bunched together. He gave them a long hard stare then he shouted, "Somers and Williams, you two get your rifles and guard these fellas and the rest of you search the camp and take your guns with yas."

Williams and Somers quickly got their rifles and stood guard while Mackay, Crearly, Beal, Collinswood and Connors went through the camp. They tore down the doorways, overturned water drums and buckets. One woman ran to her baby from the hut but was knocked down by Mackay. The baby was thrown out with the rest of the stuff. A frightened moaning came from the terrified blacks as fear began to creep into them. After a final thorough search they realised there wasn't any gold in the camp. Mackay walked over to the crouching people and prodded one or two in the back with his rifle.

"There's gold here and we want it and you people know where it is and by Jesus you're going to tell us where it is or by jingo I'll wring every one of your bloody black necks."

The poor black beggars were really frightened by now and started whimpering and kept on saying, "No gold, there's no gold here."

"Hey!" shouted Connors. "Let's send them across the creek to that cattle yard over there and really give them a working over."

"Yeah, yeah," shouted Beal in agreement. "Come on, up you get."

They all started to prod the blacks across the creek like cattle into a big cattle pen. Making sure that all the blacks were in the yard, the one entrance was locked securely, Mackay leaned over the rails and spoke once more.

"Are you going to tell us where the gold is or are we to kill you one by one before you own up to us?"

The prisoners just shook their heads and stood there staring up at them as their guns were pointing at them from various points of the yard.

"Then let her rip," shouted Mackay and started shooting.

Shots and cries rang out simultaneously and wailing broke out. Men, women and children were given no quarter. They ran round the blockade trying to get away from these terrible men. Finally, through the dust and noise, Mackay called a halt to the carnage and the shooting stopped.

"There's still some standing. We'll be back tomorrow to finish them off."

Blood-strewn bodies lay everywhere. A young boy cried out for his mother then lay still. Another gave a choking cry and then no more. Those not dead were slowly picking themselves up out of the mess and dust, too shocked and wounded to make any effort to get away. For what was once a lively bushland, not one bird called out. It was as if they all watched what went on and hid in their nests with shame.

The dust was still flying and couldn't seem to settle and the sun finally called a halt to the day. Night time came quiet and deathly. A cricket chirped here and there.

Out among the bodies on the ground, a figure stood up, looked around, then took on a crouch and began to move over to the pen's railing. It was a girl of about eight or nine who with, all the cunning and patience of her ancestors, played dead when the shooting began. She fell down and laid there till all was quiet. She didn't know how long she laid there but now was the time she felt to escape. She slowly walked around the pen here and there. Huddled figures could be seen in the dark. Some low moans came from those that lay on the ground. She closed her mind's eye to the pitiful sight in front of her. The only thought she had was to escape. She must get away in case those terrible men came back and started again. Get away, get away, she must get away. She walked partly stooped over in case one of the men was still out there. There must be some way out of these high walls. It was in the corner of the pen—a partly broken board had come loose. She pulled it back and it left just enough room for her to squeeze through. Quickly she crawled out and melted into the night. She never went to the camp but took to the bush and kept on going. She knew there was another blacks' camp some distance away and once there she would be safe. She would always remember what happened here and it will be locked in her heart forever.

Morning came bright and clear as Mackay and his savages rode back across the creek to finish off their dirty work. They had a night of rough drinking and were in the mood for another skirmish like yesterday. They dismounted and walked into the cattle pen. Only Beal and Connors carried rifles. The others thought they wouldn't need them.

There were still quite a lot of blacks alive and the drunken men started hollering and shouting. They started grabbing the prisoners and shooting them. Others they smashed up against the tree trunks. Some they just stomped into the ground.

While this was going on, a party of horsemen rode up, attracted by the gun shots and noise. Seeing the carnage in front of them, one man fired several shots into the air. Mackay and his men stopped their dirty work and stared at the horsemen as they rode into the yard.

"Oh my God! What the hell have you done here?" the boss cried. "God, what an unholy mess."

He was Cecil Dennis, a big man dressed in corduroys and boots and sporting a black beard.

He quickly got together two of his men and trained their guns on Mackay's party and disarmed the two with guns. He and his four other men quickly went around to see if anyone was alive at all. One of the party vomited at the sight and could hardly look without tears in his eyes. All were killed: babies and young children as well. Dennis walked back to where the prisoners stood.

To Mackay he said, "I've seen you men in town lots of times—even had a drink or two with you all. How could you do a thing like this? How could you bring yourself to do this to these poor people? What harm did they do? Why?"

Turning to one of his men he told him to bring the horses belonging to Mackay and his men.

"I'm placing you and your foul party under charge and I'm taking you into town to the police station. They will deal with you there," he said. He added one final word before moving off.

"You deserve to hang for this," he said.

Quickly their hands were tied behind their backs and they were seated on their horses. Then they were strung out in single file, a rope string leading from one horse to the other.

"Don't try to escape or you may be shot," said Dennis and the other men.

The cavalcade then moved off towards the township of Talcum. Who were in town shopping all stopped what they were doing and rushed out curious to see why these men were tied up and under guard by big Cec Dennis. The prisoners and their guards pulled up in front of the jail house and dismounted.

The jail only contained one cell block and office and one policeman on duty all the time. Sergeant James Burns acted as policeman, jailer and JP. Also he recorded all births and deaths in his district. He watched as Dennis marched the prisoners into the office and his face went ashen when he heard what had happened. He walked over and opened the cell door and said to Dennis' men, "Lock em in here and place some of the men to guard the jail. I'll go out and have a look at the place. Some of you men get picks and shovels: we'll have to bury them where they are."

Burns got someone to saddle a horse for him and quickly gathered a notebook and pen. When he was ready he followed Dennis and the townsfolk out to the creek.

The sight that met Burns' eyes was one of total destruction. Little children lay with their heads smashed open and shot away, broken limbs and bloodied battered bodies lay like carpet in the cattle pen. Burns wrote down everything as he seen it. He estimated that there were two hundred or three hundred bodies. Even dogs were slaughtered. When he had finished, Burns turned away quickly. "Bury them and bury them deep," he said. "Perhaps it may be forgotten in the years to follow, but I won't be forgetting it, not for a long time, not for a long long time."

For two days and nights men worked digging and burying. Already the stench was too much. Rags were wrapped about their faces as they worked. The clergyman of the only church in town said prayers upon prayers. He was only a young man and this was the first big burial he ever presided at. So distraught was he, he put aside the Bible and started to help with digging and burying. He thought he served God better this way than talking to someone who couldn't hear.

Mackay, Crearly, Connors, Somers, Williams, Beal and

Collinswood were charged with the murder of these Aborigines and were sent to trial at Sydney. The Cobb and Co. coach was ordered to take them, under the guard of Sergeant Burns and sixteen other men, to Sydney.

There, they were placed in separate cell blocks and, two days after admittance, were brought before the court. They were handed over to an English judge and jury in a trial which took only forty eight hours.

Standing before the judge, Mackay's party, one by one, gave an account of the incident.

"Something had to be done about them. We couldn't turn our backs lest a spear flew for us and they killed all our stock. Somers here had all his stock killed. Now he's broke and can't get finance."

"That's right," spoke up Williams. "You couldn't go out to the plough. There'd be a dozen blacks or more nearby to let you have it."

Each man gave his version in turn, then Burns gave his evidence as prosecutor. The defence counsel asked for freedom for the men on the grounds that ownership of property must be protected, that this is a new land and a man must fight to keep what is his. The jury was out of the room for only ten minutes when they brought in the verdict. The spokesman for the jurymen spoke to the court.

"Your Honour, we feel that these men standing before this court acted in the only way they could. We value any man's property and we stand behind any man willing to make a go of his land. Therefore we find these men not guilty."

A loud cheering broke out among Mackay's men as they slapped each other on the backs. Crearly and Williams gave a "coo-ee" and shook hands with the defence counsel and jurymen. Outside on the courthouse steps, Mackay and his men looked around themselves. They were still cheering. They were free, free to go back home and start again. All that travelling knocked it out of them and now they needed something to bolster them up. Their money, whatever the amount was, was returned to them. They spotted an hotel across from the courthouse and they made straight for it.

The city of Sydney was bustling with activity. Even here were Aborigines. Some wore the native paint and the only thing some wore belonging to the white man was the bowler hat. Many wore those. Some of the women even tried to dress up like the white ladies. Large hats and balloon dresses with trouble painted on their faces. A convict train moved down through the streets under guard. It was carrying large timber beams to the wharf to be shipped out.

The men breezed into the hotel's lounge and sat down on a table separated from another by a wall. At the other table, a group of men in the uniform of the governor sat at their meal. They looked at the men as they sat down noisily, still laughing at the court's proceedings. Beal and Somers was clapping each other on the back while Crearly and Mackay lit up cigars which somebody had given Mackay as they left the court. Williams began to grin as he leaned back in the seat.

"What a court," he said. "All this way for nothing just to be let off."

"They didn't know nothin'. These English courts are tough, Burns said to me," Connors was saying.

"Nah, we breezed through that one. They're not that tough," Mackay said.

"They could have made it a bit tougher for us. Ha ha ha. Not let us get away with it that easy," laughed Collinswood as he held up his hand to a passing waiter.

The gentlemen in the next seat heard every word said and two of them stood up and walked around to face Frank Mackay and the men. The others sat in their seats watching what was about to happen.

"So you think these English courts are not good enough for you gentlemen?"

This question startled Mackay and the others. They looked up to see who spoke. The uniformed man in front of them was asking them a question. He was dressed in the black and white uniform of the Governor's men and also he was a judge and administrator of Australian affairs.

"I ask you again, gentlemen, did you think this English court was too easy on you?"

Thinking there was no harm in it, considering they had already got out of it, Beal openly laughed again.

"Hah, they can't hurt us again. It's over now."

"Do you think so, gentlemen?" spoke up the administrator's

companion, a lieutenant of some sort. He had a stripe so he must have been important to stand with this other uniformed gentleman.

"This gentleman is Sir Nevil McKenzie, Judge and Administrator of Australian Affairs," the young man said, "and I am Assistant Controller to the Australian Police Force. Apparently you wasn't satisfied with the results of the court this morning. Perhaps you may be satisfied with an Australian court tomorrow. Arrest these men and lock them up. I'll make immediate arrangements for a new trial. Frankly I wasn't satisfied with the way the court went. This calls for justice and if we are lying side by side with these people of this country then we must be fair in all things."

This was the longest speech this young Malcolm F. Lubeck ever spoke but he spoke with feeling and sincerity. Police were called for and the men were locked up once again.

"Hey, you can't do this to us," Mackay said. "We were tried once and got out free. You can't do us again."

"No," countered Sir Nevil McKenzie. "You yourself said you weren't satisfied with the court's proceedings. You said they went too easy on you."

"See how you fare in our own court, gentlemen," said the young Lubeck.

Still protesting and arguing Mackay and the other men were locked up and arrangements for a new trial began. On the following day, the first day of the new trial, the men were brought before a judge and jury made up of all the Australian citizens. Burns once again acted as prosecutor. He explained once again how he went out and saw what the accused had done to so many poor ignorant black people, the carnage, the bloodshed. He never left out one bit of evidence and demanded the full penalty for such a wrong. Knowing they shot their mouths off too soon the accused men started to lie their way out. They said they only killed the blacks in retaliation for what they did to their properties and stock. They said they only did what others would have done if their homes was in constant attack from these savages. After summing up the case the jury went out and then the verdict was brought in. The men stood watching the juryman as he spoke. They all had grins on their faces. They were sure they would walk out again just like last time.

"Guilty your Honour," said the juryman. "We could not let this most foul deed go by only to be repeated somewhere else. The useless slaughter of so many young lives was not called for. Therefore, we ask for the full penalty for such a deed."

The Judge looked to the men and spoke in a low tone.

"Gentlemen I feel that the sentence I put on you this day is justified for the case and will bring together a feeling of bondmanship between the two races. The white settlers to this land and the black people who own this land. Therefore I sentence you Frank Mackay, Leslie Beal, George Crearly, Leslie Frederick Somers, Bill Williams, Edmund Connors and James Collinswood, at four o'clock this Thursday, Eighteenth of March, 1885 to hang by the neck until you are dead. May God have mercy on your souls."

The judge stepped down and walked out of sight. The men were locked up and shocked into such silence, they could not utter a word. Nobody saw them hanged and nobody saw them buried. On that Thursday a priest was seen going in and after a while he departed and went his way.

Mission Truck

M. Thorne

It was hay-cutting time and all the Aborigines were camped alongside the roadside because it was miles to the nearest reserve, and they daren't make a camp in the fields for fear of the cattle bulls. Children were screaming everywhere, not because they were being hit, but because their mothers were washing and dressing them and getting them ready; it was Sunday and the church people were coming out to teach them about God and the Bible. Actually they were all excited, even the adults, who love to listen and sing the hymns with the elderly churchman, his wife and young son. The man would play his accordion, it was beautiful to see everyone at peace singing under the gum trees and she-oak trees as if they never had a care in the world. Someone called out just down the road. "They're coming. They're coming." The excitement grew, mothers were calling the children to come and sit down and get ready for the visitors.

As the vehicle grew near enough for them to see, their peace and happiness was shattered, and fear took over. You could see it on their faces as they were running here, there and everywhere crying out, *"ali-wah* (mission truck), *ali-wah*, run hide. Run or they'll get you and take you to the mission." People scattered. Only the men who had already been told they had jobs on the chaff cutter stayed behind. Some of the old people and children who couldn't run stayed. The mission truck pulled onto the roadside.

Out jumped the man who ran the mission about eighty miles away. He and his helpers stood outside the truck, which was a cattle truck provided for him to pick the Aborigines; no matter who, old, young, married people and their families. They all had to be cleaned up. Cleaned up meant that they were taken to the mission. Lots of people who were taken there tried to get out or run away, only to be hunted down and returned to a life they all hated and could do nothing about. They only ran away from a place they did not ask to be taken to in the first place. The men ran around like mad until they got a few people into the mission truck. They were all crying and sitting in the cattle truck.

A short while after they had left, the people started to come back, where they found out whose family and friends were taken away. They all sat in a heap and cried. They were still crying when the church people arrived. When everyone had settled down and told them everything that had happened, the church people said, "Come brothers and sisters, let us pray that one day soon you will all be free."

Well, life went on in the camp, but they were always on the alert. Finally the work was finished and everyone moved on. Some went to another job on the farms, and others went back to their native reserves. The camps were round huts made of bags, tents if they could afford them or just wind-breaks made of bushes. After all, the men were paying for their rations on the few pounds they made. With their few pounds, the men would give most to the women, except a few bob to buy their tobacco papers and matches. The men would buy food consisting of a bag of flour, potatoes, onions, tinned milk, butter, sugar, tea and salt. They were the main items of food until the next job. There was plenty of kangaroo and rabbit, but you had to go out and catch them. They couldn't afford any luxuries. Lots of women would buy material and make clothing for their children, and one or two dresses for themselves.

The Aborigines did not drink because they were not allowed any alcohol. Not that they could afford it anyway. They couldn't even afford to buy enough bedding, mattresses they never had. Mothers, fathers and their children slept in a bed made up on the ground. The women would sew a bag with needle and twine. This was called a *wagga*, and it was used to make a tent, a round hut or a blanket to keep them warm. The *wagga* was also used to make a shower or bathroom, even a toilet. The shower was made by putting a tin tub with a tin overhead and having the *wagga* around, and for their toilet they'd dig a hole, put in a square kerosene tin with a handle on, so they could get it out to empty, they'd make a make-shift seat from fork limbs of a tree and the bag around. The water was carried from a nearby dam if anyone would allow them to take it. It was very hard at night, the adults would gather around a big camp fire telling yarns. The children sat around listening too. Or else they would make a big camp fire and have a dance, dust flying everywhere, or they would just have a sing-song. Fights between the adults, men and women, were settled with the opponents using a ring of people. When the fight was over the opponents would shake hands and all was forgotten. Children were told to obey their elders.

The Aborigines moved from place to place, farm to farm, clearing fields, post cutting, root picking, wool sorting or just farm work. Men, women and children, you name it they did it; but no matter where they were and what they were doing, they stuck together and made the most of their hard lives. They had to be out of town by dark. After a time the Aborigines were granted exemptions, only by going to court and proving that they were good enough. If they did get it, then the holder of the card was allowed to go to the pub and have a couple of glasses, but they were not to buy any bottles, for fear of supplying their fellow men. That would mean jail. The bearer of the permit was supposed to be able to have a glass of cool drink or a meal in cafés, but a few with exemption cards still weren't served.

Time went by and the mission truck stopped coming, and the men and their families moved around a bit more freely. Then, from the Exemptions Bill came the Citizenship rights. Quite a few men and women were granted Citizenship in their own country, hard to believe, but it is true. Then finally there came full granting of equal rights for Aborigines from the Labor Government. At first they were afraid to go in the bars because they didn't know what to ask for. In the cafés Aborigines didn't know whether to sit at a table for fear of being told that they weren't allowed, same with the picture theatre. After a while they did get the idea, and it was good to sit at a table without being told, "You, you're not allowed, you can't eat here. Get off the street!" The Aborigines will never forget these things. Now they didn't have to use their *wagga* bags or carry water from dams or wells or sleep on the ground. Now that they were free to move around or live in a house they got a few luxuries.

White Fantasy — Black Fact

Jack Davis

The bus driver was tired. He had been awakened several times during last night's hot summer hours, by the crying of the baby. His wife Anne had walked around with the child seemingly for hours. He hoped she had taken the child around to the Clinic today. After all it was the first summer of the child's existence, and it was really hot. Really hot.

The bus churned along the narrow bitumen road. He heard the slap, slap of the overhanging branches of roadside gums on the rooftop of the bus. His gaze fitted automatically to the approaching bus stop. He slowed the bus, but seeing nobody on the seat, he pushed the gear lever in a quick interchange of movement between foot on clutch pedal and hand on gear lever. The bus growled and surged ahead, sweeping back onto the centre of its laneway.

His mind slid back to the baby. They had called it Peggy Sue after Anne's mother. Anne had been so grateful when he had agreed with the name of their first child, Peggy Sue. He wondered what she would be like when she grew up. He knew she would be pretty. Blonde haired, blue eyed, and with a nice figure. Both him and Anne were well-built. He wondered what she would be character-wise. Anne was a calm practical even-tempered person. While he was almost the complete opposite. He hated untidiness, people with loud voices. He disliked violence, cruelty to animals. Both he and his wife sent money to overseas missions. He thought of the starving millions in Asia, and the resultant death and disease. Cholera, hook worm, sleeping sickness. His mind flitted through the explanatory brochures that he recalled to his mind, which were sent to him and his wife by the overseas mission people. He was glad that he lived in a country that was white, where there was plenty for all, where nobody starved, and everyone was equal. He saw the next bus stop ahead of him and he imperceptibly guided the bus off the bitumen.

As he drew almost level with the stop he saw the small group of people. There were eight of them.

One man of indeterminate age, but old, was drunk and coughing, softly but violently. The paroxysms of his coughing shook his bony frame. He was accompanied by a man and woman and five children. The man was also affected by liquor. They were all scruffily dressed and untidy, and a faint whiff of body odour wafted into the interior of the empty bus. The bus driver stared blankly as the small group began gathering their belongings. The old man, his coughing subsiding into sporadic bursts, staggered forward and placed one hand on the bus door. The bus driver looked at the gnarled brown dirty broken finger-nailed hand. He had a mad kaleidoscopic vision of unparalleled sickness right there within the bus.

He thought of little Peggy Sue, her fair skin scabrous with sores. He thought of Anne her body broken, lying in the back-yard. He thought this must not happen, this cannot be. The old man began to heave himself onto the bus, the others ready to climb aboard behind him. The bus driver bent forward and spoke hoarsely, "You are not allowed on this bus, let go the door." The old man glowered at him, replying, "Why aren't I?" The woman lifted her head and stared at the bus driver, she spoke loudly, shrilly. "Why ain't we allowed, we're people ain't we?" The other man evidently her husband chipped in, saying: "Driver you can't stop us from gettin' on that bus. We got money don't worry about us," he opened his hand to show a crumpled two dollar note.

The bus driver rose from his seat and pushed the old man's hand quickly, but firmly, from the frame of the door and then grasping the lever he closed the door. He wrenched the gear stick downwards, and the engine snarled as if in protest against the unexpected call for power. The bus lurched back onto the bitumen sending a cloud of dust and leaves over the little Aboriginal group left standing at the side of the road.

Molly looked at the rapidly receding bus, tears of angry frustration in her eyes. She had to get the baby to the children's hospital that afternoon. She glanced at Peter, her husband, and the old man, her grandfather. She harangued them angrily, her voice rising high above their denunciation of the bus driver. "I told you to stop drinking," she said. "Now if the baby misses her appointment you'll be the one to blame, not the bus driver."

She looked at the long stretch of bitumen, it would be hours before another one traversed the road. The baby began to cry. Molly looked at the four other children. Three were her own. The eldest, Katey, a child of eight, was a parentless stray belonging to some distant relation who through circumstances had become part of her and Peter's brood. She had not wanted to bring them on the long journey from Geraldton to Perth. But as she had no one to leave them with she had been forced to bring them. They also had to bring the old man, grandfather Joshua. It had been his pension day when they had left Geraldton, and his money was needed to assist the group on the long journey. The old HR Holden had travelled well. But near Caversham in attempting a short cut to Guildford it had given up the mechanical ghost.

Peter and Joshua had pushed the car on to the side of the road. After gathering their essential belongings (Joshua carefully retrieved his remaining flagon) and locking the rickety doors, the small group had made their way to the Guildford road and the nearest bus stop. Two-years-old Tandy began whimpering for water. Molly surmised there would be water in the small creek some 159 metres down the road. The old man and Peter lay in the shade. She looked at them in disgust, disregarding her husband's half-hearted offer to obtain water. She emptied the collection of half-eaten food from a can and with the baby on her hip, and the children following, she made her way down the road where a small trickle of weed-covered water meandered slowly under a culvert then through the paddock bordering the road.

Molly and the children stood at the edge of the culvert. She looked dubiously down the sloping reed-covered bank. She spoke softly to Katey, "Looks like you'll have to get the water Katey Doll." The eight-year-old stepped forward eager to help. With the can in her hand she slithered agilely down the bank, her mother and the other children calling directions and encouragement. Katey stepped into the mud her feet making delicious squelching sounds as she wriggled her toes in its coolness. She looked up at the small group above her, white teeth flashing, brown eyes full of merriment, enjoying her endeavours. She stepped toward the roof of the culvert where the water underneath was cleaner, deeper. She placed one slim hand on the woodwork to steady herself, and glanced to find a place to grasp the culvert ledge.

Then for one terror filled second her fingers were a fraction of an inch away from the snake. Her reflexes were instant, but even as she snatched her hand away, it struck, and with such blinding speed and force that its fangs became embedded in the back of her tiny hand, and swinging off balance, Katey Doll screamed and flung the snake in an arc, where it landed some two metres away. Then slithering in the water it vanished among the reeds. Molly saw it all as if in slow motion. She tried to call out but her voice choked off. With the baby in her arms she leapt down the bank. She grabbed the trembling Katey who stood frozen clutching her hand to her crotch. Her eyes were enormous, dilated with fear. "Mummy," she cried, "it bit me, it bit me. Will I die? Oh, Mummy will I die?" And realising the horror and the enormity of it all, the woman and the child screamed together.

Peter heard the screaming. With one leap he was standing on the road. He saw the way the children were running towards him, something was amiss. "Gawd," he muttered. "What's happened?" he ran. Upon reaching the culvert he sprang down the bank grabbing Katey. He saw the two long tips in the skin of her hand. He did not hesitate. He pulled the now mute child to a sitting position, and knelt beside her and gripping her wrist tightly, he began sucking hard and deep over the ragged perforations.

Joshua stood on the road, looking at them aghast. Molly handed the baby up to him. She struggled up the bank, calling to the old man. "If a car comes flag it down." Even as she spoke they heard the hum of an approaching vehicle. Molly standing on the road stood waving her hands frantically. The car came fast. Behind it another. Molly screamed her plea. "Stop! Please! Help! Help!" Both cars roared past, the drivers looking at them with the curious detached look of the unconcerned.

Molly sank on her knees and cried, "O God, please help us." The children were all crying. Peter began pulling the trembling Katey up the bank, still endeavouring to suck the poison from the small frail body.They all knelt at the side of the road. They heard the purr of an engine. Joshua thrust the baby into Molly's arms. He stood almost in the centre of the road, his arms waving wildly. Molly breathed a gasping sigh of relief as she saw the car slow to a crawl. It came opposite the old man, who stepped forward to speak to the driver. Then with a screech of tortured tyres it leaped forward, and an epithet, mingling with the sound of laughter, sprang at them like barbed wire from the interior of the speeding car. The old man stood crouched at the side of the road crying hoarsely, "Aw, you bastards, you bloody, rotten mongrel bastards!" Tears of anger flowed down his thin cheeks.

It was obvious now that the poison and shock were having an effect on Katey Doll, her eyes were closed, her breathing shallow, and a small trace of vomit lingered at the corner of her mouth. Peter knew he had to keep her awake. He shook the child hard, her head, arms and legs were marionette like, limp and flaccid. The old man crouched on the road verge, his voice keeping low, in the beginning of a death chant. Molly turned to him and said fiercely, "Stop that! Do you hear me? She can hear you and that'll make her worse." Suddenly, the little group became aware of a sound, a strange almost frightening sound. Now the noise was around them. The motor bikes were black and gleaming and the riders helmeted, goggled and dressed in black leather. The whole thirty of them has the skull and crossbones emblem stenciled on their jackets. The roar of the bikes began to lessen, becoming staccato as if wolf-like they had to snap and snarl at one another. A thin blonde-haired youth was the first to dismount from his machine and he spoke to the frightened Molly. "What's wrong lady? Are you havin' trouble?" Pointing to the tableau of Peter and Katey Doll, Molly replied "My, my little girl, snake bite!" The youth swore softly and and yelled: "Christ, where's the Doc? Get him someone, this kid's been bitten by a bloody snake."

A towering red-headed, red-bearded giant of two metres or more threaded his way swiftly through the mass of machines, he knelt beside the exhausted Peter sucking the back of the girl's hand. He clasped one huge paw on Katey Doll's wrist and spoke softly to Peter, "Come on let's have a look, mate." There were calls from the riders now watching intently. "How she doin' Red Doc?" The man called "Red Doc" (two years at medical school had given him that unofficial title) gently picked up the child. He spoke quickly, quietly. "We have to move fast. Go Bo, Slit Eyes, get going to the nearest phone box, and ring for an ambulance. Tell them to bring anti-venom and to meet us on the northern highway to Perth Hospital."

Three bikes leapt to life and with a full-throated roar, they swept down the road in a blinding acceleration of rising speed. Big Red Doc climbed onto his enormous Harley with Katey Doll cradled in his arms, her hand with a tourniquet applied, suspended by a belt tied around his neck. He looked at Peter, grinned and said, "Right mate, on the back." Red Doc spoke to the others. "OK you guys, you organise getting a car and get the rest of these people into town, better bring them to the hospital."

A half dozen of the bikies with Joshua and the children sat in the waiting room. Everybody was tense not knowing how Katey Doll was faring. The doctors had guessed correctly that the snake was a death adder, usually fatal. They saw the doctor with Peter and Molly walking toward them, and they knew suddenly, everything was alright. Peter spoke first, his hand groping for the massive paw of Big Red. "She gonna be OK. Thanks fellas, thanks a million." Molly began to cry quietly as reaction set in. The doctor smiling, spoke: "She's going to be alright. She is a lucky little girl, the only reason she is alive is because she had prompt attention."

Molly looked at the group of leather-jacketed men and smiling, spoke softly. "You know when you all came down the road this afternoon, I thought you were a pack of devils, but instead you were all angels on chariots, surely sent by God." Old Joshua looked up and cackled, "And it's the first time I reckon, they rode motor bikes."

Slit Eye spoke cheerfully, "Now that's why we got kicked out of Northam. It was all that 'upstairs guy's' fault." And in the late hour of the evening, the hospital waiting room echoed their laughter.

My Brother Harold

Jack Davis

My brother Harold was a serious type of boy and an avid reader. He disliked being interrupted when indulging in his favourite pastime and I usually had to speak to him five or six times before he answered. Then he would gaze at me in a bemused fashion, his mind full of galloping horses and run-away trains depending upon the contents of the book he was reading. Mum's method of making him hear was to snatch the book from him and yell "Harold!" I couldn't very well do that as he was older and much bigger than I; also, I depended on him for a lot of assistance throughout a day. One method he used successfully to make me behave as he saw fit was to refuse to make me a shanghai or bow and arrow or help me with my homework.

Ours was the usual large Aboriginal family and as the family grew, my Dad, who was a good bush carpenter, added rooms here or there or enclosed another section of the verandah as the need arose. My brother Harold was reading in the kitchen on this night. I was in bed. Our bedroom was next to the kitchen. Directly behind my brother Harold was a window which was luckily, that night open. Three of us boys shared a double bed, and this bed in our bedroom was directly under the window also.

We had at that time a particularly amorous tom-cat who was always fighting the other toms in the area over various love affairs. I did not know that then, as I was only ten years old. I forgot to mention that my brother Harold was reading a book late that night which gave a graphic description of a ghost which went around a castle cuddling its head under its arm and continually moaning, "I should have kept calm. I shouldn't have lost my head. I shouldn't have lost my head." I missed my brother Harold's presence in bed beside me. My younger brother, like everybody else, was fast asleep and I kept calling out "when are you coming to bed", but I might as well ask our tom-cat to give up his lady loves. But strangely enough it was our cat who was responsible for my brother Harold deciding to vacate the kitchen.

Suddenly, and I mean suddenly, the quiet of our peacefully sleeping household was split by the most blood curdling shriek you could ever imagine. Our tom-cat decided to fight one of his rivals in love right in our kitchen and right under my brother Harold's chair. In a micro-second of time, my brother Harold's yell caught up and blended with the screeching of the feline battlers. I told you before, lucky that bedroom window was open, because my brother Harold flipped over off his chair not bothering to use the bedroom door. He dived headlong through the window and landed a quivering mass of terrified boy, tail up in the air, right on top of my chest.

Then came Dad's voice, "What the dickens is going on in there?" My Dad never read Dickens but this was a favourite expression of his. Mum came into our room and seeing that everything was all right and after murmuring a few soothing words went back to bed.

I told the story next morning at breakfast and our old house fairly rocked with laughter. Our tom-cat was curled up on the window sill, catching up on some sleep. And to this day I'll swear he looked at me and grinned malevolently. Anyway, my brother Harold certainly glared malevolently at the cat.

Pay Back

Jack Davis

Munda had been trailing the party of three whites since early morning. He hated them. Yet within this hate was a mixture of fear. There were reasons. At the last moon, a party of white men had poisoned one of their centuries old water holes and several members of his group had died in agony. But these were not the men actually responsible. He had photographed the heavy foot marks of the men in his mind of those who had killed, and those imprints would remain in his mind forever. But he knew they were the same type of man. He also knew the party was heading into waterless country.

The searing summer heat burnt into the very minds of the white men. Liles' party headed in the direction they were travelling four weeks before them. Although they had zig-zagged across the desert for nearly two weeks they had been unsuccessful in cutting across the other exploring party's tracks. Wargoton, the leader of the group, knew that to survive they would have to find water within the next twenty hours. He was a tall man, bearded, lean and sunburnt to a deep brown. The same description applied to his two companions, Lorrest and Wicknell.

One of their three camels had died a week ago. All their possessions, cut down to bare needs, were now being carried by their two remaining beasts. They made camp in the middle of the day's heat. They were wise in the ways of the desert, and knew it was better to conserve their energy, by travelling in the early morning and late afternoon.

Wargoton shook the canteen containing the last of their precious water. He looked at his two companions crouched together with him, in the six feet of shade thrown by the ledge of rock under which they crouched. He spoke hoarsely.

"Well we're down to about four mouthfuls of water each."

Wicknell replied, "I've had a feeling all morning that the blacks are trailing us, why the hell don't they show themselves."

"Why should they?" said Wargoton. "They'll trail and watch us keep watching until we perish then they'll spear the camels for food then share what we leave."

They lapsed into a moody silence. The sun began to move on its downward path, but the day was still viciously hot. The small patch of shade began to diminish.

Wargoton groaned between seared lips in his attempt to speak. "If we're going to sit in the sun, we might as well move." They struggled to their feet. Wargoton poured out three measures of water and said grimly. "Last drink until sundown and God help us tomorrow."

Even as he spoke, the three men saw the black, standing no more than twenty yards from them. At the sight of him they knew their immediate need was solved. He was of average height, thin build and stark naked. In one hand he held a hunting spear pointing carefully downwards. In the other he held a nulla nulla. In a hair belt around his left arm was a blade of quartz and around his forehead, was a belt of hair tied low. He stood looking at the three whites with an almost bovine expression on his bearded face.

It was Wicknell who broke the long sounds of silence. He raised one hand and pointed to the canteens strapped to one of their camels. "Water, where is water?" he said. Munda pointed to the sun then swept his arm half way down from its destination. "Good," said Lorrest. "The bastard understands us. That looks to be about two hours from here." "What if he's lying?" replied Wicknell. "No," said Wargoton. "He's telling the truth, but I think we should take care of ourselves, by the simple method of making him need water as much as we do."

Wargoton offered Munda the compass. His curiosity overcame his caution, he stepped forward, eager to take the offered object. They grabbed him. He offered little resistance, but moaned and jabbered in his own tongue as they bore him to his knees in the red desert sand.

Wicknell finding untapped energy ran to one of the camels. Rummaging quickly in the pack saddle he returned with a double cupped handful of salt.

Wargoton and Lorrest held the pitiful figure firmly, while

Wicknell rammed the salt into the bearded mouth.

It was as if he realised their intentions, because he did not struggle. They let him go. He lay on his side in protest as the salt bit into his throat. He began retching, the spasms doubling him up in their intensity. Lorrest stepped forward, kicked him and pointing at the sun, said hoarsely, "Water, and bloody quick." Wicknell aimed his rifle in the black's direction. Munda climbed painfully to his feet clutching his throat, and the strange procession began.

The three whites finished the last of their water. They knew now that the black was their only chance of survival. Their victim was now nearly two hundred feet in advance of them. They let him lead. Once when he widened the distance, Wicknell slowed him with a rifle shot fired skyward.

They came to a claypan some quarter of a mile across. The black stumbling, headed across it with the men still trailing him. At the claypan's outer edge the black suddenly veered sideways. He stopped, then pointed left to a spot where long low sandhills ringed the claypan.

Wargoton spoke hoarsely jubilant. "We've won, we've won. I can see the ground damp from here." They ran forward eagerly. They saw the black running for the safety of the sandhill. Wicknell stopped and raised his rifle. Wargoton still running forward, called out, "Let him go we've got what we want."

The three men flung themselves down at the soak's edge gulping the tepid water greedily, and splashing it over their faces. They lay on their sides allowing the two camels to quench their thirst.

It was Wargoton who felt the first swordlike thrust of pain. Then agony struck Lorrest then Wicknell. Wargoton looked at his companions' eyes bulging. He gasped, "Liles, that bloody Liles has been here before us. He's always trying to wipe out the blacks, the soak has been poisoned."

Munda looked dispassionately at the scene below him. His woman came walking along the ridge of the sandhill, a kullamun of water balanced on her head. Munda drank and together, turning their backs on the scene of death below them, they walked down the sandhill and into the distance of their land.

Bidjibub

Tracy Bunda

Bidjibub was absolutely fuming by the time she got home.

"That bloody bitch of a mongrel guts of a teacher. How dare she! HOW DARE SHE!"

Bidjibub had had a great day at school, that is, until the last period with Gordy (Miss A. Gordon—"A" for Anna) that miserable, aggravating woman. Bidjibub could hear her now.

"You'll need to change your attitude, Miss King."

Bidjibub had cringed at the time, she really detested being singled-out, for good or for bad. "When you're out there in the wide wide world, not many will employ black people, especially someone as brazen as yourself."

"Christ! Wait till Mum hears this one. She'll fix Gordy for saying that," Bidjibub mused over the thought. "There ain't no stopping Amelia King when she's wild and definitely no stopping her when her children need protecting. Ole Gordy won't know what hit her." The last thought put a twinkle to Bidjibub's eye.

Her smile soon faded as she entered the front door. She could hear her mother scream back, angrily to her father's booming voice.

"Lordy, what's he doing home? Must be looking for a fight."

Bidjibub let her school bag fall automatically off her arm as she ran down the hall. By the time she reached the kitchen at the rear of the house her stomach had flip-flopped all the way to her throat. In the kitchen doorway, Bidjibub could see her mother and father arguing. Her father raised his hand but as he swung Amelia King sidestepped the blow, and her daughter (thinking to protect her mother) received the whack across the face instead. Amelia had not even known her daughter was in the house until a flash of school uniform blurred past her, and there she was now, dripping down the cupboard door.

"Come on Bub, let's go." Half encouragement, half demand.

Bidjibub didn't need much prompting. She picked herself up off the floor, wove around her father and a few empty beer bottles to make her way out of the kitchen, into the hall, grabbed her bag and bolted. Her mother kept pace with Bidjibub all the way. Jumped fences and kept on running till they reached the station.

A quick check on the finances, two dollars and fifty cents between them. Enough to catch the train to Aunty Win's and then a bus to school in the morning. "Shit!" her face was aching. Oh well at least she had saved her mother from one thump up. Bidjibub rinsed her stockings and shirt at her Aunty's. That night her mother and she, shared the single bed in her cousin's room. But she didn't sleep well, her face hurt her and she couldn't stop crying. Bidjibub felt sick when she thought of all the years of drinking and fighting. No more, she couldn't stand it any more. Bidjibub planned to leave after this last year of school, job or no job!

At school the next day, not many noticed the bruising. Thank God. She didn't want to explain to many people. Anyway, the bruises only showed as faint green lines around her eye and along the jaw line. But by mid-morning the bruises were darkening and by fifth period, more obvious.

"What happened, Lucy?"

"Aah nothing, had a fight with a bedroom door. Come on, I can't stand around chit-chatting, Gordy'll kill me if I'm late!" Bidjibub held her face down, although this position was more painful, so as not to invite any further questioning.

Twenty minutes into the lesson, Gordy noticed however.

"So, Miss King, I see you've been fighting."

"But..."

"Don't tell me you haven't, I know your kind. Can't help themselves, can they? Most aggressive race I've seen. You're no different. "

Well that was the last straw. Bidjibub walked out of the Art room.

"And where do you think you're going, young miss?"

"I don't know Miss Gordon but I tell you one thing, I'm not going to stay here and listen to this crap."

Bidjibub's friends found her huddled in the basement. She had cried so many tears the front of her tunic was damp. They didn't have any good news.

"Come on Luce, you've got to go to the office. Just tell Miss Lawson your version. She's OK. You won't be in trouble. She'll listen."

Surprisingly Bidjibub had found that Miss Lawson did listen and before she knew it, Bidjibub was telling her everything. The fighting and drinking, everything. Miss Lawson was most concerned, she was sincerely concerned. Bidjibub's spirits were raised a little at least now she felt that Gordy wouldn't be stepping out of line too often. That left her father, and that was not going to be a problem either in another six months, as the RAAF would be effecting his transfer. Bidjibub vowed that alcohol was never going to rule her family's life.

The Way Forgotten

Hyllus Maris

Kuringai and Parramatta awoke to a beautiful morning. The bush and the sea were covered with mist and the sky was painted in pink and gold. And soon the sun would arise.

Parramatta lay in his mia-mia. He could hear the birds all chattering to one another and calling to one another: We must awaken, the day has come, there is much to do!

He stretched and yawned and sat up and looking out he could see some of the Elders sitting around a big fire talking softly to one another, planning the day's activities.

He stood up, breathing in the beautiful morning air. Stretching his arms he wondered if his friend Kuringai was awake. Picking up his weapons, he strolled down to where Kuringai's family had their mia-mias.

When he got there Kuringai was already up and about. "About time you arrived, lazy one," he said to Parramatta. "You would sleep all day! Come, I will race you to the beach for a swim." Immediately he bounded away, running swiftly towards the beach, with Parramatta close behind.

They both dived into the water together. How cold and refreshing it was to their skin! It made you come alive. They swam a bit, and then Parramatta said "We must go down to the rocks and do some fishing. The others must be hungry." "Yes—let us go now."

Coming out on to the beach they took their weapons and began to walk towards the rocks. The sun had risen now and began to warm their skins. There were other people already fishing and collecting shellfish.

"Tonight," said Kuringai, "there will be a great feast to mark the end of the initiations. The young men have just completed their training." "How proud they will be!" said Parramatta. "For is it not that which links us to our land and to our ancestors?"

"Yes! They will then take their place among us. Proud as warriors. They have reached a point in life that is very important to them and the people, and it will be good to celebrate with them. Kuttabul is our greatest dancer and he will present to them a new dance tonight. Come, let us hurry up to those rocks where we can see, for great shoals of fish are coming through the gateway to the sea this day and the people have already caught many."

They stepped among the rocks, careful not to walk on the sharp edges the sea had worn away, when all of a sudden Kuringai said "What is that strange-looking thing floating on the water?" Parramatta said, "It's the mist." "But the mist is already gone with the sun," said Kuringai.

It floated towards them, flashing brilliant colours in the sunlight, and gently bumped against the rocks, "What is it?" said Parramatta, stepping back. "I don't like this. I've never seen anything like it before."

"Mmm ... help me lift it out of the water," said Kuringai. Parramatta hesitated for a moment. "Do you think that would be a safe thing to do?" But Kuringai was dazzled by the colours that flashed from this strange thing. "Help me," he said.

So together they carried it on to the beach. They sat and looked at it. "Can you eat it?"

"I don't know"

"Is it a boat?"

"I don't think so ... but it's very pretty!"

"Look at all those beautiful colours coming from it when the sun shines on it! It dazzles you!"

Parramatta reached out his hand and touched it. It was sticky. "Smells nice ..." He put his finger to his mouth. "And it tastes nice."

"Let me try it! Mmm ... sweet. Mmm ... sort of honey taste. Makes your head go round!"

"Let us take it back to the camp and show it to the people."

So together they carried it back to the camp. "Look what we have found!"

And the people all gathered around, looking at it, talking about it, prodding it, and tasting it. "What is it for? What will we do with it?"

Days passed. The people still wondered about the strange thing, that seemed to be growing, getting bigger day by day. The elders were concerned. "This thing has had a strange effect on Kuringai and Parramatta! Look how they sit around, not wanting to join in the activities of the tribe. This thing has made them sick!"

By this time the people were beginning to break great pieces off it and eat it. And they were beginning to forget the abundant food around them. No longer did they want to go down and fish. The canoes just lay on the beach, and no one went out to hunt.

Then the people forgot The Way.

And this thing grew, and covered the hills. It dripped off the trees and ran down the rocks and into the rivers. And the smoke mist from it rose high into the sky, blotting out the sun.

And Parramatta and Kuringai died, as did many of the people.

And all the people throughout the land ate some of this thing that had spread all over the land. And they too became sick. As they ate, it made them think this food was better for them. It shut their eyes and their ears to life around them. They heard only what it would let them hear, and they saw only what it would let them see. It made them believe that The Way that had been laid down for them by their ancestral heroes was stupid for children to follow, to play. And so the people turned their backs on The Way and followed this thing.

And it led them into confusion.

The Concrete Box

Hyllus Maris

We're standing on this big heap of keys—a small mountain. And just over from it is this big box. It's marked "Blacks". And I can hear them all moving around in this box saying it's dark and they're hungry. There's no food and a lot of them are sick. And they've got no clothes, no shoes. And a lot of children are dying.

And there's a little window in this box with bars over the top of it and they can put their hands out and sometimes they get food, sometimes they get clothes, but not enough for everybody, not enough food for everybody. Sometimes they get beer, wine.

But there's no light in there. And it's dark and they're stumbling around. And it's crowded, there's not enough beds—they lie anywhere, they and their children.

And over this pile of keys there's one that fits in the lock that'll give them their freedom, peace of mind, their health. And there's some Aborigines looking for the key and they're running over and trying all the keys in the lock and throwing them aside...

When they first started off there used to be a lot of people but gradually they've dropped out. Now there's only a few that keep trying to unlock the box.

And on top of the box sits this white man and he knows where the key is because he's the one that put the people in the box and hid the key. Every now and then the white man changes masks. Sometimes it's benevolent and sometimes it's indignant. But always the persons underneath remain the same no matter how many times he changes his masks.

And he can hear the people move around, and hear them whispering because they're too afraid to call out or to talk loud because the white man's been sitting on the box so long. And they're afraid he might hear them calling for help because every time they do he uses some weapon against them.

His weapons he invents himself but usually they're in the shape of money. And there's a little hole in the top of the box where he drops in coins. And the money drops into the box and the people reach up to catch it. They can see the light coming in with the money. But every time they reach up it slips out of their grasp and it falls through some holes in the bottom of the box. The white man knows this—he's made the box so the money'll drop straight through and no one can catch it.

And sometimes the Kooris looking for the keys try to lever the lid up and put their hands in to help the people to come out. But the white man slams it shut and tries to chop of their fingers. And the people inside are afraid to take the hand in case their fingers get chopped off too.

Outside the other Kooris are still looking for the keys amongst all those thousands of keys. And the white man sitting on the box smiles because he knows where the key is.

But one day they're going to try all the keys and they're going to find the right one and unlock that box and the people will go free.

Joey Comes to the City

Hyllus Maris

Joey walked the last mile to the city. It had been a long three hundred miles from the little town in the west of NSW. His thoughts went back over the last week. The cops had kept him in jail for two days for being on the "Vag", but where the hell could he get a job in that lousy town? It was the same for most of the blacks there, except for jobs like driving the night-cart and a job now and then on the Council pick and shovel, that was about all. He started to laugh about how he had given the cops a "sad" story, but it still didn't make any difference, they were after him because he was a blackfella and anyway it saved them cutting the lawn and cutting wood.

He looked about to see where he was, trying to remember the directions he'd been given to get to the pub where he was to meet Russ and Spunky. But he'd lost the bit of paper he wrote it on. Damn!

Anyway, here comes a gub, I'll ask him. "Scuse me mate, can you tell me how to get to Smith Street?"

The white man's cold blue eyes looked at him, up and down. And all of a sudden he felt every mile he had come. His clothes were crumpled and his shoes scruffy, down at heel. The white man paused. "That way," he said, and pointed back over his shoulder with his thumb and walked on.

"Bastard! Can't even talk proper to me, they're all the same."

He walked quickly now, wanting to get there as soon as he could. And at last there it was, a big red building with faded green paint on the windows and the name "Sands Hotel".

He pushed the door open and walked in. The sound of music and voices hit him first, and the smell of beer. The air was thick with cigarette smoke. He stopped and looked around. The place was jam-packed with black people, talking, laughing and dancing. It just swept over him. A girl pushed past him. "Hi handsome!" He smiled at her but she walked on across the floor. His eyes went around the room. Tables all around a little dance floor. Didn't seem to be any sign of Russ and Spunky, then all of a sudden he saw them with two girls in a far corner. He pushed his way through the crowd. "Hey, you two rats, I've been looking for you!"

The two boys at the table turned around.

"Well I'll be damned! How's things? Look who's here, bloody Joey Ryan! How's things? Come and sit down here, have my beer, I'll get another one." And Russ Jackson, his brown eyes smiling, grabbed a chair out of a stack and slammed it down. "Sit here, mate! Spunky, get a jug."

Spunky Brown got up, laughing. "OK, but keep an eye on Betty, we know what Joey's like with the girls!" And off he went to the bar, pushing his way through the crowd.

For the first time Joey was able to look at the two girls. The one with Russ had dark brown skin, nice black hair, but boy, she had mean eyes! When she looked at him she just said "Hi" and went on talking to Russ. That look said "No money, no good."

The other girl smiled. "Hello, where you from?"

"Same place as these two, Walgett."

"Oh, I've never been there, but from what Spunky says it's not much of a place."

"Here we are, a nice cold jug and some clean glasses!" Spunky put them on the table, grabbed a glass, poured it full and handed it to Joey. "This will help wash all that dust down. Here's to ya!" he said and downed half the glass.

Just then, music started. "Come on, let's dance," Russ said, and they got up and began to dance to the music booming out of the jukebox.

Joey felt lonely sitting there. He was the only fella without a girl. No hope of that the way he looked. Wish I'd brought a clean shirt with me, he thought, watching the couples on the floor.

"Hello," said a girl's voice, "Wanna dance?" And he turned to look at a small girl with brown skin, smiling eyes and curly hair.

"Sure," he said, "let's go!", and taking her hand led her to the dance floor.

It wasn't going to be a bad sort of a night after all.

Stolen Car

Archie Weller

In 1978, as editor of Identity *magazine, Jack Davis advertised a short story contest which was open to all Black Australians. Over fifty entries were received and the winning story, written at the time under the psuedonym of R. Chee, was "Stolen Car". This was Archie Weller's first published story, a success which prompted him to continue writing both prose and poetry. An abridged version of that winning entry is reproduced below.*

He was eighteen years old, thin and dark as an ancient snag hidden in a river. Golden laughter of the sun shone from his yellow eyes and melted into his blond curly hair. His eyes were the first thing anyone noticed about him. Gentle, in half crescents of laughter, sometimes wide with interest, sometimes sad. But the colour was quite strange, and within them if one was kind or quick enough, one could see a spirit of restless searching and unsureness that was the very soul of the boy.

He had hitched a ride with a truckie that morning from the country to the ragged outskirts of the city. Red and white houses pimple the hills that circle it like a sleeping snake. Orchards have tamed the crude wilderness, but now a new savageness, the city itself, squirms like the awakening pupae of some cruel, giant insect, between the hills and the ocean.

He stood under the tree trying to thumb a lift. A grotesquely ugly, yet beautiful old red-gum, covered in clusters of sweet smelling blossom, clinging tenaciously to the edge of the rushing highway.

But the tree and he are the same, out of place in this brick and bitumen world. None of the cars stop until an old Holden skids to a screeching stop beside him. A grinning dark face, minus one front tooth, peers out of the window.

"Hop in mate," a nasal voice croaks, "Ya won't get a lift 'ere mate, unless a Nyoongah comes along. Them white bastards too good for us," continues Gap-tooth conversationally.

He wrenches the gear stick around, pushing the accelerator down. They spin off in a cloud of flying gravel and dirt, bowling along the grey intestine leading into the bulging stomach of the city.

They swap names. Johnny Moydan, lived all his life on a farm near Katanning, come up for his first look at the big smoke. Benny Wallah, known as Wallaby. Brags about the girls he knows and the "breaks" he has done.

Dusk. They shoot up onto the top of the hill in Shepperton road and Johnny takes his first look at Perth.

Buildings scar the purple, pregnant sky. Anguished, tortured silhouettes, rearing from the darker mass below. Holding the dying sky and the living city apart. The claws of the city rip open the clouds. Blood pours from the wound and night comes slipping over the too truthfully cruel city, sending the day people scurrying for home and dragging the night people from their holes and ditches. Park the car in a dark, dead-end lane in an empty industrial area. Streets full of people, flat black shadows, dancing in the lighter grey of the night. Fluttering dank, dirty, moths gathering in little clusters in pools of light on street corners.

"We'll go up to Zigi's first, see if me woman's there" says Wallaby. "Might even get you a moony too. Plenty of women 'ere for ya."

City youth, wise in the ways of his world, treading the streets surely. Johnny follows, shy and confused. The sun, his sun, has quite gone now, and he is cold and a little afraid in this dead place that seems so alive.

Music from the night club throbs hypnotically, escaping through its gaping red mouth and crawling painfully across the air, beaten out on drums and lacerated by whining electric guitars. The club's pale face shows neither pleasure nor annoyance, only suffering blankly. An air conditioner protrudes like a gray wart, dribbling into a pool on the street. People are spewed out of the fluffy red mouth, gathering in chattering groups on the street. Stumbling people, happy people, angry people, Aboriginal people. This is the Nyoongah hang-out.

Around the corner, dark and full of lanes, Aboriginal people talk quietly and laugh softly. Sometimes voices rise and a family quarrel that erupts into a brawl. Then the police move in like a pack of hungry dogs.

Police car always squatting in the road outside Zigi's. Big, cold-eyed policemen striding the streets, pushing the stray people around.

Wallaby leans against the glass window of the Pizza bar next to Zigi's and fishes in his pocket for a smoke. A voice from the dark cries out.

"Hey, Wall, when you get out of 'Illston?" and they are surrounded by a crowd of boys with a few girls clinging to muscular arms, afraid they will be swept away if they let go.

Dirty, sly, wary, children, with eyes that look at, yet away from, strangers.

Where is the soil that spawned their ancestors? Only bitumen and cement here now. These are not spirits from the bush, who hide in the bodies of humans, or trees, or rocks, or bound joyously to the stars. They are like the leaves of yesterday's yellowed newspaper, with yesterdays news, whirling aimlessly in dirty streets.

"When ya get out, well? Ya only bin in 'Illston a coupla munce unna?" asks a slouching youth, paler than the others, blank, humble eyes and a twisted smile. A kicked, stray dog, tail between dusty, dungareed legs, and a whine.

"I ran away, Billy. Me an' Froggy Moore. Froggy got caught, but."

"Well, what ya standin' on the streets for Wall? Bloody demons 'll 'ave ya d'rectly. Flog piss outa ya then," rasps a bedraggled boy, cheerfully.

"Not me, Eddie. This is th' Wallaby 'ere, look!"

Bursting into the cocoon of male security, two short solid girls push their way. They are sisters with blonde streaked hair, lively flat faces, and happy brown eyes.

"Wallaby darling. Where ya been ya stroppy bastard?"

"Ah, just 'anging around, Junie," a wink at the others, an arm over her plump shoulder and he has found his woman.

Her sister Jody looks at Johnny. Big warm eyes and fleshy boldness. Shy Johnny looks away.

"Well," Wallaby hitched up his trousers, "Oo wants a ride in me car?" "Go on! Where's ya car, ya bullshitter? Ya just run off from 'Illston an' buy a car, like that, or what?" sneers a youth on the outskirts.

"Don't believe me then," cries Wallaby, ego shattered. "Ya c'n ask me mate, Johnny 'ere, if ya wanna, Charlie Moran."

To own a car is the dream of all of them. In a car one is King of the roads, going anywhere. Down to Albany, up to Geraldton, even across the Nullarbor. A car opens up limitless boundaries of adventure. Squeal around the dull streets, impressing the girls. Shout out to lesser mates who have to walk. A car is a throne for Royalty to sit in and observe, in arrogant splendour.

"If none of ya wanna come, me an' Johnny's goin' up to Balga to roll some drunks."

"Truth is ya jus' wanna show off Wallah. Ya c'n roll drunks jus' as easy in Supreme Court Gardens," jeers Charlie and Wallaby thinks it's time to be going. The Morans are enemies of the Wallahs, through some long standing family feud. It would be just his luck to get in a brawl with drunk Charlie, be arrested, and returned to Riverbank for escaping custody.

He swaggers off, Johnny and the two sisters in attendance. Back to the car, lurking in the shadows. Scramble in, happily anticipating adventure.

"All of ya ready for one ride ya never goin' forget," Wallaby cries. "Orright, then, 'ere we go."

Let out the clutch. Slam foot on accelerator. Alley fills with smoke and the smell of burning rubber, wheels spin on the spot, car leaps out of its cave, glad to be free.

"Jus' leave me trade mark," Wallaby laughs. "Now, you mob, this car's 'ot, so if we get caught jus' say ya 'itch 'ikers, orright?"

"Let me out, Wallaby ya mad bugger. Ya drive too fast, an' in a stolen car too. That's askin' for trouble," cries Jody, then shrieks as they just miss a bus.

"You shut up, ya stupid bitch. I'm a good driver."

Then they hear the triumphant, maniacal, wailing of a police car behind them.

Spin the car around the corner where the bridge sags over the line, near the station.

Wallaby is out and running as it jerks to a stop. As though he is a magnet, the girls cling close behind, Johnny last.

Up towards Zigi's they belt, desperate and afraid. Round the corner into James Street Wallaby is out of sight. The girls run up a lane that opens bedraggled arms for them. Johnny follows.

Then a thin young policeman runs up beside them and drags Johnny down. "Come on!" he orders.

A van speeds swiftly and smoothly down the rutted lane.

Bundled in the door.

Before he can even sit down a torch probes in. The beam rests on him. A finger of doom.

"Come here son, the sergeant would like a word with you."

Torch beam hauling him out, like a fish on a line. Pushed into the back of a sleek police car. Hunches into the corner, miserable, confused. The young driver's face, pale, humourless, looks around at him.

"Steal a car, did you?"

"No," he mutters.

"Hah," Face laughs, nastily "I'll bet you didn't."

Then the sergeant gets in.

Middle-aged and thin. Greyish hair, a little curly. A hard, lean, bony, face. A slit for a mouth, and cruel, dark eyes boring into the youth, alight with a madness that frightens and paralyses him. The sergeant leans close and speaks in short, hissing bursts.

"Right, sonny. Now you're going to tell me a little story, aren't you?"

"Me name's Johnny Moydan, an' I never knew th' car was stolen," stammers Johnny.

The sergeant leans closer. The excitement in his eyes whips the quivering youth.

"Now listen, I haven't been a demon for ten years for nothing. I'm giving you five seconds."

"What—what ya wanna know? I never done nuthin'."

Poor Johnny. Confused, terribly alone. Peaceful, gentle, Johnny, who liked to muster sheep and breathe in their greasy smell; who liked to pick the first blossoms of the red-gum, or Christmas trees for his mother; who liked to listen to the magpie's call or the parrot's cheeky whistle.

A fist slams into his face, just under his left eye. He doubles up in shock and pain, covering his head. He is pummelled in the side of the stomach, and punches thud on his thin back. Then the sergeant is savagely pulling his blond hair, his gift from his sun. All the time the hissing voice continues.

"You stole the car, didn't you. You stole it from Innaloo last night. Come on, who were your mates?"

"No, no! I didn't steal it," cries Johnny.

"Don't lie, you little black bastard. You stole it, didn't you. Speak up."

Jerk his head up and down.

Johnny's brain snaps. He becomes a loose, ragged spineless, wreck.

"No, no! God's honour mate, It was Wall 'oo stole it," he blubbers.

"You said you didn't know it was stolen!" comes the driver's triumphant jeer, and Johnny hates him as he has never hated before.

The sergeant seems to love the feel of Johnny's hair between his fingers. He pulls it more and jerks Johnny's head up and down as though trying to break it off.

"Wall who? Where's he live?"

"I don't know. Oh, I don't know. Please don't hit me any more boss. I'll never get in trouble again."

"Hit you," says the sergeant, surprised. "Listen, I've only just started. By the time I've finished with you, you'll be stretched out on the ground. And when I get tired there's a younger bloke waiting to take over."

The car rolls to a menacing stop in a vacant block and the sergeant suddenly opens the door and pulls Johnny out by the hair. The boy collapses onto the cold, earthy smelling soil, his soil. A green, untidy vine stares sadly him from the fence. A light winks in the old CATS building beside the empty army barracks.

Scream and bring people running.

But nothing, except a sick grunt, and another as he is kicked in the stomach.

"Too many houses and people here," one of them says.

Pushed back into the car. It is too late. His chance of escape is gone and his soul dies.

The sergeant gleams at him, triumphant and victorious.

"Have you got your baton there?" he asks the driver, watching Johnny's face. But Johnny has learnt in these last five minutes what he should have known since the day he was born, to keep a shutter always between himself and the white man. He stares blankly at the floor. Face expressionless. Only his mind knows the weak terror within him which will stay there forever.

"Yeah," comes the driver's flat reply.

"Well we'll find some dark lane. I'll hold him down while you give him a few whacks in the crutch. Might help his memory."

Move off slowly and surely around the corner and down the hill. Turn left into a lane of grey dirt, bordered by grey fences. Rubbish bins, startled awake by the stark, harsh glare of the headlights.

Turn them and the engine off.

Silence.

The two men stare at the youth, hungrily, with their not quite human eyes.

Then— a voice crackles over the car's intercom.

"Detective-sergeant Maxwell would like to see the prisoners now."

Hesitation. Then the car starts up, slides like a snake out of its hole.

The sergeant leans over Johnny.

"Listen sonny. This Sergeant Maxwell is a big man, and a friend of mine. If I find out later you told him anything you haven't told me, I'll come looking for you. You understand, you little black bastard?"

Out in the main road again. Cars and lights, people and reality.

Past Zigi's.

Johnny looks up with his new, dead eyes, and sees two Aboriginal youths leaning against a car watching him with the same dead eyes. He is truly one of them now.

Drive to Central, a towering glassy building that curves beside the Swan River, like a scorpion's tail.

Statements, fingerprints, photographs, then led off to the cells.

Iron bars, flat yellow walls and floors. Pale light from passage gently brushes his face. Lie on the hard mattress, smelling of vomit and other people. Pull the grey blankets up over him and momentarily stare at the hump in the next bed, wondering who it is.

The feeling that it is all a nightmare slowly dies away.

Shiver with shock, exhaustion and the reality of it all.

He had always been a "good boy". It had been like a medal for him and a trophy for his parents. The Moydan family had worked for Mr. Williamson on his farm for years. Betty Moydan was proud of her neat little house and the whole district knew and liked quiet, gentle Johnny, a good worker and a good footballer.

Fall into an uneasy sleep, and dream his ordeal all over again.

Next morning.

Thin and afraid in this wooden, shiny, court, before the bored, bespectacled eyes of the magistrate. Only the legal-aid man isn't his enemy. Even him he doesn't really trust.

Gape around the room, while the lawyer speaks.

". . . good boy . . . up from the country . . . never been in any trouble . . ."

What is the use. He's speaking out-of-date words.

Pompous, mechanical voice of the magistrate discharging him. Led out, signs book, receives his envelope of belongings.

Then he runs from the building.

Wallaby and Billy in a pool-room. Wallaby grins at him.

"G'day, Johnny. They catch you, unna?"

"Yeah," flatly.

"I was watchin' ya from behind a tree. Then demons flashed their torches at me, but they never seen me, look. I 'ad one big piece of pipe there. I'd 'ave given it to them monyach bastards too," he growled.

Empty bragging. A pitiful attempt to prove a manhood that doesn't exist. Stamped out of existence by generations of white men. Roll a cigarette and silently offer his tobacco to the others. Slit his eyes against the smoke, gaze around the room.

This is what he had come to Perth for. Enjoy himself, then go home. But he can't go home now. Restless, uneasy and bitter like the city that has adopted him.

"'Oo give ya th' black eye, cood?" asks Billy.

"'Oo d'ya fuckin' well think?" snarls Johnny.

The two boys stare at him, shocked by the hate in his voice.

"I'm complaining about them two cunts," he continues.

"Hey, look out Johnny," Wallaby whispers, scared yet awed,

while Billy looks fearfully around. "Don't drag me into it, anyrate. I'm on th' run, remember."

"Nor me," says Billy. "More better if you just forget about it, cood?"

"No." Johnny's voice is flat. "But you don't 'ave t'worry you two. Only me, all by myself."

Ring up the legal-aid man, who helps him write out a complaint. Two weeks pass. Staying at the Wallahs' house in West Perth and watching TV with dark, happy Raymond and Wallaby's sister Ethel. A knock on the door. A deep voice.

"Johnny Moydan home?"

"Dunno. Might be." Mrs. Wallah flusters.

Walks into the hall, followed by Raymond and Ethel.

"I'm Johnny Moydan."

A giant Inspector, shiny cap, snowy white shirt, row of coloured ribbons displayed on his jacket. He senses the other Aboriginals staring at him and knows he is alone.

"You made a complaint, I believe?"

"Yeah," Johnny shuffles.

"I'd like you to come to the station with me. Make a statement. You understand?"

So he has begun. Can't stop now. Wallaby is angry.

"Ya too simple Johnny. Jeez, ya can't tell ya nuthin! Now ya got th' cops sniffin' around Mum's 'ouse, gettin' 'er upset. An' what about me ay?"

Night.

Billy and Johnny ambling home. Billy spots the slowly moving car, pulling to a threatening stop and nudges Johnny. They lean against the charcoal-coloured wall, while three plain clothes men descend upon them.

Two of them close around the fearful Billy, eyes opened wide so the moon reflects the whites. Third one beckons to Johnny who follows warily.

Pushed into a corner. Big red face leers down at him.

"Where's your switch wires?"

"What ya talkin' about? I got no switch wires."

"Yeah! Supposing I search you, then?"

Beefy hands whip over his thin frame then the man straightens up and takes out his note book.

"What places has your mate broken into tonight?"

"None, 'e was with me."

"Well, what breaks have you done?"

"None. Leave me alone."

A sudden slap across the face breaks his lip. The detective's mate calls from the alley entrance. "Righto Wal, this one's clean."

"Right, Allen." Luminous eyes peer down at him "What's your name, anyhow, smart-arse?"

"Johnny Moydan."

"Yeah?" the man stares at him a minute longer "Well, piss off." Raises his hand. Johnny cringes. Hates himself and the man. Hurries away with Billy.

Next day.

Rings up the same legal-aid officer, and complains. Can't understand Billy's fear and that of the other Aboriginals. He sees it as his right. Urges the others to complain too. Talks loudly to the lawyer about the wrongs his friends suffer. Advised in apathetic tones to get them to put it in writing. Other Aboriginals frightened of him. He is different. Begin to drift away from him until only a cheeky Wallaby and Billy are his friends.

One evening, they wander aimlessly and happily down the street. Once again a police car slides to a halt. Two uniformed men get out, relaxed in their confident authority. One points to Johnny.

"You— come here."

Johnny is spat out of the group. Shambles forward.

"All right. What's your name?"

"Moydan. Johnny Moydan," he pouts.

"You mean you're the smart little nigger who's been rubbishing the force?"

Johnny says nothing. Digs thin hands into pockets. Where will he be flogged this time? The words of his friends drum in his mind.

"Look, cooda, if ya black ya got no chance. It's natural aint it?"

"Monyach blame us for most anything, then beat piss outa us, but aint nothin' ya c'n do 'bout it, 'cept keep outa their way."

"Can't even take a slap in th' face look."

"That Moydan is one wild boy, 'e's mad I reckon."

Glances into the policeman's face, then his eyes slip sideways.

Murky eyes, dull, muddy coloured as a river in winter. Angry as one too. So much dirt in the water now, no one can see the ugly snags that will impale a man.

The policeman's mate wanders over to Johnny's side. He says gently. "Listen Johnny, you may as well own up and give up."

"What ya want with me, well? Ya always pickin' on me." For a moment his eyes flash fire before the flood puts it out.

"No, Johnny, you've got it all wrong. You were identified, see?" Brings a pad from the car and reads from it. "Young Aboriginal, blond hair, thin, brown coat, bare feet. Fits you exactly, Johnny."

"So where's the wallet, sonny?" growls his mate.

"I never got no wallet."

The quiet policeman treads on Johnny's bare foot, squashing it to the pavement.

"Johnny, you don't want us to flog you, do you?"

Remain silent, staring at the ground. Keep the pain from his foot from showing in his face.

The policeman sighs and removes his boot.

"Well, suppose we show you to the old man you robbed?"

The old man looks him over and shakes his head.

"You can go then. You were lucky tonight Johnny, but just keep out of trouble in the future, see," says the disappointed policeman.

How can he keep out of trouble, when trouble waits around each corner to seize and roll him in the filthy mud of petty persecution.

Then Wallaby is recognised, picked up and returned to Hillston. For a week Johnny stays indoors at the Wallahs, brooding.

Wander back down town at last.

Long, low, pool-room, glass windows staring onto the street. Red door gaping stupidly open wide, a lipstick mouth. Juke box mumbling words of love. Pool tables, flat and green—plateaux of dreams where a man becomes a hero or a loser, able to spin the balls into ideas of his very own. Around the walls pin-ball machines clack and tinkle.

He is about to spend his last twenty cent piece on a game when he is hailed.

"Me ole cooda, Johnny. 'Ow are ya then, mate?"

"Goodoh. Run outa money but, Billy."

"Come out 'ere bud," Billy hisses. Around the corner into the covered car park. Hands the startled boy a handful of crumpled notes.

"What's this then Billy?"

"Well it aint shit," Billy grins. He is high and happy. He and Crabby Unkel have busted the easiest store of all, and stolen over a thousand dollars. Billy thinks of all the clothes he will buy, the wine he will drink to forget what he is, the friends he will have. But his laugh is sliced in half by a blinding spotlight.

"Hold it right there, you two," a voice shouts.

Billy gets nine months, and despite his denials and Billy's insistence that he was not involved, Johnny gets six.

He is released in the autumn.

His face is thinner than ever, hard and angry, picked bare by experience. Quieter than ever, with bitter golden eyes staring like a savage dog. Catches a train from Fremantle into Perth to slide his body into the tepid, stagnant swamp of people.

No one he knows anywhere. Wallaby inside again, Billy still in Bunbury. The girls, like fat little brown moths, have fluttered off to other lights. Wander down to Supreme Court gardens. No one there. Coloured leaves dance frantically in the wet wind, drying, dying. Perhaps like him they wish they still had something to cling to.

Squeeze into a corner by a brick wall. Roll a cigarette. He shivers and wonders where he'll sleep tonight.

A car pulls up beside him. But it isn't the police.

A boy gets out of the car. His own age, in a neat clean, suit, warm ruby-coloured shirt and white tie. Gold cuff links show as he straightens his immaculate hair. An expensive watch circles his wrist. A chain shackling him to the rich life he leads.

"Come on darl. We're running late."

Now a slim girl gets out. Beautifully dressed. The prettiest girl Johnny has ever seen. They clasp hands and hurry up the street, leaving the keys in the lock.

Something deep down in Johnny's tortured heart breaks. The strange white boy has so much, while all he has is a bad name, lying among the weeds of society like rotten fruit, eaten away by white maggots.

The car is a smooth blue sports type. A prostitute, flaunting her body sensually. Teasing and tempting him. He desires her. Be as good as the boy who owns her.

Out of the shadows, into the comfort of the car.

Turn the keys. The car purrs instantly to life. A good clean engine, just like the owner.

Squeal down the street and around the corner, past the immaculate boy and his beautiful girl. Honk the horn, laughing, leaving them standing there stupidly.

He wishes Billy and Wallaby were there, to see him commit his first crime, and share with him the joy and beauty of his car.

Drive out to the ocean. Whirling around corners and up straight stretches. Push the car until it whines in agony. Rejoice in the speed and power he controls. Turn on the heater, to warm his frozen body. He finds a packet of cigars and sticks one jauntily in his mouth. Turns on the radio.

He reaches West Coast Highway and turns up it. Black and mysterious ocean. The light from Rottnest flashes regularly across its dark, oily, undulating back. The sea is his father, the earth his mother. He is remote from man. Safe and warm and sheltered in the pulsating body of the machine.

The police find him near Scarborough.

He sees the light coming up behind him, hears the murderous howling. Thin face pulls into a dingo grin, hard angry eyes shine with excitement. He feels no fear. He has no feelings at all. They were beaten out of him in prison.

Slender hands grip the wheel and he pushes his beautiful blue being to its limit. The police car's blue cyclops eye flashes into the blue-black night. People get out of the way to watch. For the first time in a long while Johnny Moydan isn't being pushed around. He is in control, he is free, he is supreme—he is someone.

But at the corner he couldn't control the creature he had created.

He was touching two hundred kilometres an hour when they hit the sand dune.

Someone?

Pathetic Johnny. The shadowy, formless people watch from the footpath. Watched you and the banshee-wailing police car rush past and away, leaving just a wind in your wake.

And who remembers the wind?

A Letter from an Aboriginal Mother

Ruby Langford

13 January, 1987

Dear Sir

I am writing on behalf of my people. I'm an Aboriginal and I don't know much about your white system of justice as I've never been in trouble with the law. But I have sons whose fathers are white men and have been involved in prison and police custody since they were children, and in boys' homes. Now I'm not only talking about my sons, but the sons of every mother, be they black or white, who have ever run foul of the law.

I went to court on the eighteenth of December, 1986 to hear my son's bail application and I was thoroughly disgusted with the attitude of the Magistrate or Judge that heard his bail application as he was, in my opinion, a very opinionated judge. And after the Crown Prosecutor produced evidence which I thought was not admissable anyhow because it was bought up about him absconding from the boys' home twice when he was a child and here he was, now a thirty-one year old man, and the courts were still judging him on his record when he was in boys' homes.

When he was seventeen years old, this son of mine whilst in the company of another youth, aged sixteen and a girl fourteen, and also very drunk, was driven to my home in Green Valley, as he'd had a breakup with his girlfriend and had gotten drunk and asked the sixteen year-old youth to bring him home to me. What he didn't know was that there was a gun under the seat, the sixteen year-old was driving negligently and the police chased them, then the girl opened up and fired shots at them. I know my son and the only

violence in him is against himself. The Police had to have a
conviction: he being the eldest was the one that ended up in Long
Bay Gaol at seventeen years old, when he should have been in
juvenile custody, along with the other two. The girl went Crown
Witness and blamed him, after the police promised her they'd be
lenient with her. She and the other sixteen year-old youth went into
childrens' homes and my son went to Long Bay where he served six
years of a ten year sentence, so where is the justice in that? And here
it was in 1986, fourteen years after his childhood evidence was still
being used by the system against him, he'd been out of gaol eight
years and was a rehabilitated man, worked constantly, as a matter of
fact was a workaholic and met a nice lady and lived together with
their two children and between them both working applied for and
got a $58,000 home loan from St. George Building Society, and they
don't give these home loans to bums.

Then came the death of a loved brother at twenty-eight through
drugs and his world started to crumble around him. This is what
gaol has done to him, he believed he should be the one dead, as he
said "I'm the criminal. Why didn't God take me? Not David." He
proceeded then to go downhill and have a nervous breakdown, lost
his job, was battling to pay the home loan off and he was even
ripped off by the solicitor who was handling the home loan for him,
to the tune of $1,400. He tried very hard to cope with everyday
living, but eventually went down in a screaming heap, he was
missing for a couple of days and his wife and I were frantically
looking for him and we found him out at David's grave, lying across
it, and brought him home.

The next episode of his breakdown was when he was found by
police lying in the middle of the road wanting the traffic to run him
over and kill him; he wanted to be with his brother and instead of
the police taking him to a psychiatric centre for counselling, they
took him back to gaol and bashed him. He came out looking like the
Elephant Man. These were his own words, so you can see these
actions were a cry for help, but no one listened. I encouraged him to
go to Brisbane, to my sister's place, to try and get himself together.
Coming back he was flagged down by the police, and him with no

licence, thought "Oh God, I'm going back to gaol," produced a gun that some great mate had given him for his protection, and this mate even supplied the car, and fired at the radiator to stop the police car. How ironic, here he was doing the same thing what he was supposed to have done fourteen years ago, but didn't do, but he still served his time in gaol for it, six wasted years. So can you tell me, where is the justice here?

I'm going to get a petition going, to protest against the bringing of evidence against people who have already done time in custody for things done when they were young and all the courts being able to bring up past evidence up as far back as childrens' homes, as I don't think it's fair and I guess, so do a lot of mothers like me. And I for one don't want my son, to become another statistic of Aboriginal men dying in police and prison custody.

Ruby Langford

The Trials of Nobby

Ruby Langford

Today the ninth of November 1987, I'm going to court for my son Nobby, he's been in and out of boys homes, since I lost my two eldest children within eight months of each other in 1969 and 1970.

The two deaths had a bad effect on him, he was brought to his sister's funeral in handcuffs, accompanied by a policeman, when he was only thirteen years-old from the boys' home.

He was with me when I found his eldest brother Bill drowned in a bath tub, through an epeliptict fit, since that, he's been unable to cope with the sorrow of losing loved ones, he wouldn't let anyone talk about them for years, he'd just pushed it all to the back of his mind. My youngest daughter Pauline picked me up, she was the only one with a car, then on the way we picked up my daughter-in-law Shellie, Jeff my youngest son couldn't come owing to work.

When we arrived in town, we couldn't find parole court number twenty-six, there were parking spaces where the Judges left their cars, so we left it there, hoping not to get a parking ticket.

We turned into Macquarie street, and asked directions from a lady, and went in behind a big museum behind RG Office—Nobby's lady, Bella, was waving to us, we'd finally found the court, I asked directions again, and took off for the nearest loo.

Kath Barton, Nobby's solicitor, and the shadow attorney general, who was representing my son for nothing, because us blackfellas have no money and some gubbas you couldn't knock, only they were few and far between. Kathy introduced Mr Dowd, and I shook his hand, thanking him for his representation of my son, and feeling embarrassed, because we had no money to pay the man.

I hadn't been to see this son of mine for a long time.

Fifteen years ago, he was convicted of a charge of firing at police, he was seventen then, I thought back to that time, while in the company of a another youth, aged sixteen and a girl age fourteen, and also very drunk because he had a breakup with his girlfriend, he asked the other youth to drive him home to where I lived in Greenvalley out at Liverpool.

What he didn't know that there was a gun under the back seat, because the youth was driving negligently, the police chased them, the girl opened up and began firing shots at them.

The girl went crown witness, and blamed Nobby, after the police promised they'd be lenient with her. The police had to have a conviction, so my son wore it, he was nearly eighteen anyway.

Six years of a ten year sentence, he served for something he didn't do. So I only went once to see him, and I couldn't go anymore, it broke me up to see my son behind bars like a caged animal.

I had major surgery on my stomach in March 1987, it left me with a lot of stress and depression too, I was doing rewrites of my book I'd started in May 1984, writing up the deaths of my children. And also the death of my son David, through a drug overdose in November 1984, added to my stress.

I started to feel real crumbly, I couldn't understand what was happening to me, I'd start crying at the drop of a hat.

Six weeks after I was discharged from hospital, I had to see my surgeon for a check up. While waiting in the surgery, he came to the door and beckoned me, I burst out crying in front of everyone, and couldn't stop. "Now, now, Ruby it's not that bad, your wound has healed splendidly, I'm real pleased with it," he said.

I thought to myself, what about all my other scars, the battle for life and the struggles I've had to contend with, I knew he couldn't heal that, no-one could, only me.

I said to him "I don't feel well, and I can't stop cryin', what's happening to me doc?" He answered, "It's not unusual to suffer from stress and depression for anything up to six months or twelve months after major surgery, it will pass, give it time." Easy for him to talk I thought to myself. I called him Mack the Knife. Maybe that's why I burst out cryin' as soon as I saw him, I could imagine him cutting my gut. Yuck. "Never again will I let anyone cut me up." Famous last words, I'd made that promise to myself six years ago. "Oh well, that's life." And the iron bars in front of me, brought me back to the present. My son was behind those bars again, going stir crazy, he had the shits with all of us, like if we could do anything for him. I was told this was a natural procedure, nothing's natural for him anymore, he'd been jailed for something he didn't do. Now he was thirty-one years old, and this great white justice system still had him in its clutches. But I was told that every prisoner goes through this agony, every time they are fronting for parole or sentencing, so he was no exception, just another jailed ABO.

I'd never given up hope that, that things would go right for Nobby one day, I prayed often for him, I'd been living at Allawah Aboriginal hostel at Granville since the 11th of August, 1987. Allawah in Aboriginal means stop, sit down and rest awhile. How appropriate, I sure needed this place to rest and recoup, and get well, and lift myself up spititually, it's very peaceful here, and there's always someone to talk to. Goodbye loneliness, I whispered to myself.

One night we had a sing-song with some christians who came to the hostel. Brother Peter and sister Maria were people of mine, Bundjulung people, he was my mother's nephew, and had read the service over my son David when he'd died.

After the sing-song, he asked if anyone wanted prayers said for anyone? "Yes," I said "Please pray for my son who's fronting parole court on Monday," he prayed beautifully, "Please Lord Jesus you are the good spirit, who cares for all your children, just reach down and open those prison gates and let sister's son free, like a bird, we ask it of thee Lord, amen."

I felt so good afterwoods. Then Kathy's voice brought me back to reality. "You can see Nobby through that window over there," she said pointing, we rushed over to see him pacing up and down with several other prisoners, he could hardly see us for the sun glare on the window, and when he did, he hung his head and looked like he was crying.

As we were waiting outside the court room which was two flights up, and very small, Nobby was being bought up the stairs in handcuffs, accompanied by two young gungabuls, he went to walk past us, Pauline called out "Give us a kiss," I got one too, then we filed in to the little courtroom.

To the left of us four parole board members sat, old dignified men, and the Judge was seated up front with his glasses sitting on his nose. Then John Dowd spoke on Nobby's behalf and gave all the court particulars and produced photographs of his home, with all the landscaping he had done.

Next Bella, Nobby's lady, spoke. She said his home was the only landscaped home in the whole of Woodvale Close, Plummton, and that he was a good worker and provider, for her and her children. Mr Dowd next read Nobby's parole officer's report, and said "Mr Mustard is not a qualified psychiatrist to give his opinions of the prisoner's psychological problems, he is only a parole officer." Mr Mustard's face turned a vivid shade of red.

This parole officer was an ex-Buddhist monk, and was very predjudiced in his treatment of Aboriginal prisoners. Nobby told me, "Mum I was classified as a black activist because I drew our flag, black, red and yellow, and hung it in my cell. The screws came and ripped it down, and I wasn't allowed pen or paper for weeks." This is just another example of treatment of Kooris in custody.

I was thinking Mr Dowd sure was a brilliant barrister, work reports of Nobbys were talked about, he had six work references, he was a fork-lift driver, a picture framer, a storeman and packer, he was a good worker. The parole board adjourned for ten minutes and came back.

Nobby's time for questioning; at first his voice was barely audible. "Could you speak louder please, we can't hear you," the judge said.

"I know I've got problems, I couldn't accept the fact that my brother was dead, and the nature of his death, he's the father of two little kids. Someone gave him smack and it killed him, he was only twenty-eight years old, and me and him were real close, I do realize he's gone, and I have to go on with life, not only for my sake, but my family, who I love dearly and don't want to hurt anymore by breaking the law, and going back to jail, they have stuck by me through thick and thin, and if you give me parole I will see a psychiatrist and attend regular with my parole officer, and get work so I can pay my home off and stay out of trouble.

After he finished speaking the board adjourned again, this time it was for three quarters of an hour, by this time I'd seated myself directly behind Nobby, I whispered "Don't give up hope son." I

could see the tension in his face, then Pauline came over and started
to tell him some of her sick jokes, he was laughin' and so were the
two gungabuls besides him. I whispered, "Don't loose your sense of
humour either, because you're stuffed without it."

"Yeah mum, I know," he said.

A hush fell over the room just as the board came back, Nobby
stood up and faced the judge, who said "Your record is very bad,
you've been in and out of trouble since your youth." And with that
my heart sank, Pauline and Bella took off out of the room, the judge
rambled on and on, and I was close to tears; he's not going to get
parole—"My God." Then he was saying, "The whole board voted
unanimously, that because of your work record, you be given
another chance."

Then the tears came out, and I wept unashamedly before the
whole court, everyone stood, as the judge left the room. Shellie took
off down the stairs to tell the girls the good news, I could hear
Pauline's voice echoing up through the stairway, "Good one, Good
one, Right on, Right on."

We kissed him good-bye, he'd be home for Xmas to live free—
"Thank you Lord the good spirit, for answering our prayers."

Pauline did get that damn parking ticket after all, she was lettin'
go with some obscenities, I said "Shut up Porkie pie?" that's her
nick-name, "You'll get pinched for bad language."

When we were in the car going home, she said, "Can you hear
those church bells mum?"

"No, I can't hear anything?"

"You must be real deaf?"

"I heard three bell tolls, suppose to be a good omen?" she said. I
smiled to myself, I did hear them, real loud too, and knowing they
were bells ringin' from our hearts.

Nikky's Story

Gordon Langford

For Nichole

"Good day my little Devil.

"Here's a special little story for you, so Mummy can read it to you before you to go sleep. It's about a little girl and her blanket. The little girl in the story is named Nikky, so really the story is about you."

No-one is really sure when Nikky made friends with her blanket, but it was a very long time ago, because she couldn't say very much. Every time Nikky woke up she would get hold of her blanket and it was very hard to make her let go.

When she had her morning bath (which she enjoyed very much), she even wanted to take her blanket into the tub with her. And when she was being dressed, it was always difficult for Mum, because she had to put Nikky's clothes on while she was holding the blanket.

Sometimes she would put her blanket over her head, and pretend she was a ghost, and say, "OOH OHH OHH OHH!" and frighten everyone. Then she would come out from under her blanket suddenly and laugh at her old Dad who was scared of the "Ghosty".

Every so often the blanket had to be washed, because Nikky would drop milk and biscuits and dinner and chocolates and jellybeans all over it. Maybe she didn't drop these things by accident. She might have been feeding her blanket!

Anyway, when the blanket was in the washing machine, Nikky's

Mum had to watch her very carefully. Otherwise she might have got into the washing machine also. Imagine what it would be like to be washed and spun dried!

Of course the blanket had to be spun dried by the time Nikky went to bed, because without it she wouldn't go to sleep. And there was Teddy and Dolly and furry animals to think about. They couldn't go to sleep unless they were wrapped up in the blanket with Nikky too.

Every night, when our two little children were fast asleep, Mummy and Daddy went from bed to bed to make sure their special chaps were nicely in and warm as toast. Especially in winter, during weather when Jacky Frost is around, and as we tucked that blanket, that very special blanket, under Nikky's chin, she would snuggle down until we could only see a mop of hair showing.

"And that is the end of my story, as I know it. I hope you liked hearing it. It made me happy to write it.

"Lots and lots of love my dear Nikky.

"From Daddy."

Gelam

Lydia George

*Listening to stories was always popular among the young children
of the Torres Strait Islands. Stories were highly respected in the
creative world of the Torres Strait. There are many stories, but
among my favourites is one about about a boy called Gelam who
turned into a dugong. Often this kind of story is performed in island
villages. As I adapt some of the text from the original Meriam
language of the Murray Islanders of the Torres Strait, I will reveal
the characters of the boy Gelam and his widowed mother Atwer
(this name means 'criticisms'). I will try to represent the true image
of their relationship and their characters. The story of Gelam was
told to many children in the villiage of Morgor in Erub from the
1950s and 1960s. I remember this story being told to us as children
and to the grandchildren of the late Mr Kailu and Mrs Perina
George, my beloved Gizu Ata, Mrs Mary Anne Simbolo and my
surrogate mother, Mrs Akazi George, who have spent many
wonderful days and evenings labouring their love to my brothers
and sisters. I dedicate this story of the legend of Gelam to the
preservation of the heritage of the Torres Strait Islands.* — L.G.

The Relationship Between the Mother and the Son

Gelam grew up on a small village called Bulbul on the island of
Moa (St Paul). He lived with his widowed mother, Atwer. They had
come from a place called Wabada in the North, near Fly River.

Atwer was left to bring up a teenage son on her own. Alone, she
must face the task of raising her son in the proper way, the way that
is acceptable in their society. Many months have now passed. Atwer
was ready to teach Gelam the art of shooting with boonara (bows
and arrows). In a few months Gelam had became very good at
handling this boonara. Each day, he would go into the sou (inner

beach forest). He would shoot and hunt the pigeons.

THE SCENE: Near the village house, there were two separate fires burning. Every day Gelam would be returning from his hunting trips with the pigeons. That's what he would do, he would give the pigeons to his mother to roast in the fire. Then it was the time to change, Gelam could now tell the differences between the roasting pigeons by the taste of them after they were roasted. Soon, after each hunting trip, he would give his mother the smaller pigeons with less fat and he, himself, would keep the fuller one, which was much fatter. So one day, Atwer noticed that Gelam had kept the best pigeons to himself and gave her the poor pigeons, the one that is less fat. Atwer must have felt very sad about the way Gelam was behaving towards his mother, so she decided that Gelam must be punished in a certain way. Greed is not an acceptable way of life in their society. Making up her mind that Gelam must be punished, she followed Gelam into the sou to study his activities in the bush. Then the next time, Atwer would frighten Gelam as he ventured on his hunting trips. So Atwer had planned for herself to apply charcoal dust, clay and mud paste all over her body. This sounded good. And this is what she must do to frighten Gelam out of his wits.

On this particular day Gelam had told his mother that he would go hunting with his boonara. Often, he would shoot with his boonara as he walked into the sou. He would aim with boonara at the prey and would never miss. It was Gelam's favourite pass-time, crouching near the pigeons traps he had made and waiting for the diba-diba (Torres Strait Pigeons). On this day he was lying very still and waiting for the game to come to drink near the traps. While he was lying there very still, he heard a ruffling sound come from the bush behind him. Suddenly, the noise began to grow louder and louder and then BANG BANG and WHOO OO ! There was a great black shadow hovering over Gelam. Frightened by the sound of the mysterious noise, Gelam began to run for home. He was so frightened and he forgot to pick up his boonara. Stumbling over large stones and logs, he ran for home.

Meanwhile Atwer had taken the shortest route back to the village of Bulbul. She had known for some time about the creeks with flowing streams to wash all the charcoal dust, clay and mud from herself, before going into the village. Quickly she made her way back home. Putting fresh clothes on herself and pretending that nothing had happened. Here comes Gelam hopping, madly onto the verandah with his scratches and bruised knees. Atwer quickly went to his aid. Picking a herbal plant from her garden. Chewed the leaves and applied it onto Gelam's bruised knees. Atwer began to ask Gelam about the whereabouts of the pigeons he had hunted, only to be told that he had dropped them, when he had to run away from the noises in the bush. The incidents did not frighten Gelam for long. The next day, he went again on his hunting trip. Many months later after similar incidents, Gelam sat down to supper with his mother. After supper, when it was time to go to bed, Gelam asked his mother to tell him some stories. While listening to her talking, Gelam moved quietly towards his mother, for he had noticed that there were small bits of charcoal dust, clay and mud on the inside of her talinga (ears). Watching his mother very closely as she was telling Gelam about her days and the stories, Gelam had noticed this strangeness about his mother and quickly he jumped up and said "Ama it was you, who had frightened me, all this time." Then there was a long silence.

The Dreams

Gelam: Suspicious and upset. He was so furious towards his mother, not only for frightening him but betraying him as well. He had become so obsessed by his anger, furiously and sadly he was unable to forgive his mother, Atwer. That night Gelam had a dream, in his dream his father had appeared to him. His father appears before Gelam in dreams to give him advice. The dreams foretold Gelam to go and find a suitable floating wood, and carve out a dugout canoe in the shape of a dugong. And when this is completed, he must leave Moa behind and go to another island.

Searching for a Floatable Wood

Each day, Gelam would tell his mother that he had to go to the sou to hunt. But, instead he would search for a floatable wood. Now, he had ventured into the sou and began to cut down the wapad tree.

This is the light wood that can be found near the beach. After cutting down a branch of the wapad tree. Gelam would carve it into a shape of a dugong or sometime a fish. He would placed it on the water and attempt to float it. But the timber is far too light to float, for it surfaced on top of the water. Every day he would go out into the sou and search for more floatable wood. His spare time would be spent finding the right wood and carving it, and then trying to see if it could float. Gelam had tried many varieties of trees. He tried the iutarkub (a wild cotton tree). But it was too heavy. So therefore it is not the right type of wood at all. By now Gelam had tried three types of trees. He had tried the garagatulu (a blood wood). But it was not heavy enough to float. Feeling discouraged Gelam went home. That night, his father had appeared to him in a dream again and advised Gelam that the best and easiest way to find the right type of wood is to go and tap on every tree he could see in the place. The only clue would be that the trunk would make a "pii" sound. Then this the right type of wood that would be of suitable use on the water because it would float so well. Another clue would be that there are flocks of little black birds nesting on its branches. And when you tap it the little black birds would leave their nests and fly away. This is the correct type of tree.

Early next morning, following his father's advice, Gelam set off to find this correct floatable tree. Walking and singing to himself, Gelam went and tapped as many tree trunks as he could. At last, he heard noises of little black birds among the trees. Tapping the trees as he walked along, he has finally found the right sort of wood he had waited for for so long. (For Gelam, patience had been imbued in his nature, but sad to say it had not touched his heart in forgiving his mother.) It was the baidamtulu (bloodwood). Cutting it down quickly and with a small piece of the tree, Gelam would try to see if it would float. Jubilation for this young man—he was so proud of himself and of his unseen contact with his father. He dragged the wood down to the sea and attemped to float it. The wood did float. It would have been a real joy to see this young man's facial expression.

The Journey

Unable to forgive his mother, Gelam had by now made up his mind to leave Moa. Each day he would gather the various species of plants, fruits and vegetables from their gardens and pack them into the carved replica of the mulu dungal (Dugong of the Eastern Torres Strait: It is black, heavy-bodied and very dark in colour. It can stay under water for a long period of time and surfaces only once for breathing). Gelam was planning to go to Mabuiag, an island in the Western Torres Strait. But he remembered the stories that his mother had told him about how she had to escape from Wabada, the place where there were serious battles and disputes among the nearby villagers. The battle led to the death of his father. Who was once a great warrior. The thought of going to Mabuiag discouraged Gelam. As he looked into the distance between Mabuiag and Moa, he said to himself that it was too close for him, that his mother would come to visit him there. Gelam had planned to leave Moa for many, many months by now.

One day, Atwer told Gelam that she was going to the reef to catch fish. Gelam was very happy for the opportunity for him to launch his dugong. Finally, he said to his mother: "When you see some big fish out there, sing out to me and I will come and spear it for you." Meanwhile, Atwer was out onto the reef. By now, Gelam hurried to his dugong and pushed it out to the sea. He swam inside it towards his mother and circled around her. At home, that evening, Atwer told Gelam about the friendliness of a dugong who came so close to her out on the reef. Smiling quietly to himself, Gelam was thinking of his next plan, when his mother would go out to the reef. Many months later, Gelam was preparing to leave his mother. It was the time of the year when the sagre winds blow. Atwer left the gardening and went to fish in the lagoons. As she was casting her nets into the sea she saw this thing floating towards her. Amazed by the friendliness of the sea creature, she gently stroked it. The dugong came so close to her and opened its mouth. To Atwer's amazement, it was Gelam. Gelam said to his mother, "Ama, many times you have tricked me and pretended to be a ghost, while I was out hunting. Today, I am going to go far away from you and will never see you again." After that Gelam closed the dugong's mouth and swam away.

Atwer was very sad and she began to weep and called out to Gelam. "Bakiu au mu Mer ge, au lewer lewer ged ge esigemerau." (Go and lie down in Mer [Murray], an island rich in food)

In his stubbornness, Gelam had now swum out to sea and came to the island of Nagir (Mt Ernest). Turning around, he could still see his mother standing there weeping. Gelam told himself "I must not rest here. It is too close to my mother and she will come and visit me often." He turned around and saw Lama (Yam) island. Swimming towards it to rest, he could still see his mother Atwer standing on the reef weeping. He could not rest for his father had told him that if he rested he would turn into a stone. Turning around to the east he saw Sasi (Long island), Poruma (Coconut Island), Masig (Yorke island), Ugar (Stephen Island). He tried to rest on these islands, but he could still see his mother weeping. The sun was setting and his ballast was getting heavy to carry. He was also getting tired so he swam to Erub (Darnley Island). He beached himself on beautiful Garsou lagoon and unloaded most of his plants, vegetables and fruits. Gelam must look elsewhere to rest. His father who had appeared to him in his dream several nights ago told him that he must go far away from Bulbul. Gelam found it uncomfortable resting in the lagoon because he could still see his mother as a tiny speck on the horizon. As he turned away from his mother, he saw Mer (Murray island). "That is where I am going to rest and make my home," he said to himself.

So he left the beautiful lagoon and swam to Mer. Arriving there, he beached himself facing the north-easterly wind (Naiger). As it blew hard up his nostrils, he turned around and faced the south-west. He spat out two "wada" seeds and they became the islands of Daur and Waier. With his left hand, he threw out all the species of plants, vegetables and fruits that he had carried from Moa.[1] He rested for a while before going to sleep. While resting, Gelam saw sharks attacking Peibri. Peibri left her home in the reef of Mebgor and came to live with Gelam.

Mer was once a small island. The arrival of Gelam and Peibri, had turned Mer into large, rich volcanic island as it is today.[2]

On the island of Moa today, a rock stands where Atwer stood as she wept Gelam goodbye. On low tide, she can be seen standing with fresh water trickling from her eyes.

[1] *Seeds and plants include: sorbi (a tree which bears rich edible fruit on its trunk), kud and wais (which bears edible red fruit).*
[2] *The rich red soil of Mer is said to be brought by Gelam from Moa. Moa as a result is now deprived of that rich alluvial soil. It now has poor, loamy and sandy soil.*

Pigeon Story

Banjo Worrumarra

Now—
PIGEON—
Pigeon START OFF—
him bin—
I talk to you—
with the Pidgin English, Pidgin—
white man tongue, Pidgin—
he bin start off got—
breakin' in HORSES—
him bin SHEARER—
shearin' sheep—
with a BLADE—
not a machine—
'cos those days they had a blade—
so he bin work on that one—
shearin' blade—
he bin work Quanbun—
Noonkenbah—
Liveringa than he went back to Kimberley Down—
he work there—
an' he went back to p'lice camp—
then he start p'trol—
he went for p'trol—
look around some BLACKFELLAS inna bush—
he tracking—
—
(long pause)—
What they done?—
they killed two white man—
in Mount Broome—

then p'lice went up to find him—
so they pick-im-up—
Pigeon the outlaw—
they take-im in—
up on the range—
then Pigeon walk up—
an' he got a MOB—
an' he bring them back—
SOME was there—
right one—
that bin kill the white man—
but he didn't know who he was—
take him to Windjana Gorge—
tie them there—
they turn around tell 'im Pigeon "alright you wanna get a—
kangaroo"—
"for us?"—
"we can't jus' sitting down here stave hungry on the chain"—
"you bin bring us"—
"so you mus' FEED us"—
—
So—
Pigeon turn around and see boss—
the boss—I wanna get a—kangaroo for these prisoners—
"Alright you know where the rifle"—
so he went up and get the rifle—
'stead of he go for KANGAROO he shot his boss—
in Windjana—
Lillamaloora—
that was a p'lice station—
—
(softly) Anyhow—
he went there—
got the mob—
take-im off the chain—
an'—
he bin—
go in the hill—

everyone followed him up there—
but he the one done all the FIGHTING—
an' this OTHERS didn't understand him—
(softly) they never have-im fight—
—

Anyhow—
he went across to Ninety Two—
he shot one white man there—
then he went to Oscar—
Oscar Range—
station—
he shot one white man there—
early mornin'—
then he went down to Plum Plain—
he see MOB comin-up gotta horse—
stockboys and the p'liceman they ALL come—
look for Pigeon—
then he take off—
from that big plain—
Plum Plain—
they chased him—
when he got into the HILL country—
he look back he knock that hats off the p'liceman—
take his hat off—
(knocks table) one bullet—
he asks that p'liceman he says—
"You want you life or wanta dead"—
p'liceman said "No I wanta life"—
"you get back"—
so he just taste-im but if he wanted-im he hadda kill-im then—
anyhow he let-im go—
he went to Brooking Gorge—
corner of Brooking or Leopold—
an' he went toooo—
—

(long pause)—
—

he went to King Leopold—

an' he went tooo—
he get a mob of blackfella there big tribe—
they start fight there—
they take-it-away one woman from there—
young girl—
they couldn't fight-im—
they couldn't foller-im—
went back to Windjana—
be bin fight for SIX YEARS—
and ah—
governor or government went up there and said—
he went up he get up he's there Pigeon "You there?"—"Yes"—
"I'm here"—
Ah—
"Well we all friend now you'll have to come down"—
so Pigeon didn't take a risk—
so he knock his hat—
said "You better go off"—
said "Ah I don't want to (inaudible)—
knock his hat off this government bloke whatever he was—
anyhow he went back agin—
so (laugh)—
stay there too long—
anyhow they follered-im up—so LAS' he felt himself—
he was—
he was losing hope—
they can put a bullet right across here—
shootin-im in here—
nothing can come out—
not even water—
not even a drop of blood—
(softly) nothin' doin'—
no matter how many shot he used to take her nothing doin'—
THAT didn't put him back—
anyhow—
one—
maban blackfella witchdoctor—
come from ROEBOURNE—

they used to call'im ah Minko Mick—
he got onto the boat—
in—
Roebourne—
or Onslow—
boat call—er name ah—
Koombana—
three funnell—
come right up to Derby landed—
anyhow blackfella got onto—mail coaches—
they take-im to Meda and from Meda to Kimberley Downs and from
Kimberley Downs to Fairfield—
then he ride across with horse—
horseback—
went to Tunnel—
he SLEEP one night there—
he didn't go fast—
but next mornin'—
they stirred-im Pigeon up—
so he got up—
to start shooting—but this bloke seen his life—
soo—
witchdoctor told them boys—
"Alright"—
"I know" he said—
"I take jus one bullet in my rifle," he said "I'll kill im 'an you fellas
can go an' pick 'im up"—
cut his HEAD off—
so this Pigeon went up aaah—
Minko Mick—
followed the river up—
he got into the boab tree—
he look up—
upwards—
Pigeon was right on top in the cliff—
so he FIRE ONE shot he knock him in his thumb—so he fell down
an' he sing out—
"I shoot-im you can go in and pick'im up whenever you want"—

very fright they said, "NO we can't run up to pick-im up"—
"NO—you go in an' see-im"—
"he's finished"—
"alright"—
oh well they didnt argue with 'im all them fellas round up there—
and see—
sure enough Pigeon laying there—
smashed up—
is thumb—
(pause for tape change)—
so when Minko Mick—went up there he looked 'is—thumb he
found a little—
little heart—
like a fish—
in his thumb here (shows thumb)—
that where he shot—
an' that was the end of the old Pigeon story—
(SM: Oh good)—
it's from Banjo—
Pandanus Park—

(Transcribed by Stephen Muecke)

The Great Journey of the Aboriginal Teenagers

Robert Bropho

Robert Bropho tape-recorded the story "The Great Journey of the Aboriginal Teenagers" for his granddaughter, Dotty; a transcription of that tape is reproduced here.

The days of old, back there in the yesterdays, in the past ... for us, Aboriginal teenagers then, in the fifties, in the late forties, up into the early sixties ... back there in the past.

Today is the closing stage of the day ... it's eight o'clock pm in the evening, twenty-third of the first month of nineteen hundred and eighty five. I decided to make this tape in the darkness, in the quietness of the evening. I'd like to talk about us, the teenagers, the Aboriginal teenagers ... then ... in the days back there in the past. Of what we encountered and what we went through, being teenagers.

My family was living in camp life ... it was really bad in them days for us. The teenagers today, they're of a different generation ... white and black, they songs and musics and they beats of today is entirely different, it's fastened up. They in a different time and age now. But for us it was really rotten, really bad. We used to be bored with ourselves, nothing to do, no work. There was hardly any social services around in them days for us, the teenagers then. If we found ourselves in a starving situation, we'd have to go and steal. Oranges, fowls from the white man's fowl pens, this is after hours in the darkness. Steal bread, milk, we had to do it to survive. There is many times that we sat around the campfires, where our camps was—in the scrub, in the black, dirty filthy sand. Dry. When the east wind would blow the dust, the black dust from the sand would hit our eyes and out of that would come sore eyes, watery, red, sore and overnight the matter would build up and your eyelashes would clamp together. We'd be drinking bitter tea ... if we had no tea we'd burn sugar till it's brown in a spoon and then put it in the boiling water and drink that.

It was idleness then for us, there was nothing for us going. That then caused us to do what we did then, to go around stealing. It got that bad that we used to get in mobs and go. One such occasion I'd like to talk about now is ... it's a big great journey of ours which ended in disaster for us. The long arm of the white man's law, elastic law that stretched so far across the breadth and length of this country—grabbing up and snabbling up Aboriginal people who put their foot wrong in the eyes of the white man's law, the Ten Commandments.

Anyway, the great journey started off with us pinching an old Vanguard van and doing a real tour of the metropolitan area after hours, early hours of the morning. Breaking into pubs, stealing large quantities of whisky and rum, beer and wine, all kinds, and barrels of wine and picking up money if we could out of the tills. On this occasion we took all this stuff. The strangest part of it all is I was senseless drunk to some extent, before we started off on this thing and all through this breaking and entry for all this white man's spirits—which is the wine and things—I slept right through it until I woke up in the morning surrounded in the back of the van with bottles of wine and beer of all kinds all around me ... and cigarettes and things. When I became wide awake we was parked in the scrub. All my mates was with me—William Bodney, Man Mippy, Ted Bropho (Gubbi's his Aboriginal name), and Donald Wallam and his brother, the one that's noortch, dead now, who's laying in the South Guildford Cemetery who died young, twenty-eight. Anyway, the police got the wind of it that we might have been connected with the crime. So we said (this is at the Lockridge-Eden Hill area now where the camps was) "Oh well, we'll give them a run for their money now."

So we waited till the late hours of the night, in the darkness. Just before twelve o'clock we drove the van down to Bassendean station and abandoned it there and then got onto the station and under the darkness got onto the train and went down to the East Perth area where the line branches out and goes to Bunbury. We waited for the goods train to come then. We had a bit of swags rolled up, a few rugs with a bit of rope tied around it. We made some sort of a shape of a handle with the rope, chucked it over our shoulders so it'd give us two free hands and two free legs and free movements of the body when the train'd come. Anyway, the goods train rolled up, with all the coal trucks, pulling the coal trucks to go down to Brunswick Junction (the junction that's about seventeen miles out of Bunbury) and there the train would automatically change lines and go back through to Collie. We all boarded the train, climbed along and got into one of the empty train trucks, made our beds down and laid down and went to sleep, for some part of the journey right down through to Brunswick Junction ... arriving down there in the early hours of the morning before daybreak.

We went up into the hills to my auntie's place ... and had something to eat very early and went back further up on the high points of the hills so that we could get a good view of all around the flat lands. We knew the cops'd be after us. Yes, end of the day we seen them coming to the camp, to Donald Alfred Wallam's camp, to his mother's camp, who was alive then, his father. So we went down and asked after they (the cops) left and they said "Yes, they came looking for youse." So we decided to stick to the hills and the valleys. We walked from Roelands right back along the scrub, under the cover of the scrubs, and waited on the Collie line at a big hill and the train came. It was coming up the hill at a slow pace to climb the hills, and we runned along the side. Each and every one of us we knew exactly what we had to do, we was experts in jumping trains—we could jump onto a moving train, we could jump off a moving train—that's the hardships of being born what you are, in poverty. Anyway, we rode the train through to Collie, arriving there still under darkness, and we decided to steal a car from there.

The car we picked was a Holden ute. We got onto that, and went right through Darkan, through Williams, right down to Pingelly. My brother who's dead now was living then, was working for the PWD, the water supply, down at Pingelly. He got the job through an office in Perth here and was stationed down there. We called on him early in the morning, got some food and than had a feed. Went up to the bush and hid until darkness—we always travelled under cover of darkness, that was our protection, that was our strategy that we used

... travelling through Corrigin, right through to Bruce Rock. Arriving there, Bruce Rock, still under darkness and seeing Bruce Rock Co-op was there, we all decided to go in there and store up with whatever food we could snabble up from the supermarket. It was our choice to pick what we wanted. We got into the place there and the first thing we looked for was torches. Everyone had a little torch, and it was strange ... the bloke who was left outside to watch, to keep nick and see if anybody was coming, he told us after that, he said "You was all like ... you could see all little lights walking around in the darkness, in the darkness of the supermarket." So we got tins of meat, and fruit, and smokes and things, and cool drinks and cordial and water bags, and we dumped them in the ute, loaded up and went through. We had to pass through Merredin before the daybreak.

We moved along very quickly and pulled right off the road down from Bulla Bulling at the siding just down from Southern Cross, and we got into the bush there. We decided to lay off all day, playing two ups for cigarettes, just lazing around in the scrub there. We was well hidden off the main highway. When it was time to go we decided that we must leave now and try to get along ... it was getting near sunset. Just after dark started to fall we found that we had a flat tyre and no spare, so we had to abandon the ute there. We rolled up a few of our belongings and a bit of tucker and we decided to Shank's pony—that means walk—along the line, we wouldn't hitchhike on the road. We walked up to Bulla Bulling siding. We arrived there and were sitting down in the darkness, spelling ourself waiting for a goods train to come. Yes, we could hear it coming, from the Merredin area. They had steam engines then, the whistle blowing, you could hear 'em coming from a long way. Anyway, when it arrived at Bulla Bulling it wasn't going to stop, it slowed down to pass through there. So what we had to do was run along the side at the speed of the train, which wasn't travelling too fast, and board the train. To board a running train you must pick where the joining of the empty rail cars are 'cos there's always a foothold there and a handhold. That's the way you board a train. But you don't abandon a moving train from that position because it's pretty dangerous between the trucks. You must alight or jump from the centre of the train trucks when you're getting off a moving train and always fall away from the train. Anyway, we arrived in Kalgoorlie early in the morning just before sunrise. We didn't ride the goods right into Kalgoorlie, we waited until it slowed down coming into town and then we jumped from the moving train on different sides. And (when you do something like that) always explain where you're gonna head for, where you're gonna meet. That's the main thing because if you get split up then you know exactly where everybody's gonna meet.

We got off the train and was all standing together in the scrub deciding what to do and we could see this smoke rising a little way down the line, away from the line. We went down and it was an old Aboriginal man and his wife sitting down there. They had a fire going and was just finished cooking a damper in there and had a black billy of tea. So we walked up to the camp. Straightaway they offered us a drink of tea and a piece of damper each. We sat down for a while talking to them and then we decided to move further back into the scrub and wait for the cover of darkness again. So this time ... it was a big town, Kalgoorlie then, a fairly sized big town ... so we decided to send two people down to search for a car. The persons that had to go down was Man Mippy because he was the driver, experienced driver, and another physically fit young bloke with him, Donald Wallam's brother. So they went down and we sat and wait. After a while we could hear a lot of bloody shouting going on and cars whizzing up and down there. Someone had surprised these two fellows (Man Mippy and Donald Wallam's brother) who were trying to steal his car, and they ran up the lane, they got away from him. While the police was looking for them this end of the laneway they was further up. They went right up the top on the other side and pinched a car up there, drove back down, picked us up and we headed north from Kalgoorlie, past Broad Arrow. We had to move fast to get to Menzies because the daybreak was getting close. We decided that we'd pull right away from Menzies out in the scrub and wait there until darkness again so that we could go down and see if we could pinch a bit of petrol. So we hid the car.

Through the day we was, we got on a high point east of Menzies so we could see down. We could see the road coming in from Kalgoorlie, we could see it going out towards Leonora. So we waited there, the pinpoint we could see all the movements of the trucks and things, and cars down in the town. We had binoculars that we pinched—and that helped a little bit so that it would give us the distance away and we could see things from a long distance. Anyway when night fell we went down and found a depot. We got in there and there's drums of petrol up on these stands. So we filled the car up, filled the small drums of petrol and put them in the car and then we headed for...Wiluna now...we went through Katherine Valley. That's a little place but it's long-gone now, it's closed down. We passed through there and we got to Wiluna. Again, we pulled off the road before we got to the town and waited. And we cased that joint again and we seen a surveyor's truck—we didn't know it then, but it was a half-ton truck—seen it parked, the truck in the yard. So we decided we would visit that place under cover of darkness and try and get that, to give us two—a half-ton International truck and we had the ute then, the ute from Kalgoorlie. And anyway, we succeeded in getting that half-ton truck, we loaded that up also with a forty-four gallon drum of petrol. And then we was looking for a rabbit proof fence ran through Yandl station heading north—it's supposed to go right up to Port Hedland.

We got on the rabbit proof fence and we followed it through, we went through Yandl station and Roy Hill and Bonny Downs. And there was many times we got bogged in creek beds. If the Holden ute got bogged and the half-ton International truck was stronger than that and would get through the bogs, we'd have to unload everything, pull that (the ute) out. We'd go on to the next creek bed, we'd get bogged again. It was a full day going along like that. We'd come to a big water tank where the windmill was—where the sheep's supposed to come—and it was really stinking hot. And in this International truck that we stole there was one of those long binoculars like those olden day pirates put out ... right out. So we got up on the windmill then, we sent one bloke up there to keep nick from the top of the windmill and we give him this long spyglass and he could see right back miles down the track where we'd been, and right ahead. He'd be scanning the area for dust—dust was sign of movement, whether it be cattle, kangaroos or cars or whatever—while the rest of us stripped off and had a swim in the tank. After having a swim we decided that we'd move along now and find a camping spot. So we drove along as fast as we could, we got a flat

plain where all was hard clay, but dusty. And the boys started to
have a bit of fun with the half-ton truck and the Holden ute,
zigzagging through the trees and making the dust rise. We did this
for a least an hour or so, having a bit of fun, and then we went right
along. We came about sundown to this spot where all the ghost
gums was, flat country ... and the place was full with kangaroos. So
we decided to camp there.

We sent the Holden ute around, chasing the kangaroos around and
they knocked one over, brought it back and we skinned that and we
ate a meal of kangaroo and some dry biscuits and things. We all
bedded down. We made a big fire and let the coals die down so that
there wouldn't be no light. We though it'd be safe, that far out. Plus
we could see any lights coming if any cars were coming along the
fence where we came, or if there was cops looking for us, trailing
us. We was all sitting down around the coals of the fire, talking and
planning out ... and talking about where we came from and how far
we travelled and what we did. But you must bear in mind that we
had no drink, we wouldn't touch the drink. We could hear these
camel noises in the distance ... and I know from experience of my
Dad and what he's told me about camels, if a camel knocks you
down he'll lay on you until you stink. So everybody started to get a
bit scared and so they all decided to climb up on the half-ton truck
and all squeeze in there. Made beds and laid down there.

We got up the next morning and we headed for Port Hedland. We
got so many miles out, travelling in the dark, and we took a chance
on getting bogged and running into difficulties through the night.
We drove for endless hours and we lay down and we went to sleep.
And it was the early hours of the bloody morning and we didn't
know we was close to the gravel road, where the rabbit proof fence
come in. And the Holden ute was hidden out of sight but the
International truck, half-ton truck, was in sight. And one white bloke
going into Port Hedland seen it. He didn't come near us, he went
and told the bloody cops. Anyway, this was unknowns to us, the
fugitives. We was laying there sleeping and I came out of my sleep
and I could hear this "Bang!" ... this bloody rifle shooting. When I
woke up there was a cop standing there pointing a rifle at me.
"Don't move" he said, "you black bastard. You the bastards we've
been looking for." I could hear the rifles going off. "Bang!" getting

further and further into the distance. They were chasing Johnny Wallam and Donald through the spinifex. They came out of their sleeps seconds before the police got out of their cars and they started running across this red sand with the spinifex, the spinifex was all this sharp grass in different spots but not all over the ground and they never had time to get their shoes and they bloody runned. They runned so many miles, so what the bloody cops went and done they brought in some black trackers ... and those buggers was cantering along on bloody horses tracking Johnny Wallam and Donald, followed by cops on horses until they found 'em. By the time they found em I was already taken into custody, put into the Port Hedland lockup. Man Mippy was with me and William Bodney. Then they brought in Donald and Johnny handcuffed, blisters all on their toes and on their heels and soles of their feet from this hot sand. Gubby (my brother Ted) was already in there with us.

Anyway they kept us there for days on end until the magistrate came, the visiting magistrate. In the meantime they had us out working like bloody horses—cleaning all around the gaol, outside, cleaning around the sergeant's house—but they gave us freedom, they wasn't standing over us watching us. They'd just open the doors up and say "Alright, work now today." When it was getting near twelve o'clock they'd call us back, we'd go in and leave the doors open. We'd go in and have something to eat, the sergeant's wife used to cook it—a very thin meal. Same applied to suppertime and then they'd lock us up for the night.

It went on for a while there and we decided that we'd make a break from there. We opened the side gate with a knife, got out, went down to the bloody jetties. Before going to the jetty we broke into the bloody pub and got some beer and wine. We'd decided "Okay we'll have a bloody ... we'll have a spree up now" (that means have a good time while it lasts). We all got these cans of beer and things and then went down to the mangroves ... because when the tide goes out the mangroves become higher, you're standing on the dry ground then. And we stole a little rowing boat. "Righto, we're going to row to Singapore now." They loaded everything on the boat. And the best part of it is, everybody else could swim but I couldn't. So I explained it to them and they said "Oh, you'll be all right. If the boat goes down we'll save you." So we got in the boat and started rowing out. We got a bit of distance from the shore and the waves started to get rougher. Each time a wave'd hit a certain drop of water would come into the boat and they started emptying it out with a tin. And I said "Turn back, I want to go back." "No you'll be all right, Singapore's not far away." Anyway while this was going on we heard some shouts from the foreshore—it was the bloody sergeant and the two constables, the black trackers and a few civilians from the town—and the sergeant's voice was singing out "Come back ... Co ... me ba ... aaack." So we decided to row back. We rowed so far back. The sergeant red face was chest deep in the water coming out, trying to paddle out to us ... and the two constables, they couldn't wait until the boat got into shallow waters, the moment they got us in arm's reach, they started wrestling with us. William Bodney, they handcuffed him to me. Of course William started pushing the constable and the constable started pushing him—because William Bodney was a bit of a fighter—and me at the same time was tiptoeing because each time they'd wrestle they'd go down a bit, and I was tiptoeing to keep my head out of the water.

And anyway, they got us all back into the cells and double locked the doors and they gave us our sentence then, took us to court and gave us our sentence. I ended up with thirty-two month. The rest of them twelve month and six month and whatever.

They put all us on one of the old DC planes with the propeller engine and brought us right back down to the Guildford airport. Arriving there ... and the police paddy waggon van was still going then, was waiting there, and the police constable. Out of the plane, into the van and down to Roe Street and down to Fremantle Gaol. And that's where the journey of the teenage Aboriginals—that's us—in the late forties through the fifties and early sixties ended up ... and that's what us the teenagers in them days went through.

(Transcribed by Sonya Jeffrey and Matthew Holden)

Reflections on a Black Childhood

Leanne Hollingsworth

We lived at Twenty-nine Mile Crossing, a couple of miles out from Walloon, which is outside of Ipswich. I was living with my "real" family at the time. Our house was the only one around for a couple of miles. We lived in a very old, two-storey house near a railway line, surrounded by bush and a river.

It was here, at the age of five, that I experienced embarrassment and humility but learned pride.

Being always the last one in the family to make a move, I remember lying drowsily on my mum's bed, one eye open, watching everyone else scurrying around, getting ready to catch the train to Brisbane for a day of shopping. I remember Mum repeatedly telling me to get a move-on if I wanted to go. It was really no big deal to stay home on our own; each of us had at one time or another. Besides, we had the television to keep us company! But as I lay there, my decision whether to go or not moved more positively towards the excitement of the big city, lunch in a cafe, lollies, and persuading Mum to buy this or that.

Busily chewing the decision over, I didn't notice everyone leave the house, yelling half-hearted farewells in their hurry for the train! Its whistle blew loud and clear as it rounded the bend! Man, did I move!!! I rushed around at blind speed trying to find suitable clothes. Of course, the inevitable occurred—I couldn't find any! So I grabbed Mum's old house dress from the end of the bed, slipped it on (inside out) and raced out in time to see Mum talking to the conductor, obviously asking him to hold on a second. How she knew I was coming, I'll never know. Maybe it's that thing that all mothers are supposed to have—intuition?

I raced down the front steps and took a short cut through the barbed wire fence, snake style, on my belly; but I didn't flatten my bum on the way through. Hmmm! you guessed it! I ripped Mum's dress, my panties and scratched "it"! Ouch! But I was in too much of a hurry to notice pain! I reached the train with great relief.

I climbed the stairs, facing the knowing smile of my mother. I remember the quiet humoured whispers of the other passengers as they noticed my bared piece of anatomy; and do you think I was going to show them how utterly embarrassed I felt? No way baby!!

I turned to them and smiled my best toothless smile with an air of poise as if I was wearing my best blue dress with the oversized bow at the back!

Nanya

William Ferguson

William Ferguson first heard the story of "Nanya" as a young man and later met Harry Mitchell, one of the trackers sent out to bring in the "lost tribe" of Scotia Blacks. This is the story as told to him by Harry Mitchell around 1920.

A long time ago, before the white man came to this country, the Aborigines used to make their camps along the main rivers, and on any site close to permanent water, hence we find at the time our story opens, groups, or tribes of dark skinned people scattered at different distances along the Darling River. Each tribe conducted their own social affairs, by means of a local committee, with one man as the head, but all tribes and committees and head men, were subject to one mighty Law, the Bora, or Bulbung.

The Bora controlled all Aborigines throughout Australia. By means of the Bora the Aborigines have been able to keep the race clean, without mixed marriages right down through the long ages, for many thousands of years, which in itself is a great achievement. I can't say very much about the Bora, only that it represents a powerful secret society, but I will explain as much as I dare, and be truthful. Any writer, White or Aboriginal, who dares to go further than I, is either a lunatic or a liar, because all the secret rites of the Bora are known only to those who have been initiated, and have never been divulged to outsiders. I know several old men who had been through the Bora, confirmed old drunkards some of them were too, and I spent much time and money trying to get the desired secret information, but whether drunk or sober, they guarded the secret well. They told me that if they said the things I wanted them to, their life wouldn't be worth living, some of the tribe would find out, and the punishment would be swift, nothing less than the spear. As far as I could find out, the Law centred around one word, Meat, and it is the hardest word in all the different Aboriginal dialects to pronounce. I can pronounce it, but I cannot find letters to spell it, so I will spell it Gingue. The Aborigines with their belief in reincarnation, believe that every soul is born and re-born, each time in different forms. Every baby born therefore, represents some animal or bird, and the marriage laws are fixed, in order that only those named after certain meat can marry only certain other meat. It is very simple, although it may appear complicated.

An illustration—a family of Kangaroo in the far north, say Darwin, start to move south. Thousands of years later they are spread right across the country. A stranger walks up to a camp, and the first thing they ask him "What meat you?" "Kangaroo," he answers. "Alright," he is told, "you my brother, that's your wife over at the next camp," and so it has always been.

If he didn't tell the truth and said he was Emu, and they let him marry his own meat, that would be breaking the Law, and although his lie might go over for a while, he would be sure to be found out sooner or later, and then the spear.

Our story opens on an ordinary scene at that long forgotten time. About twenty youths are gathered around the camp of the head man, or Chief, and he is speaking to them. The Chief is an old man, and still shows traces of his once fine physique. He is tall, about six foot two inches, and in spite of his years, stands very erect. Rather thin, but strongly built, grey hair and whiskers singed short. The boys grouped around are listening attentively to what he has to say. Their ages are about sixteen years. "Now you boys, you are going away today to the Bora. There you will be told all the mysteries about life. You will be taught how to hunt for food, how to track animals, and man, how to make all kinds of weapons and tools, and how to use them. You will be told how to respect all people, particularly women, and how to devote your lives to love and not to hate your neighbours. You will go now with the old men who are waiting for you, and stay away until they bring you back." The boys knew he had finished speaking, and all turned and walked away into the bush, following the six old men who took the lead.

The old Chief watched until they were out of sight, his old eyes following to the last one boy in particular, whom he watched until they were swallowed up by the Bush. Then he sat down beside his fire, and thought: who knows what he thought, but we suppose it was of the time when he as a boy many years ago, went to the Bora, or was he thinking of his own son, who had just left for the Bora, and who was to take his place as Chief of the Tribe when he became too old? Nanya was the boy's name. He was about sixteen years of age, tall like his father, of powerful build and could run faster than any other man of the tribe. Not only his father, the Chief, but all the tribe loved Nanya, old and young, and why shouldn't they? He was always helping the older men, fixing their mia-mias, carrying wood and making them comfortable. Even as a boy he speared more food than any of the others and shared it among the tribe. He was to be seen playing with the children, and making them laugh with his antics. He would carry them on his broad shoulders for miles, and never tire, his endurance was simply marvellous. He had been known to run all day, as a stick carrier. On one occasion, he ran from his camp, about where the Menindie Aboriginal Reserve now stands, six miles above Menindie Town, to another tribe at Cuthrow Station, about 40 miles down the river. That means that Nanya travelled fortymiles to Cuthrow and forty miles back in twenty-four hours, without rest.

The Aborigines matured very early in life. A boy of sixteen was as much a man as he ever would be, and girls were women at fourteen—some even younger. They were given in marriage when very young, and often went to live with their older husbands, but the husbands never had intercourse with their wives until they matured to womanhood, about thirteen or fourteen. Among the girls of this tribe was one whom we must turn to for a while. Mimi was fifteen years of age, and she watched with others of the tribe, the departure of the boys. Like the old Chief, she too had eyes for only one, and that one was Nanya. Love shone in her beautiful big eyes, the full young love of a lovely girl. Mimi knew that her love was returned, because Nanya had told her. But oh, the tragedy of it all. They both knew that she was the wrong Gingue. Mimi was not for Nanya, because they were both the same line of Gingue, both belonged to the Kangaroo. She was given when very small to an old man, who died before she was old enough to be his wife. Her next husband elect was among the boys now proceeding to the Bora, and when they returned, the Law said he was to take her. Hearts were not consulted in Aborigine marriages, and it's just as well so, because if they had been allowed to choose for themselves, they would have degenerated hundreds of years before. The one chosen as husband for Mimi was not a very desirable person. He was bad tempered and selfish, short of stature and fat, like all selfish greedy boys are, but the Bora Law gave to him the most beautiful girl of the tribe for wife.

Nobody knew, or even suspected the secret love of Nanya and Mimi, except God, the great master, who knew everything. When the little band of boys led by the old man vanished into the bush, the light died in Mimi's eyes, she knew her life was doomed to emptiness, there would be no happiness for her without Nanya. She turned away from the rest of the people, and walked down by the river, to sit and dream of her sorry plight and perhaps to talk and commune with her friend, the black Swan, who swam majestically across the river to where she sat in tears. Whatever the Swan told her is not known, but when she joined the other girls she was her usual self, jovial and bright, and none knew of her hopeless love. She even chaffed with the other girls about their marriages when the boys returned. Although their stay would only be a little more than six months, on their return they would be men and qualified for marriage.

We now follow the boys into the bush. They walked on and on till near sundown. It was springtime and the bush was teeming with life. The ground everywhere was covered with beautiful flowers, the boys enjoyed the walk, and when the old men told them to get some food for supper, they all tried to outdo each other in spearing emu and kangaroo and possum. When they had sufficient food, a place was selected for camp, fires made, bough breaks made and supper prepared. Choice bits of food were given to the old men and the boys ate what was left. After supper they all sat around the fire, in their most comfortable positions and listened to the old legends told by the old men. Great old yarn tellers they were, and they talked and talked until one by one the boys fell asleep. They were roused at daybreak and started on their march, which continued until late in the afternoon, when they arrived at the Bora, about fifty miles from the camp, and situated in a wild scrubby place, well hidden from curious eyes, because the Bora and all pertaining to it is sacred to

Aborigines.

The Bora ring is a place in the bush made similar to a circus ring. It is about fifty yards across the ring and worn down to about a foot deep from the tramping of bare feet of many Aborigines over a long period of years. This is the place where the actual ceremony takes place. The knocking out of the two front teeth we know of, but the other part (riding the goat) we know nothing. We won't even try to guess, beyond saying that for six months or more, those boys, who are being trained by the old men in bushcraft during the day, spend the greater part of the night in Sacred Corroboree in the Bora ring. So we will skip over the months and come to the last day of their schooling, and we find a different lot of boys. From continual and careful teaching, they are now experienced men, able to make tools and weapons to perfection, and use them just as perfectly. They have learned how to prepare for and go into war, how to track and kill game, and other mysterious things such as pointing the bone and witchcraft. Only special ones are selected for witchcraft. Those selected are known to possess supernatural powers, inherited from their ancestors. Among this line of gifted men is our hero Nanya, who came from a long line of Wirrugar, or clever men. The Wirrugar is a spirit man, who has been endowed with supernatural powers, given direct from the sky, and anyone with this power, can change from a man to an animal. If his meat or Gingue be a Kangaroo, then he will take the form of a Kangaroo, and his power will take effect for good or evil over any distance. For instance, if a man offends a Wirrugar, he will get a warning, and although the one offended be many miles away, the offender will take sick and die. I suppose it is the power of mind over mind. It is one of the things that the white man makes fun of, so we will leave it to the learned white man and not trespass too much on something sacred to Aborigines. The old men who were in charge of the Bora were Wirrugar, and they imparted some knowledge of spiritcraft to Nanya.

So now on the eve of their return to camp, we behold a different lot of boys, and especially a different Nanya. Almost the perfect man walking, with long springing steps, head slightly thrown back, apparently carefree, but with a deep resolve to marry the girl he loves, with the full knowledge of doing wrong. Great was the jubilation on the night of their return. A big feast was given, and a big Corroboree, natives from hundreds of miles around, had been gathering for weeks. We can imagine the scene. All the mia-mias clustered around, hundreds of camp fires, men in groups talking earnestly, women talking of the coming marriages and children playing at their noisy games. Many a night I have witnessed such scenes.

But there was no happiness for Mimi. The next day, after the Corroboree, all those girls promised in marriage would be claimed by their husbands, and Mimi would be the wife of the man she detested. She cast many a covetous glance at Nanya. It was not allowed that she could walk up openly and speak to him, that would be against the Law, and Nanya avoided looking at her, but I suppose it was instinct, or nature asserting itself, that told them both that they would meet as soon as an opportunity offered. It came just before the Corroboree started. Nanya walked towards the river, Mimi happened to be near the river too. Others were close by, but not close enough to hear Nanya give a command; "Be waiting for me near the Warwee hole just before dawn." Mimi just bowed her head, and passed on.

The Warwee hole (means the place where the Bunyip lives) was over two miles from the main camp, and just after midnight we see Mimi walking quietly towards the meeting place, wondering what did her lover mean. She did not belong to him, but she did not care. She would just wait and trust to his wisdom. It might mean just one sweet hour of love, and then death for both.

At the camp all the men painted and decked out with feathers. This was a special Corroboree, which marked not only the return of the Bora men, but also the induction of Nanya as the next head man of the tribe, to succeed his father. Many fine speeches were made and Nanya's name was mentioned often. He was held up as a model of manhood, one whose example could easily be followed to advantage, one who was sworn to obey and uphold the Law, and one day he would be Chief of the tribe. He took his place as leader of the Corroboree and did his part well. Never did a man shake his legs as did Nanya. The people were amazed at his quickness. He seemed to excel at everything, every movement perfect. Like some great actor, he held the people spell-bound, right through to the finish of the

Corroboree, when everyone retired to their camps, to rest, and be ready in the afternoon for the big marriage ceremony.

Nanya hurried to the trysting place, his one desire to see Mimi. Her quick ears heard him even before he came in sight. She rose to meet him, before she knew it Nanya had her in his strong arms. No word was spoken between the law-breakers. They loved, and when did ever love wait for Law.

"You belong to me Mimi, we both know it is against the Law and that we must both suffer death."

"What does it matter now Nanya, so long as we both die together."

"It is one thing to love and die for each other, but what about loving and living for each other?"

"Impossible," said Mimi. "We can't avoid the spear now."

"Not so impossible" said Nanya, "we will flee together."

"We can't get far" said Mimi, "they will overtake us."

"No" said Nanya, "they can't catch us, come on, we will go into the desert. No one can follow us there, they can't get water." And so commenced one of the strangest elopements known in the history of the world.

Back at the camp, the people are starting a new day. The fires are being poked up, and long spirals of smoke make their way into the sky. Men are calling out greetings to other men at other camps. Women are busy preparing breakfast and children are starting to make a noise. The old Chief scans all the camps within range of his quick eyes, and not seeing his son, calls out to his neighbours. "Did you see Nanya?" "No," and he asks one of the young men, "Isn't Nanya awake yet?" "I don't know, he didn't sleep with me last night." "Well go and wake him wherever he sleeps and tell him I want him." A search is made and Nanya can't be found. "Oh, never mind, perhaps he wanted to be quiet by himself." At another camp, Mimi's mother and father are concerned about her absence. She might have gone to another camp—a search is made, but without any results. The camp is now all commotion. Whispers are started. Nanya and Mimi are both missing. A council of all the elders and Chiefs of the tribes is called. Witnesses have been called, those who made search for them and the only logical conclusion they can arrive at is that they have broken the Law. All eyes are turned towards the Chief, Nanya's father. How will he act? Will he try to shield his favourite son? The old man stands up bravely and looks them squarely in the eyes. It seems as though he could read their very thoughts. He spoke quietly. "It is said that my boy, whom you all know is everything in the world to me, has broken the Law. I command that he and the girl be brought to me. If they can't prove their innocence, we will deem them guilty, and although it will break my old heart, the Law of the Bora must be carried out and both will be speared to death tonight—now go."

And so was given a decree that never was carried out.

Down the river, the runaway pair were making for the desert, which is now known as the Scotia country. This country is a vast scoop of barren waste, sand and mallee, extending from the Darling River out beyond the South Australian border, and from Broken Hill to the Murray River. The Aborigines had never ventured far into this desert. They told legends of strange animals and spirits who lived out there, but no man had ever lived there. There was no water to keep anyone alive. Once a man had gone into investigate and five days after he was seen walking and reeling like a drunken man, and when he got to the camp they found he had gone raving mad. He said he met the Mirrie-youla (dog Wirrugar) out there. He died that night and the Mirrie-youla was seen in the river that same night. Nanya had often heard of the spirits that lived in the desert, and as they ran along hand in hand, he told Mimi all about it. "Don't Nanya, you make me afraid." "Have faith in me Mimi, I am not afraid. I, too, am a Wirrugar. I am young and strong, and just as powerful as any spirit or Wirrugar in the desert." "But we will die Nanya, we can't live without water." "We will die for sure if we are caught," said Nanya, "but we have a chance of living if we get into the desert. I have been thinking of this day for the last two years, and preparing for it. Ever since that day when I first told you of my love for you. I studied bush law and signs, I learned how to find water when others couldn't find it. I can travel all night by the stars and not get off course. I can throw a spear straighter than any man living. When you feel tired, say so, and I will carry you because I never get tired." Mimi believed him.

They had reached a point about twenty miles down the river when Nanya, who had been looking back watching for a signal, at last saw a thin line of smoke rising, followed by other thick black smoke, then repeated. He knew what it meant, and had been expecting it. It meant that their tracks had been picked up, and was a signal for others down the river to intercept them, and hold them, or kill them. The same signal was noticed and interpreted by a party of Aborigines a few miles further down the river, and only for fate interfering, and altering the course of the fugitives, this story would not have been written. Nanya showed Mimi the smoke and laughed to think of them trying to catch him, Nanya the Powerful. He said, "There is no camp nearer than twenty miles, we will leave the river just this side of the camp and make for the desert." Hardly had he spoken when right in front of them they saw the strangest sight ever seen by Aborigines.

The sight that startled them was what appeared to be men, with white faces and hands and their bodies and legs and arms covered with something. Even their head and feet were covered, and they were sitting on big four legged animals, unlike any known animal in the bush, and were moving towards the place where Nanya and Mimi stood. Instinct told them to hide in the long grass and they moved on all fours nearer the river, until they found shelter in a big hollow tree. From their hiding place the runaways watched the strange procession, the white men riding the strange animals, and more surprise, two men of their own colour with their bodies and legs partly covered, also sitting on the strange animals and driving other loose animals with packs on their backs following the tracks of the white men. It may have been the Bourke and Wills party.

"What is it?" asked Mimi. "Wirrugar," said Nanya. "Come, we will cross the river here, and head straight into the desert." This resolve saved them from running into the party of Aborigines waiting just a few miles further on. Here they said goodbye to the river forever.

We cannot but admire the courage of Nanya, when we take into consideration the fact that he was venturing into a wild, unexplored desert, with no other equipment than a strip of Kangaroo skin about his waist in which was stuck a small stone tomahawk. Nothing more. They were both as naked as when they were born and up to that time none of that tribe wore covering, not even the loin cloth. We cannot help comparing the outfit of Nanya and the party of white

men. The fugitives ran steadily till about noon, having covered
about fifty miles from the main camp. Although it was late summer,
the days were still hot, and they were glad to have a few hours rest,
so crawling into a low bushy scrub, they lay down and slept till late
in the afternoon. Although they had not eaten since the previous
night, they felt no hunger and so they continued their flight through
the night, mostly running, sometimes walking, having in mind all
the time that those who were trailing them were also endowed with
great endurance. Nanya left nothing to chance. When Mimi told him
she was thirsty, he told her how he could get water by cutting the
root of certain trees, many of which they passed in the night, but he
advised her to suffer as long as possible until it started to hurt her,
then he would give her water. He did not want to let his pursuers
know that they would live—the best way to safety was to make
them believe that they would perish for water, and his reasoning was
right. The two men who were following easily followed the tracks,
and they too got quite a scare when they ran into the party of white
men, but unlike Nanya and Mimi, they were seen by the whites who
tried to speak with them, which only added to their fear, so they ran
and dived into the river and swam across to the opposite side, and
continued down for about a mile, and then crossed back, but it was
hard for them to pick up the tracks, as the horses had been over
them and they could only pick them up here and there, until they
came to a place where they lost them altogether, and it was just
before sundown when they accidently found where they crossed the
river.

So they decided to camp until morning, and take up the trail
again. The following morning, as soon as it was light enough, they
started on the tracks and at noon they reached the place where the
runaways had rested just twenty-four hours before. After talking the
matter over, they decided to give up. They reasoned that Nanya and
Mimi couldn't last long in the desert. If they got water from the
roots, the Wirrugar would get them, so why follow them? Anyhow
they might turn back and someone would get them in the end, they
can't dodge the Bora. And if we go too far we might die, so they
gave up the chase and returned home. Their reasoning was accepted
by the tribe, but Nanya's father, the old Chief and medicine man,
knew different for he had communion with his Wirrugar. As a

consequence a big old man Kangaroo could be seen travelling after the law-breakers, not to wreck vengeance on them, but to safeguard and protect them for all time. The old man lay dead. He was buried next day in the old burying ground near the mission.

So ended a long line of head-men of that tribe. A meeting of the old men resulted in a new Chief, who counselled and advised the tribe, till owing to the advent of the white man, the Bora was finally discontinued altogether and then commenced the degeneration and demoralising of the Aborigines, which has ended in what we have today, a race of unwanted half-castes, who have been deprived of the old Bora Law and given nothing to replace it, refused the rights to proper education, and shunned by their fathers, the white man.

We now return to the fugitives. Mimi was getting thirsty, and from the way she was walking Nanya knew she was tiring. They did not waste much time in talking. The Aborigines are silent people, they convey to one another by means of signs anything they wish to communicate. So, although there was a lot of love and understanding between our two runaways, they spoke little, but each could almost tell what the other was thinking about.

Nanya knew that there was enough distance now between them and their pursuers, so he kept a look-out for suitable trees, but they were travelling over a stretch of sand and spinifex. The sun was just rising. It was the second sunrise since they left home, and they were now a long way from the river, about forty miles into the desert. When Mimi stumbled, without making any complaint, Nanya lifted her on his shoulders, and carried her. The most precious burden he had ever carried. "I will save you. I won't let you die," he said. Mile after mile, and hour after hour he walked until he sighted a clump of young needle-wood trees in the distance. He walked straight up and we don't know if he was surprised or not, to see a big red kangaroo lying in the shade of one of the trees. He placed Mimi in the shade of a tree, and at once proceeded to cut a coolamon (a piece of bark off the bump of a tree). He then found the right roots and cut them and by placing one end of the roots in the coolamon and leaning the other end against a tree, standing them almost upright, he soon had about a quart of clear, sweet water. Not until she was told, did Mimi drink. There was plenty of yams growing about so they had their first meal since leaving the camp. Nanya cut more root and cut a larger coolamon, and they rested there all day and that night. Through the night Nanya heard an emu drumming, so early next morning they both set out to find the emu. They both wanted meat. They had not gone far from their first camp, when on looking behind, they saw the big kangaroo go to the coolamon and drink. Did Nanya leave the coolamon full of water for that purpose? And strangest of all, two dingoes—a male and female—both had a drink and started to follow them at a distance of about a hundred yards. Just behind the dingoes came the kangaroo. Nanya had taken his bearings from the sound of the emu drumming in the night and he judged the direction, also the distance so exact that he knew just when he would be close to the emu's nest. Telling Mimi to walk carefully and keep directly behind him, he started to stalk the emu, which he did so effectively that before the emu had time to jump from the nest, he threw the stone tomahawk. His aim was so true that he broke the emu's neck. Great rejoicing. Plenty of meat and nice fresh eggs. Nanya now set to work and dug a hole in the sand. He next filled the hole with pieces of wood and started a fire by rubbing vigorously two pieces of wood together. When the fire burned down, and only coals and ashes were left, he scooped the hole out with a stick cut for that purpose, placed the emu in the hole, and covered it over with coal, and put sand on top to keep the heat in. The eggs were placed in the sand and fire too, and what a feast. The future which but a short time before looked so gloomy, now took on a brighter aspect. Plenty of water, plenty of food and a Kingdom of their own. The dingoes came closer, perhaps the smell of meat coaxed them. Nanya threw some scraps a long distance out, and the wild dogs came nearer, until before the day was through they came quite close and ate up all the scraps, but always retired to about a hundred yards distance. The kangaroo fed on the plain and camped in the shade of a nearby tree by turn, never out of sight. They camped at that place for a few days till they ate up all the meat and eggs, then they moved on. Later on the dingo's howl at night brought other dingoes and later still, the dingoes used to chase the emus and kill them, but always waited for Nanya to cut a piece off for himself, before they would eat of it. Nanya was always close to the kill, for he could run as fast as an emu himself.

So they wandered and lived until once when Nanya had been

away all day hunting, on nearing the camp, he heard a strange noise, a baby crying. He just flew over the last few yards. "Yes Nanya, a son. He is so like you." "You alright Mimi?" "Yes Nanya, I'm alright." Not much fuss over the birth of their first baby, but in their silence they both knew they were drawn closer to each other. And also by their silence and only speaking in short sentences, they actually forgot their own dialect and learned to speak another language. After a few years their names were not spoken and then forgotten altogether. Another baby, this time a girl, followed by other boys and girls. And because Nanya himself had broken the Law, what was the use of bothering with others? None of them was named because they were all one meat. So it didn't surprise father or mother a few years later, when their first daughter was about 13 years old and the son about 15, that a baby was born to her, and so it went on, they degenerated completely. Fathers cohabiting with daughters, sons having intercourse with their mothers. Mimi was dead, and no one to tell them it was wrong. Only Nanya, and what right had he to reprimand them. Hadn't he set the example in the first place? And so we leave them in their misery, poor unhappy wretches, for surely the way of the transgressor is hard.

About the year 1890 a party of men were erecting the border fence separating two States, South Australia and New South Wales. The border struck through a portion of the Scotia Desert. Water was carted in two four hundred gallon tanks on a bullock wagon. Another wagon was used to cart posts and wire and netting and all the fencing gear. There was no cook but the men took it in turns for one to go to the camp a bit earlier than the rest in order to prepare supper.

One day, the man whose turn it was to cook supper got a suspicion that someone had been at the water tank. Not only was the water a lot lower in the tank, but the lid was not in its proper position. He told his mates about it. Oh no, no one lived out there. If they had been white men they would have camped for company. A search for tracks showed nothing, but the next morning the amount of water was noted and when it was found to be about three or four inches below the mark in the afternoon, they were all satisfied that someone was interfering with their water. So the next morning one stayed back to watch. Soon after the men had gone he was surprised and a bit scared to see a mob of Aborigines walking up to the water wagon. He was too afraid to meet them so he watched from his hiding place. He saw them go straight to the watertank. Some of the men climbed up and the others passed up their water containers (kangaroo-skin bags) which were filled, and as they made off, others brushed the tracks out with bushes, until no sign of a track remained. Word was sent to the police at Broken Hill, who in turn communicated with the police at all outlying police stations advising them of a tribe of lost blacks who were wandering in the Scotia Scrub. The police tried to find out from each camp if any of their number had left camp and wandered away. Enquiries at all camps along the Darling, down the Lower Murray, Lake Victoria, and in fact right around the desert, did not uncover any missing Aborigines.

Word was sent to Melbourne, Sydney and Adelaide, with the result that the New South Wales Government issued instructions to the police at Wentworth to go out and bring them in. The sergeant selected two young troopers and commissioned them to fit out an expedition, to get three of the smartest trackers possible and bring the wandering people in that they might be civilised and protected. So commenced the second manhunt with Nanya again, the hunted.

The Party consisted of two mounted police and three blacktrackers, whose names were Dan McGregor, Harry Mitchell and Bill Bell. The mounted police were both picked men, good horsemen and excellent bushmen. They took along three packhorses, with proper desert water bags, a good supply of food, besides a supply of firearms and ammunition.

For two days they travelled from Wentworth and on the third day a quarrel took place between Dan McGregor, who was the Senior Tracker and a good one too, and the troopers about the route to take. The troopers wanted to go in one direction, but McGregor, with his unerring bush instinct advised a different direction, and the troopers ordered the trackers to continue themselves and they returned to Wentworth. So the trackers journeyed on with only two pack-horses, they themselves were well mounted. For another five days they travelled right into the heart of the desert without seeing any sign of the Aborigines, but on the sixth day, without any warning they rode right onto the tribe. They must have seen the trackers approaching, and lay down in the grass to hide, and watch, and not till the horsemen were within a few yards of them did they jump to their feet and start to run. McGregor ordered the other two trackers to try to surround them. He shouted to Mitchell, "You go to the right and head them off, and Bell, you go to the left, and on no account will you shoot until I give orders." So with McGregor riding straight behind and the other two fanning out on either side, the chase began. And what a chase. The men on fast horses racing at top speed and the wild naked people on foot; running in the lead as swift as an emu was an old man with long snow-white hair and beard. He was bearing to the right, and the others following him. He continued to run for about half a mile, when he gave up suddenly and fell down exhausted. The others soon gathered around him, and all the men stood at bay with their spears drawn back ready to defend the old man and women and children.

There were in all thirty-three people. The old man was the tallest of the lot. Some of the other men were well built, others were deformed, as were some of the women. Twelve of the men carried long spears, about twelve to fourteen feet long. The old man carried an old worn-out stone tomahawk. The others carried absolutely nothing. If they had waterbags or food they must have left them behind somewhere. Bell aimed his rifle (a new Martine Henry just out). But McGregor made him put it down. Mitchell could speak many native languages so McGregor appointed him as spokesman. Nahndy wa mayjne (What black-fellow you?) he called out, addressing the old man, who still stood with his spear raised. No answer was made. Nahndy wa gingue (What meat?) no answer. The same questions were asked in many languages. Still no answers. The tribe started to talk among themselves in some strange language. The three trackers also conferred. "Did you ever hear of a man who broke the law, and took the wrong woman," asked McGregor. "Yes," said Mitchell, "I remember the old people talking about him when I was a boy. It happened when my father was a boy, about sixty years ago." Mitchell then called out in a loud voice "Nanya.". The old fellow bent his head as though he was trying to recall something.

Mitchell called again "Nanya". The old fellow repeated the word Nanya. He put his spear down and spoke to the others, who all put down their spears. Mitchell dismounted and walked towards them. They grabbed their spears again, but Mitchell put his rifle down and continued to advance. Some more talking and the spears were put down again. When Mitchell found he had started a train of thought in the old man's mind, he didn't let up, but continued to talk and talk in Nanya's own language and each word helped to revive Nanya's memory, until he remembered and spoke his own language. Mitchell explained to him that he must come back. "No," said Nanya, "the Bora—they will spear me." "The Bora is now forgotten" said Mitchell. "White men have taken our country. We got a good kind Government. Him give us plenty tea, sugar, flour and bacca, also plenty rum. Him give blanket and clothes and all the women now have white baby, no more black baby." "I think we stay here," said Nanya. "We happy here, no one to interfere with us, we own this country." "Well," said Mitchell, "Government now our law. Him tell us to go to desert and bring blackfellow in; if they no come, you shoot them." He then demonstrated with his rifle. About two hundred yards off there were some kangaroos feeding. "Look," said Mitchell, "I show you how to spear kangaroo," and he fired. The report of the rifle frightened the wild people, but they were soon quieted again by Mitchell, who called out and showed them a kangaroo lying kicking on the ground. "Look again" he said, and Bell and McGregor both fired together, and two more kangaroos dropped dead. "This feller white man spear, him kill anywhere. We not going to spear you. Bora no more, nothing to be frightened of, come and live on river in big camp, plenty fun and tucker." For a long time Nanya talked to his people, before deciding, and while they were talking the trackers were taking stock of the company. Next to Nanya in age were two old men over sixty years and one woman also old and grey. Those three were the only ones living directly descended from Nanya and Mimi. There was another man over fifty, with a crooked neck and another with a big lump on his neck, others were deformed in legs and arms, and with the exception of a few women, they all suffered more or less from deformity due no doubt to inter-marriage. Just behind was seen an old man kangaroo. The biggest ever seen. And not far from the kangaroo was a pack of about thirty dingoes. Mitchell drew the others' attention to the giant dingo. "Wirringa" said Mitchell, and they all agreed to go back. After mounting his horse and taking the pack-horse, Mitchell rode off with Nanya walking beside him talking about the tribe he had left years ago. The rest of his people followed while McGregor and Bill rode just behind them and about a hundred yards further back followed the dingoes and the kangaroo. Mitchell told Nanya to get his men to carry the three dead kangaroo for food. "No," said Nanya "that our Gingue." So they shot two emu that afternoon which was carried on to the night camp. It is sad to relate that no modesty or even moral code was observed by these unfortunate people. They acted more like wild animals than human beings. They obeyed any nature calls as they walked along. They walked in silence and spoke only by signs. Three men had sexual intercourse with one woman that afternoon. Tnere was no fixed mate for any one. Any man had connections with any woman whichever was nearest to him. After the trackers had made their camp, boiled their quarts and cooked some emu, the others just warmed their meat, some ate it raw and all lay just where they happened to be sitting. Nanya sat long into the night and talked to the trackers. He described everything that had happened in that long flight from the Bora. Right up till the time of Mimi's death. Although he must have been over eighty years of age, he could still run but not so long. His eyes were also good and he seemed just as strong and vigorous as ever. An incident occurred that first night which must be recorded. As I stated before some of the women were comely and one girl in particular was really beautiful. As previously stated no names were used for any of the tribe. The custom was for the speaker to look directly at the one addressed. But the trackers for their own convenience named them all. The one with the lump on the neck was called Tom. The one with the crooked neck was named Willie and so on. Now the girl who was most beautiful was about fourteen years old, and they christened her Ada.

From the time the tribe first halted, Bell had been watching Ada with lustful eyes and although he did not know it, McGregor and Mitchell were watching him, and while he was hobbling the horses for the night, these other two discussed the matter. "I don't like the way he keeps watching her," said McGregor. "No," said Mitchell, "and although we have seen for ourselves that these people have no moral code, I don't think it would be right for us, who are partly civilised to take advantage of them." "Just what I was thinking," said McGregor, "and I will watch Bell, and the first sign of interference with that girl, I will stop him." "Alright," said Mitchell, "I'll back you up in that."

So after the people laid down to rest and Nanya sat talking with McGregor and Mitchell about the long, long ago, Bell took his swag and settled down, not directly next to Ada, but not far distant, about eight or ten feet away. The others watched him as most of the people fell asleep, edge a little nearer to Ada, who was sound asleep. Still a little closer, now only about a yard away. Mitchell stood up and in his hand he held his rifle. He said "Bell, come away from there. If you don't I will shoot you like I would a dog." Bell tried to point out that it didn't matter to them, as they were without any moral code. "But," said Mitchell, "you are not like them. They have never been told anything about the Bora Law, or white man law. They know only animal law. You lay between McGregor and I, and if you move tonight I will shoot you. Tomorrow morning you will take a fair share of the food and leave us."

And so in the morning Bell saddled his horse, took his swag and some tucker and started for Wentworth where he arrived after five days' travel. It was he who told the world that the wild Scotia blacks had been found, and were being brought in to Pooncarie by McGregor and Mitchell. The news travelled slowly in those days, and not till a fortnight later did word reach Mr Crosier of Cuthrow Station, who with his wife and family, the residents of Pooncarie and Menindie, made up a big reception party, to meet the Scotia people at Popatar Lake fed by the Annabranch, a Back Station of Cuthrow, that being the place for which the trackers were making, and they told Bell to tell the police to meet them there in two or three weeks' time.

They had to travel slower each day owing to old Nanya getting sick and one of the women, who had one leg shorter than the other, going lame. Although they tried hard to persuade Nanya to ride Mitchell's horse, he steadily refused and insisted on walking the whole distance. Some of the children, and the crippled woman, had a ride for a few days when both the trackers walked, but it took in all ten days to reach the Annabranch, a few miles below Popatar Lake, where an old white shepherd was camped in a bark hut, shepherding sheep for Cuthrow Station.

A shepherd's life was very lonely in those days. They were put in charge of a few hundred sheep and stationed in some lonely place far removed from the home station. Their job was to watch the sheep all day and yard them at night. They saw no one from the day they left the station till the ration cart visited them once a month, bringing rations and mail, when newspapers six months old would be eagerly read. Everything contained in the papers would be news.

During the ten days journeying through the desert, Nanya and Mitchell spent a lot of time together. They walked and talked all day and sat and talked late at night. During those talks Nanya, whose memory had become quite clear again, repeated and lived again his life, right back to when he was a small boy. Mitchell told Nanya the story of his flight from the camp, as it was told by Mitchell's mother who was one of the girls of the tribe at that time. When told her name, Nanya remembered her well. Mitchell told Nanya his father died the night after he ran away. Nanya said he knew, because that day the big kangaroo, the one that was still with them, came to him and talked with him when he was cutting roots for their first drink of water. The knowledge that Mitchell already had about Nanya, and other information supplied by Nanya himself, gave Mitchell the full and true history of Nanya. There is not much more to be told, only of the civilising by kindly whites, just a short history of tragedy.

The little party landed on the bank of the Annabranch, a tributary of the Darling. The creek was in flood and with the exception of Nanya, none had ever seen water like this. They must have thought it was a level road or clay pan, for two children, a boy and girl about eight or ten, ran down the bank and jumped into the water and were not seen again. Nanya had to tell them all about the river and make them be careful, or I suppose others would have done the same, thinking it was level ground. There was no mourning for the loss of the children, so it will be surmised that the loss or death of children was common with them.

A suitable camp was chosen and McGregor rode off up the creek to see if he could find the Lake; they knew they couldn't be far from it because they found signs of sheep and the shepherd's horses tracks. He discovered they were only about four miles from the Lake. He visited the shepherd who was surprised, but pleased, to see and talk with someone. He had very little tucker, but was expecting the ration cart any day. He invited them to bring the tribe up close to camp while they were waiting for the police to come. When McGregor returned to the party, Mitchell told him that Nanya had taken a bad turn, so they laid him on a blanket by the fire, when he asked them all to come close. He spoke in the new language, the one he and Mimi made by cutting short long words and making short sounds like grunts, to convey certain messages to each other. Lumpy neck, who had learned some of the original language, told Mitchell parts of the conversation which he, Mitchell, couldn't follow. Nanya spoke as follows. "Now children, I am going to leave you tonight to join my father. When I was a young man I committed the greatest sin our people can commit. I broke the Bora Law, but I did what no other man ever did, I evaded the punishment of the spear. Your mother and I both knew we were doing wrong, but we were both young and we loved. We both thought at the time that we had done something clever, by dodging the Bora. It wasn't many years after that we both wished we hadn't been so clever, for although we dodged the spear, the 'maingue' law was too strong for us, the Bora sent Wirrugar after us, we were punished through our children. We saw you marry each other and have deformed children. Then when Mimi died, I was left alone to watch you turn into animals, not like man, but I couldn't tell you because I did the same thing. I am going back to the desert and I hope you will soon follow." The very minute that Nanya breathed his last, two big kangaroos followed by the dingo pack was seen making straight back to the desert. Kangaroo shooters and dingo-trappers to this day, tell of two old-men kangaroos which live in the heart of Scotia Scrub, and defy leaden bullets. Are they the spirits of Nanya and his father? Who knows.

On the second day after they buried the body of Nanya, the party of squatters, settlers and police arrived, not by motorcar, but on horseback, and some in horse-drawn vehicles, and spring carts loaded with all kinds of food, clothing of all kinds and blankets. Some of the squatters drove in buckboards. The squatters' wives took charge of the women and girls. They gave them each dresses and other clothing and told them by sign to put the clothes on. Some of them put the dresses on upside down, some poked their legs in the sleeves and tried to walk. It took a while to dress them. The same thing was happening with the men who put their arms through the legs of the trousers and their legs in the sleeves of the shirts. Some put both legs in one trouser leg. They jump along and fall, laughing. Everyone was in good spirit.

Food was served out, which the women had prepared with great kindness, such lovely cakes and pies, the result of this feast was the beginning of their death knell, their stomachs were not adapted for such food. The police then read a Proclamation, which none of the Aborigines understood, declaring them subjects of Her Majesty the Queen, that they would be taken to Pooncarie, and cared for by the Government. Then commenced the civilising process. After the party of white citizens left, it started to rain and continued for several days. I do not suggest it was the first rain these people ever experienced, but in all their lives they had never worn clothes. They have never seen any shelters, they had never built mia-mias like other natives, so when it started to rain, Mitchell built tents which had been left by the Government and they all packed into three tents. Mitchell and McGregor (who remained with them with orders to escort them to Pooncarie) had a tent to themselves, but before the tents were erected it rained in torrents. The people got wet through and when they packed into the tent with wet clothes and wet blankets, and lay coiled up all night and next day, it is no wonder that they contracted pneumonia and before aid could be brought three women and two children died. That made eight counting the two who got drowned and Nanya, leaving twenty-five souls to be civilised. The nice food brought by the whites and other ailments that were altogether new to them, the two trackers helped all they could. One went to the shepherd and got two fat wethers. While he was away the other got the flour of which they had a big supply and made "dampers" and "johnny cakes". He showed them how to use the white man's "tucker" and tea and sugar. The children ate the treacle and jam from the tins with a stick. Some of the natives tried to make damper as they had seen Mitchell do, but instead of making dough, they mixed it on a sheet of bark with water, and then poured it on to the coals, not knowing any better.

When the rain cleared off and they marked the graves of their eight dead ones, McGregor borrowed the spring cart from the shepherd and packed everything into it, together with those who were too sick to walk and they started for Pooncarie. They went around the lake to a place where they could cross the Annabranch, and only travelled about ten miles when another died, so they camped and buried her, a little woman badly deformed. The dissentry got among them and three more died.

A week later they arrived on the Darling opposite Pooncarie. They were taken across in a boat and poor Lumpy fell out of the boat and was drowned. So out of thirty-three, only twenty reached Pooncarie. The girl who was described as good looking was taken by a squatter and married a boy of her own colour, who was working at the station. There is nothing more to say.

Just two years saw the last of them. With the exception of this one girl, the tribe was extinct. She had one son, and died on giving birth to her second child. And so the Bora took them all. But they are only a few who have suffered by white man's civilisation. Haven't the Aborigines been civilised right down from the first advent of whites to the present day? The same protection continues, even to the half-caste descendants of the white man.

Harry Mitchell told me that the son of the last girl of the Scotia tribe, is still alive and that he is known as Mulga Fred. Others claim that the boy when very young went travelling with a buckjump show and is known as Queensland Harry. I know both those old Aboriginal showmen, both good rough riders and whip crackers, but I don't suppose we will ever know which is the sole survivor of the "Scotia Blacks".

MIRNMIRT

JIMMY PIKE

When single woman likes a man, she draws this story in the mud with a stick. When woman talks about man, talks about love, she draws this story.

When someone talks, or a man sees that story, then he goes to the woman. Then they talk marriage. Mirnmirt is the marriage law.

When man has finished the law, done everything, he can marry. He has got to learn everything. There are two laws. One for the young boy, takes several months. One for the full man, takes five or six years.

When man come back from bush after manhood, woman waiting. They have a big feast and make man and woman red with clay.

Struggling

Mudrooroo Narogin

ONE

Kevin's dark troubled eyes moved from red-bordered card to red-bordered card, from the top row down to the right hand side then up again. When he reached the last card, his eyes flicked down to one in the centre of the board. Did he really want to try again for a stint as a kitchen hand? Anyway it was past noon and was sure to be gone by now. Was there anything else? Not a darn thing! On each card, the word "experience" stood out in bold letters, and what experience did he have except dishwashing and fruitpicking. Well, he would have to come in first thing next morning and check again. He did need a job, at least until he heard from the Public Service about that examination he had sat a few months ago. It was just the sort of job he would like, and the thought caused him to stare at the public servants behind the counter of the CES office. It was teabreak. He watched one of the girls. Her little finger poked up in the air as she pecked delicately at her cup. Yes, he wanted a job like that, but would he ever get one? With a sigh he turned and went out into the street.

He stepped just outside the door. The afternoon stretched as long as the road, and he had to fill it. His life was becoming a drifting from home to dole office and back again. Well, he would do something else today. He fiddled around in his pocket and felt a few small coins. They wouldn't get him far. Just enough for the bus fare home. He turned and his eyes fell on a girl walking towards him. She wasn't what you would call a stunner, but she did have on a nice flowery frock, and from her features he saw that she too was a Nyoongah.

His stare made the girl notice him. Instead of freezing her face into a cold mask of untouchability, she flashed a smile. This threw Kevin into confusion. His eyes fell to the pavement and his body stooped as if to pick them up. The attitude of dejection was fast becoming a habit. He caught himself and straightened up with a jerk. Confusion gave way to anger, and this gave him the strength to say, "How you going?" as the girl reached him. She hesitated just a fraction before replying: "Alright—been after a job?" Then she smiled a warm smile which helped to lessen his anger. He replied: "Been looking, but not finding. You know how it is?"

"Yeah, it's pretty hard to find anything these days, isn't it?" she agreed in a soft voice.

As if they had known each other for years, or as if they were close relations, they walked off along the street chatting.

Kevin heard himself saying, "I sat for the Public Service examination almost six months ago, and I still haven't heard from them. I know that I passed it. We compared answers afterwards, but then you never know, do you?"

"Don't worry, they'll be getting in touch with you soon," the girl replied, flashing her warm smile which showed her confidence in him.

"Yeah, but the whole thing could be rigged, you know? Just like those phony job ads in the paper. You know, I went in for an interview. It was a real come-on. They told you that you could make a hundred dollars a day. I found out that it was selling things people put in their front doors. It might have been a good idea, once, years ago. I went from door to door and found out that every second door already had one, and those that didn't, didn't want one. People like me flogging last year's things."

"But the Public Service is different isn't it?" the girl answered. "It's government and they don't cheat you that much, do they?"

"Don't they? What about land rights?"

The girl shrugged her shoulders. She stopped beside a brand new car. She looked up at Kevin as he hung there, then asked: "Can I drop you anywhere? I'm heading for the uni, got a class at a college there."

Kevin had friends living in St George's College just across from the university, and quickly accepted her offer of a lift. It would take care of the afternoon. As she got into her car, he couldn't help scowling. Why, she was just his age, maybe a few years younger, and already had wheels. How could she afford to, when his chances of ever being mobile were zilch?

As the girl got behind the wheel and buckled up, she wondered about the scowl. Since coming to the city and meeting Perth Nyoongah boys, she had found them without exception to be more touchy than those from her home town. They were all like this one and got upset over the littlest thing. Anything would set them off. She guessed that this time her car had something to do with it, and as Kevin seemed nice under his city toughness, as they drove off, she explained about the car. Her kid sister had forced her to buy a raffle ticket with her last dollar. She couldn't believe it when she had looked in the local paper and saw her number. "I suppose you can't be unlucky all your life," she finished off with.

"Don't know about that," Kevin answered morosely. "Bet if I had bought every ticket except one, I still wouldn't have won." He gave a shrug, smiled wryly at himself, then changed the subject, asking her where she was from.

"So you're from Bayside? Was down that way just a few months ago. Had a job picking peas. Piece work, a dollar a bag. Then work ran out after a fortnight. They have these machines which do most of the work now, and they only take you on when one of them breaks down. You must know Joey Michaels. I worked alongside of him."

"Yeah, he be one of my cousins. You know how it is. We're all related down there. You must of heard of the Michaels. My Dad was a member of the NAC before they got rid of it. Now he's chairman of the local Housing Co-op. I'm Margaret, the youngest barring the kid sister who got me this car. You meet anyone else while you were there?"

"No, only Joey. They got us up at the crack of dawn and we picked peas to sundown. You hardly stopped to have a feed or a cup of tea, and then the work ran out, I hitchhiked back to Perth. Anyway, my name's Kevin Young. We're originally from Pinjarra way, on the Murray. Now we live in the city, in Balga."

"Pleased to meet you, Kev," the girl said coyly, as if she had just met him that minute.

They were quiet until the vehicle approached the cluster of odd-sized buildings that made up the university.

"Where do you want to be dropped?" Margaret asked Kevin.

"Anywhere along here'll do," he answered abruptly.

She glanced across at him surprised at the tone of his voice. She saw his scowl and wondered what had set him off again. To put him at ease, or at least to try and get his mind off what was bugging him, she began talking quickly about how her Dad had wanted someone with secretarial skills to do the book work at the Co-op and had arranged for her to come to the city to do a course. As she talked she pulled the car over to the kerb and as Kevin was getting out said that she would see him around as everyone kept bumping into each other. "Not enough breathing space," she finished off, smiling her warm smile as she moved off into the traffic.

Kevin stood and watched her Honda Civic scoot off. The image of her smile lingered. He hoped that they would bump into each other and soon at that. His face relaxed as he passed between the thick concrete gate posts, and went up the drive to the fake castle-fronted building in which his mates lodged.

Paul's room was on the second floor. He found the door locked. This was unusual when he was in. Half-heartedly he knocked softly. His irritation returned and he kicked at the door. No answer, and he was turning away when a voice came through: "Sorry, busy right now, catch you later, OK?"

"Hey, it's me, Kev, open up!"

"Don't know any Kevs," the voice mocked.

"Arrh, come on, stop mucking about, Elias. Is Paul in there with you?"

The lock snicked. The door opened wide enough for Paul to stick his head out. He saw that it indeed was Kevin and stepped back to let him in.

"What's with the conspiracy bit?" Kevin demanded as he pushed past Paul.

"Open your eyes and see," Paul replied, locking the door behind him. He stuck out his hand and they exchanged a mason-like clasp. Kevin looked past Paul and at the bed where Elias sat busily poking away at something.

"Up to his old tricks," Paul informed him, "and he a good Christian too. Just wait till I tell your white Dad," he yelled at the skinny youth who, wearing only a pair of patched jeans, squatted on the bed before a spread sheet of newspaper scattered over with coins. Elias tipped up a collection tin and jiggled a knife in the slot. More tumbled out. Kevin noticed a few were gold dollar coins.

"What is it this time," he grinned, "St Anthony's Home For Alcoholics, or the Odious Home For The Reform Of Drunken Delinquent Drug Addicts? That one was a real beauty. You'd think that people would have latched onto it, but no—didn't someone even give you a five dollar bill to rehabilitate the poor things?"

Elias's teeth flashed in his dark handsome face. "This time I decided that simple is best." He twisted the tin around so that Kevin could read the bold red lettering: PENNILESS PENSIONERS' FUND.

"Don't know why he hasn't been lumbered," Paul sniggered. "There must be a lot of silly people out there, though not in this room I assure you. You know, he even gets the labels printed up in the student newspaper office."

"Good for him," Kevin cut in, then added bitterly: "Wish I had some racket to supplement my dole money."

Paul saw that Kevin was down in the dumps and laughed to relax him before trying to give him some advice. "Guess it'll soon be back to school for you, me old dole bludger. These days you've got to get a piece of paper to wave in their faces before they'll take you on. Just front up here for a few years on an Abstudy grant and study sociology like I'm doing, then you'll be set for life."

"Oh yeah, and what happens if I don't play their game? Look at that Collins bloke, the one who sat in front of the cathedral for days on a hunger strike for land rights—well, he's got that magic piece of paper, and we meet at the same dole office. Education is just a heap of shit!"

"Maybe, maybe," Elias came in for his say, "but it does keep you out of the dole queue for a few years, then after that there's always a job with DAA or ADC. And don't let this tin can routine fool you—the Abstudy grant doesn't cover the cost of the books I want, so I have to make it up this way. In a few years I'm going to be a lawyer and a good one at that."

"Yeah, the way you're going, a criminal lawyer," Paul said, and all three laughed.

"Hey," Kevin called, "it's too nice a day to hang about inside. Let's get out and about."

"Yeah, life—be in it," Paul said. He flung Elias his shirt, then went to a mirror and tugged a comb through his unruly hair.

They rushed out of the room, down the stairs, raced along the driveway and reached the street, then stopped. None of the three had the foggiest notion what they were going to do. Suddenly a cyclist shot out of the university grounds and swerved into the road and right smack into the side of a passing truck. The cyclist went sprawling, his machine was twisted to a mess of junk.

"Serves him right!" Kevin exclaimed.

His two mates stared at him in astonishment. They knew that he was going through a bad patch, but the guy could be badly hurt. They watched as the cyclist got to his feet.

"Let's go over and see if he's alright," Paul urged.

"Never get involved, especially as a witness. It doesn't pay enough," Elias said. He noticed that except for a limp the guy seemed to be OK, though his bike was a write-off.

"Yeah, he's still in one piece," Kevin replied, regretting his outburst.

They turned their backs on the accident and walked to the bus stop. A bus rattled up. Without thinking they joined the surging crowd of students and let themselves be washed past the driver who called "Hurry up," in a British accent and clicked and clicked his ticket machine.

The clicking annoyed Kevin as much as did the sudden lurch of the vehicle which flung him off his feet. He stared angrily towards the driver and their eyes met in the rear vision mirror.

The driver jammed on his brakes at the city stop and Kevin and his two mates were flung towards the front. They had had enough and decided to get off. As they went past the driver he yelled: "Hey, you three, show me your tickets!"

"Pay the rent first, you pommy bastard!" Kevin shouted as he jumped into the street.

"Yeah pay the rent or get out!" his mates yelled as they raced away and down an arcade.

"Well, now we're in town," Paul said.

"Yeah, now we're in town," Elias echoed.

"Should've went to Freo," said Kevin.

"Well, why didn't you say so?" his mates yelled at him.

"Didn't think of it," replied Kevin lamely.

"Hey, I know what to do," Elias said, "let's go to East Perth. I know a couple of yorgas there. They should be home by now."

Two women in very short shorts and thin blouses strolled past. They turned and watched them walk away.

"Yeah, let's," agreed Paul, his eyes clinging to the bottom of the plumper girl.

Kevin wrenched his eyes away, then muttered: "Harlots!"

His mates glanced at him, and to avoid any problems or stupid explanations, he agreed with them. He forced a smile on his face and said: "Yeah, it could be fun."

Elias led them to a city clipper bus stop and while they waited for the free bus, Paul again tried to help Kevin without antagonising him. He knew that his mate was upset about not being able to get a job, but all he could suggest was some course of study to keep himself occupied. Kevin had calmed down enough to listen, but he didn't agree and mumbled something about a Public Service examination and how he was waiting for the results. Then the bus arrived and he rushed onto it and away from the conversation.

They got off close to the Aboriginal Council building and went between it and a hall and through a back entrance of the Nicholl's Hostel. They walked along a short passageway and into a large room in which a TV set blared. A sofa and a dozen easy chairs were grouped before it.

Kevin saw two girls sitting directly in front of the flickering screen. They were the ones Elias knew. They saw the boys and grinned up a "hello" at them. Kevin didn't know them and as he reacted in any situation he felt uneasy in, he stood there scowling. He felt a mug and out of place, then felt a mug for feeling a mug, then felt relief when Elias shouted his name at the girls and they flopped down to watch the programme. It was about some sort of intelligent wombat and they all, except himself, found it hilarious. He thought it was childish and his mind wandered away to the girl he had met outside the dole office. What was her name? Margaret Michaels, that was it.

Why, she might even be staying at this hostel. Perhaps he should ask one of the girls? He looked at the two now sitting together on the sofa.

Their names were Diana and Noretta and both came from East Coballing, but from their clothing they had been long enough in the city to make the choice between fashionable fashionable or unfashionable fashionable. Diana obviously favoured the former, unlike Noretta who wore a floppy shirt and a pair of old jeans. Diana wore loose white cotton pants and a soft cotton shirt which emphasised the brown warmth of her skin. As far as Kevin could judge, and he wasn't an expert on such things, Diana's make-up had been carefully applied to highlight her high cheekbones. Her hair was cut short in a boyish fashion which did not look good on her. He could have looked at her for hours, but was sure that if he had the choice he would feel more relaxed with Noretta who, though pretty, did nothing to make herself look prettier.

Noretta felt his eyes on her and glanced towards him. She had lovely eyes which somehow reminded him of the brown still waters of a billabong near his old home town. He remembered how he used to sit on the bank and gaze onto the water perhaps watching a leaf slowly submerging. Someone entered the room and he jerked back into reality. It was hard to believe, but it was Margaret. He stole a glance at her. She didn't have Diana's startling beauty, or Noretta's wonderful eyes, but he felt her presence fill the room.

He was afraid to look directly at her. Only flicked glances towards her, but she caught one of these. They silently exchanged greetings. As she walked towards him, he tried to find something special about her. She was on the large size, though not fat, and just escaped being ugly. But none of this mattered. She smiled, and her smile reached out to him like a caressing hand. Without fuss, she reached his chair and perched on the arm. Her nearness alarmed him. He felt himself shrinking inside, growing smaller and smaller, and more and more vulnerable. Worse, what would his mates think, if they knew?

They weren't thinking of him or his feelings at all. "Luck Of Your Life" was about to begin and the approaching event held all their attention. The girls explained how they never missed a show, and set themselves the task of answering each and every question. They had done this nine times in a row, and now wanted a perfect ten. Impatiently they waited for the ads to end.

Kevin and Margaret didn't join in the chatter. Occasionally they flashed a smile. This was enough for Kevin who was trying to come to grips with the fact of being so aware of a female. He sat very still. He could feel the warmth of her body, and knew that only a slight movement could bring them together. Then he began stealing glances up at her. He noticed a scar on her chin and wondered how it had come about. From the looks of it, it had been a nasty gash. In another glance, he noticed a mole on her cheek and saw a number of fair hairs growing from it. Then he saw the length of her eyelashes, the darkness of her pupils staring directly at him, and her nose crinkling up as she laughed: "Had an eyeful yet?"

If it was possible he would have blushed, but suddenly for no reason at all he felt at ease. He settled back in the easy chair and flashed a dopey smile up at her. "Just about," he grinned. He felt the perfume coming from her body and liked it.

"Shhh, shush, you two," hissed the others. The quiz-master bounced onto the screen with teeth exposed in a gleaming smile. He hesitated for the camera to zoom in on his face and a voice to intone a rapturous welcome: "And now, here is your host and mine, Timmy Marsh!"

Quiz-master: "Hi folks, and let me introduce my lovely assistant, Miss Jenny Victoria."

A woman pranced onto the set. The camera cut to a close-up of her smiling mouth ejecting a wisecrack. In rapid succession the contestants were introduced and seated in a row behind a button which worked a buzzer and light. Each tested his or her button. Then the camera panned from prize to prize with the most wondrous receiving an extreme close-up and a caressing hand from Jenny. The kids waited impatiently through this opening and for the questions to begin. But before this there came another batch of advertisements. They commented on the contestants during the break.

"The woman really is a sloppy dresser," commented the fashion-conscious Diana.

"That lawyer guy will win for sure," stated Elias, sticking up for his chosen profession.

"It doesn't depend on brains, only on luck," explained Noretta.

The others disputed this while the ads continued.

Except for a smile at an occasional phrase, Margaret and Kevin didn't take part in what might have developed into a lively argument, if the quiz show had not cut back. The first question came. "What is the capital of Canada?" The buzzer of the woman, a housewife, sounded. "Ottawa," called out Noretta, before the contestant answered. And so it went on with the kids giving the answer often on the sound of the buzzer. They reached the last segment of the game without missing an answer. Were they going to score a perfect ten?

"Bet we make it," Noretta exclaimed. "One of us should get on this show and show them how it's done."

"Yeah, we're just as good as any of them," Diana agreed.

"How do you get on anyway?" asked Elias.

"You should be the one," Paul mocked gently. "You've got enough gumption for all of us together."

"Maybe it should be you, Paul," Margaret cut in with a laugh.

"Not me, mate, not me, I'd just freeze up. What about you Kev? Think that you'd be willing to give it a go?"

They all laughed at this, for Kevin hadn't attempted to answer a single question. Margaret had looked at him once or twice as if urging him to get into the spirit of things, but he couldn't. Once, when he knew the answer and was just about ready to shout it out, Elias got in ahead of him and left him high and dry, like a fish gasping out its life. This made him angry with himself. They must think him a real dummy. He scowled and felt his body go heavy and inert. The laughter made him feel worse, then just as it often happened, he knew that he had to get himself in ahead of the others and answer at least one question. He pushed away the thought that if he got it wrong, the shame would kill him.

He watched as the quiz-master began. He felt his body tense, then relax.

Quiz-master: "Who am I? I was born in Plymouth, England, in June 1784. I was a career officer in the British army, serving at first in Jamaica in 1813 as Assistant Quartermaster and Acting Paymaster..."

The man continued his nattering and Kevin knew the answer. He glanced at the puzzled faces and gloated. He looked at Margaret who smiled at him. Just a few more clues. He had to be right!

Quiz-master: "He became Lieutenant Governor of Van Diemen's Land in 1824 and served two terms..."

"Governor George Arthur," Kevin said confidently. The others looked at him in surprise. They didn't have a clue, and needed Kevin to be right for them to have a perfect ten.

Quiz-master: "That was hard, wasn't it? Well, no-one gets the points this time. The answer is... George Arthur."

A perfect ten and a collective sigh of accomplishment filled the room. They had proved themselves, but why not make it twenty in a row?

"Touch and go on the last question, but we killed them again," laughed Noretta.

"With a little help from the boys," added Diana.

"We're the champs!" shouted Elias.

Kevin grinned happily. He had done his bit.

It was just about teatime for the girls. They turned off the set and while they waited, discussed what to do after. It was too warm a night to hang about inside. Just on the bell, they agreed to go to the city and maybe take in a movie. Kevin was about to agree when he remembered he hadn't enough money.

"No, I can't go," he said quickly. "I have to get home for dinner. Mum's expecting me." He raised his wrist as if to look at a wrist-watch. He hadn't one, but it might add weight to his words. He was disappointed when no-one protested. He got up to go to the door and Margaret followed him out. They stood closely together in the dusk hearing the soft hum of the traffic.

"See you soon, real soon," the girl said softly, underlining her words with her warm smile which checked his irritation at not having any money.

"Yeah," he agreed. "See you soon." She touched his arm. The soft pressure of her fingers made him nervous. "Got a baby sister, just a bit younger than you," he suddenly blurted out for no reason. To make matters worse, he heard his voice continue: "You might come home and meet her one day. Got a little brother too. Tommy, he's smart, but a little wild. Then there's Mum and Uncle..." He stopped with a shrug.

"Yeah, I'd like to do that sometime," the girl replied.

Kevin was out of his depth. He stepped back quickly into shallow water with a firm, "See you," which sounded very abrupt and final, then walked away. He glanced back. The girl smiled and waved, then went inside. He went to the bus stop. While he waited for the bus, his mind rested on her final smile, then on the touch of her fingers on his bare arm. He smiled, then scowled. He thought of his family and where they lived. At last the bus arrived, and he got on and flung his money down for a ticket. He wedged himself in the corner of the back seat and stared at his reflection in the window.

TWO

Why they called the block of flats "Mia Mia" Kevin didn't know. Often he thought that it was a calculated insult to the Aboriginal families living there. Others shared his belief and the name plate had been stolen so many times that Westhomes had stopped replacing it. Gloom seeped out as he pushed through the door and walked towards the stairway. He was lifting his foot on to the first step, when a hard voice made him freeze. Monaych!

"Hey you—hold it right there!"

A beam of light flashed out.

Monaych, cops, and instantly in a reflex action to authority, his head dropped. He waited for the worst.

"Who are you, what are you doing here? Get against the wall, hands over your head. Stretch out. Jump to it!"

Another cop held the flashlight on his mate as he ran his hands over Kevin. He was ordered to empty his pockets.

"He's clean," the cop said, looking at the few coins and the handkerchief Kevin held in his hand. "What's your name?" he yelled.

"Kevin Young."

"What?"

"K–Kevin Young," he mumbled again.

"You live here?!"

"Y–yeah."

"Flat number?!"

"S–seventeen."

The cop pulled a list out of his top uniform pocket. He ran his finger down the long list of names, and then along a line. "OK" he snapped, "get going and don't let me see you again tonight."

"Y–yes," Kevin stuttered, forcing his legs to ascend the stairs slowly. He felt like running, but forced himself not to. It would be suspicious and he knew what could happen to him if they took him down to the station.

Out of earshot, he muttered, "Pigs," but his anger was directed more at himself than the so-called guardians of the law. Why hadn't he protested? He lived there and they had no right to search him. Suddenly he lashed out a fist at the grey concrete wall. What was life? Only a struggle to survive!

He stamped into the flat. Uncle, Mum and his sister, Sue, were in the living room. They had been at it again. He could tell by their faces and the tension in the air. Without a word he stamped past them and into his room. His mother's hurt look made him feel bad all over again.

His mother had been trying to understand things for a long time now. As her children grew older, it grew worse. They retreated from her and often treated her like a strange, distant relative. She looked at her daughter and sighed. With her, she had hoped things would be different, but no, she too had become cold and distant. Still she was flesh of her flesh and she had to try and keep her straight. She sighed again as she wondered when it had all started. She tended to blame the city, the impersonal flat and all the trouble and heartache around them. It was no good and was tearing them apart just like it tore apart other Nyoongah families. How she wished that they had never left Pinjarra. She had been happy there and her family had clung together through thick and thin. It didn't matter what the Wetjelas thought about them either as they had each other, but now since moving to the city it was all different. Her family was drifting apart and becoming uncaring.

In the loneliness of his room, Kevin let his rage seep away. His mother's crest-fallen look filled him with sadness, then he thought of Margaret and he felt better. He even smiled as he pulled off his shirt. The loose change which he had stashed in his top pocket after the search fell out and over the floor. He got down on his hands and knees to collect it and noticed a pile of newspapers under his brother's bed. Tommy was doing an apprenticeship in printing and studied nights at the Technical College. Kevin knew that he sometimes took advantage of the machinery to run off things for some friends. He was being used, Kevin decided, as he picked up the top paper. The headline read: "TO HELL WITH THE PROFESSOR". It was about some bloke called Lamey who wanted Australia for the Brits. All of it, and was against any form of land rights. Just like all the Wetjelas, he thought, as he turned over the pages and came across an article headed "Marxism and Human Nature".

He read out a bit. "The reason why there is no unchanging human nature is because human beings are labouring animals who, in altering their methods of production, transform themselves and the natural world of which they are a part."

So what, he thought, and what did it mean to him as one of the jobless? What chance had he of transforming anything? With a sigh he read the last few sentences. "We live in an unnatural society where those who don't work for a living control the levers of power. We socialists are in the business to put an end to this odd state of affairs." Kevin gave an ironic cheer at these words. He was one of those who didn't work for a living, and what levers of power did he have? It was those with jobs, like the cops, who had the power. Then his eyes hit another heading: "The Dignity of Struggle". This made some sense. Keep on, mate, keep on. They think they have you down, but keep on, keep on. That was more like it, and even Tommy would learn that for all his printing up of trendy lefty newspapers, nothing much would ever change in the Land of Oz. Life was a struggle and that was that!

He tossed down the newspaper and continued searching for the rest of his coins. One had rolled under his bed next to his case. As he searched for it, he saw that his case was unlocked. How many times had he told Tommy to leave his things alone? He opened it and pulled up the sheet of paper lining the bottom. His magazine was still there. It was a porn book he had found blowing along the street, and the pictures of men and women making what they called love had made him hang onto it. And to hide it, he thought, in the bottom of his case. Suddenly he felt shame and then his anger hit.

Why had he kept it? If only he had his own room ... why? So that he could be alone to look at dirty pictures! The thought disgusted him. Savagely he ripped the magazine into shreds and flung the pieces across the floor. Hurriedly he gathered them up and flung them back in the suitcase. Next time when he went out, he had to take them and fling them in a street rubbish bin. No, better still, strew them along the street so that everyone could see the filth that was printed these days.

He felt grubby. He wanted a shower to wash away the dirt. As he went into the bathroom, he glanced into the living room. The rest of the family sat in front of the telly. No one spoke. The hissing hot water relaxed his body. He felt much better. As he combed his hair, he made faces into the mirror. Was he handsome? How did Margaret find him? His lips mightn't be too thick, but wasn't there a shifty look about his eyes? Would you trust this young man and give him a job? Would you, would you—what was it—give him a job to enable him to change his human nature and his natural world through labour? God, he had to find something to do, he had to! With money coming in, he might even get a flat of his own, though he didn't want to leave his mother. Well, he could do other things, like taking Margaret out, like starting to enjoy all the things that they said over and over on the telly they were lucky to have in Australia. Yeah, lucky as long as you had the money!

He left the bathroom and stopped in the living room to see if dinner was about ready.

The tension still hung in the air. His mother still glanced at him, than back to the screen. Sue sat slumped in the chair. There were four streaks on her cheeks and a stubborn expression on her face. Uncle as always looked somewhat stern and righteous, except that a slight quivering of the lower lip showed his anxiety. He looked up at Kevin and in a soft voice asked him to wait for a moment. "Is Tommy in?" he asked. "No," Kevin replied.

"Well, pull up a pew. Dinner won't be long."

Kevin flung himself into a chair. He stared at the screen for a moment, than watched his mother go out to the kitchen. He felt a deep concern for her. She had always put the family first. She came back and he saw that her eyes were red and swollen. He recalled that they often were like that. It was as if she was always on the verge of tears, or had just finished crying. For how long had they been like that? As long as he could remember, or at least since Dad died. Before then she had always been cheery. What was the song, she had often hummed?

He couldn't remember it. It had been so long ago. He turned his eyes on his uncle. Had his nature been formed by his labour on the roads? A nasty accident had put him out of the work force and onto a pension which kept the whole family going. Still, he managed to keep himself active, and spent much of his time down at the

Numbarra Workshop trying to rehabilitate drunks. It took a drunk to help a drunk, he often declared, and had bored Kevin silly with tales of how bad he had been before he had given the booze away. Still Kevin respected him for his work. He was keeping up the struggle.

Uncle caught Kevin's eyes, and began to speak in a serious voice. "That Tommy is getting a bit out of hand, ain't he? Never here at all. God knows what he's getting up to. Next thing you know he'll be in trouble with the police."

Kevin nodded. Until recently, he had been more than a little wary of the man. All the stories about his drunkenness and fighting weren't all gammon. He was a huge man and at one time had been a boxer in one of the troupes which had toured the country taking on all comers. Though that had been long ago, and now he was soft and flabby like most city Nyoongahs living on chips and meat. Still, once there had been something there, something that held Kevin. No thought of this as he replied: "You know Tommy's working days and studying evenings. He really works hard to keep up with it all, then he told me that he's standing for some sort of post in the student union at the Tech School. No wonder he's hardly in."

"That may be, and I'm not complaining about that. He's a good worker, but he can't study that much in the evenings. Night after night, he comes home after midnight. It's no good to be out all the time. He should spend more time home with his family. What's the use if he becomes a big shot in his student union and forgets his family?"

"Arrh, you know how often the buses run, and then there's that study place which has opened in Wellington Street. He goes there a lot," Kevin answered, coming to the defence of his brother. "Teachers volunteer to help kids keep up with their studies. You know how his marks have improved over the last few months?"

"Yeah, and I know all about that study centre of his," Uncle retorted. "I've heard that our kids are picking up some pretty funny ideas there. It's not right, especially when it's funded with our money."

Kevin guessed his uncle had been listening to the gossip at the Workshop. He tried to gloss over it in his reply: "Arrh, well, you know, all they do is talk a bit about politics and things like that. Nothing much. I've been there a few times. It's harmless. Only kid stuff."

"And what about your sister? She's going the same way," Uncle suddenly declared, getting onto what he wanted to talk about. He was determined to bring everything out into the open and involve Kevin in it. After all he was almost an adult and ready to do a bit to keep the family together.

Kevin briefly wondered what his uncle thought about his behaviour, before thinking about his sister. What could he do about her, he thought? She at least had a decent enough job, put a few dollars towards the rent, and even helped occasionally with the housework. Once they had been very close even though they fought like cat and dog, but over the past few months, she had stopped confiding in him. It was most likely because she had a steady job— but then she was an attractive girl and when she wanted to could twist men around her little finger. It was little wonder that she was working, he thought, resenting her inner certainty and energy which he felt he lacked. Still, this didn't excuse her behaviour. She should spend more time at home. It wasn't fair on their mother. Then how could she afford the expensive clothes she was getting around in? They weren't cheap stuff from K Mart. She had told them they came with the job. That might be true. Still, it was part of the problem. She walked into that shop job without really trying, and her boss, some sort of European, didn't exactly treat her as just another one of the workers. Why, he even drove her home in the evening.

Kevin recalled that it was not the first time that Sue had been mixed up with an older guy. It had happened in her last year at school. A teacher had taken an interest in her, for her well-being he had said. And what had happened? She had found herself pregnant at fifteen and had turned to him for advice and help. He had taken her along to the Aboriginal Health Service and they had arranged an abortion for her. That was over a year ago, and it was from that time, he realised, they had begun drifting apart. After that she had taken up with a local boy who lived in the next street. His name had been Ralph, a Wetjela who thought he was a big man. He couldn't stand the guy and had told him to leave his sister alone before socking the sneer from his mouth. He also had ordered Sue not to see him again, but she didn't listen. Tommy had seen them going into the local pub. He rushed home and told him. They rushed off to the pub. His sister was under-age and had no business there.

He found them sitting at a table in the saloon bar. Ralph, who always wore a black leather jacket in all kinds of weather, glared at him with a sneer. Sue stared away into the distance. At last she glanced up at him, took a sip from what appeared to be rum and coke, and simpered: "I was in town waiting for the bus back and Ralphy came along in his car. I had been waiting hours and he offered me a lift, then as I was feeling thirsty we came here for a drink." He looked at his sister, trying to keep his temper. He didn't want to start a fight on the guy's home ground. There wasn't another Nyoongah in the place either. He had to control himself and get the guy later. With an effort he managed to smile. Ralph even offered to buy him a drink. He ground his teeth together and accepted a beer. Later he even agreed to a lift home. A few days later, Ralph came before the court on some charge or other. He was sent to gaol, and to Kevin's relief that was the end of him.

"What's Sue been up to anyway?" he asked in a quiet voice, trying to be rational and adult. He looked at his sister, but she avoided his eyes. She stared at the TV screen, but he noticed that her eyes were smudged from crying. He looked at his mother. She too was gazing at the screen. He switched his eyes to his uncle, who told him. "That bloke she's working for—she's seeing far too much of him. He's old enough to be her grandfather. One of my mates came across her going into his house. He has one of those posh terrace houses going up in Northbridge, right near the Workshop you know. Well, she's been going into his place with him when his wife and the kids aren't there."

Kevin was anxious to prevent the row from starting up again. Anyway it wasn't much to go on, and so he came down on his sister's side: "Most likely it was about something to do with the shop. Sue's told me he keeps some of his stock there. I think he even has some women coming in to do sewing."

"It hasn't only been once or twice. My mate lives in one of the last boarding houses in the area and he spends most of his time on the front veranda. Why don't you ask her? Go, ask her," Uncle said, raising his voice.

"I haven't done anything wrong," Sue suddenly shot out. "He's my boss and I do what he tells me. He does keep things in his house and sometimes he takes me there to model a dress for him. There isn't any harm in that. No harm at all!"

"Yeah, I bet he watches you getting into them," Uncle answered with a sneer.

Mother entered the conversation to stop it exploding into a row. "Let's keep things quiet," she begged. "You know how thin the walls are. If we don't watch out it'll be all over the block by tomorrow. You know what those Jacksons are like next door? Then Sue's a good girl, I know she is, and she's got a good head on her shoulders. Sue, you wouldn't lie to us, would you?"

Kevin scowled at this pampering of his sister. It had always been like that. She had been the pet of the family and been spoilt rotten. It started with Dad, and Uncle had done the same. What was it to him what she did, or didn't do? Suddenly he felt as if his head was splitting and to end the fuss, he spoke to underline his mother's words. "Mum's right, you know. Sue wouldn't lie to us. Sue, no one's accusing you of anything. Uncle's just concerned about you. You have to be careful what you do. Your boss is so much older than you and has a wife and kids. Sometimes you have to watch out for guys like him, you know?"

The girl turned from the screen. Her hand went up to brush a curl of hair from her forehead as she darted a scornful look at her brother. "I'm not a liar," she declared. "He's harmless, not at all fresh like some others I could name. No harm in that. Then, what's it to any of you if I do go to his house?"

Kevin tried to remain calm for his mother's sake and because of his splitting headache. He knew Sue expected him to flare up and shout at her. He wouldn't, he wouldn't!

He managed a strained smile as he forced the words out quietly: "No one's accusing you of anything, or him for that matter. We just felt we should warn you."

"Just because I model a few dresses," Sue began, glancing at her Uncle so that he could see the tears welling in her eyes.

"What about the other girls in the shop? Can't they do the modelling?" Kevin said, his control slipping.

"What—them?" his sister replied scornfully. "They haven't got the figures for it. You should see them," she smirked, sitting up straight and running her hands over her slim body.

"So you his favourite?" Kevin shot out in resentment.

"Don't know about that," his sister smiled complaisantly. "The others are cows and he has to have someone good-looking to show off the clothes, that's why he lets me wear whatever I want from the shop."

"Yeah, and what does he get in payment?" Kevin retorted.

Sue's eyes flashed and it was on. "What do you know about anything? What do any of you know? Just look where we live. It isn't safe to go out into the corridor, let alone the street at night. He knows how bad this suburb is, and that's why he drives me home in the evenings. It's all right for you," she shot out at Kevin. "You're at least some sort of a bloke and can take care of yourself. It's different for a woman. If you're so concerned about me, why don't you get a car and pick me up from work. That would be OK."

The dig about the car and what it implied made Kevin see red. "So Miss High and Mighty eh—you and your stupid job in a stupid shop run by a dirty old man."

Mother came and took his arm. "Kev, leave off," she implored. "Don't let it upset you. You know how upset you get. Sue didn't mean anything."

"Like hell!" Kevin shouted. "All she's good for is rubbing our noses in the dirt. She doesn't care what she does, as long as she gets what she wants."

"Yeah!" Sue yelled back, "at least I've got a job. All you do is hang about with those grubby mates of yours. I could tell you a thing or two about them, if I was a telltale. Anyway what right have you to tell me what to do? I pay my share of the rent. How much do you pay? Not a cent! Why don't you stop bludging and go and get a job. You're such a know-all, aren't you?"

"Shut up you little bitch!" he shouted back. Beside himself with fury, he jerked forward as if about to rush at his sister and lash out at her with his clenched fist.

Kevin's rage frightened his sister. She had gone too far. All at once she fell back in her chair and began sobbing.

This always caused Uncle's heart to melt and now was no exception. Although he had been the instigator of the whole row, he broke in to calm things down. "You know, Sue, we all didn't mean anything. We've only been a little worried, a little worried, that's all.

We wouldn't be family if we weren't."

She sobbed out in a little girl voice, "Mr Wiseman's a nice man. He's only interested in teaching me the trade, that's all."

Kevin fought to regain control. A red haze clouded his vision and his temples throbbed in time to the aching in his head. He felt like shouting out that if Wiseman was so good, why had he taken on someone without experience when he could have gotten someone better, but then he couldn't be bothered. It was all too much! "Mum," he said to end it,"you know I'm waiting on the results of that exam I took. I know that I passed it. When I get the job we can get away to a better place in the suburbs. There's some nice houses in Coolbellup and it's quieter there."

But his words had the opposite effect to what he had intended. She stared at him and he saw the tears start to her eyes as she wailed out: "But we've lived here ever since we came to the city! I know people around here. I couldn't go and live among strangers. Just wait a bit and everything'll turn out alright. Just wait and see."

Kevin couldn't find words in reply. How could anyone ever become attached to a crummy Housing Commission flat in a block in which fights occurred every night? Why, a bloke had been murdered just down the hallway a fortnight ago, and worse, the cops harassed you whenever they felt like it. His irritation returned and he looked at his sister and told her that she was not allowed to go to Wiseman's place again. "I won't allow it, I won't!" he said hoarsely.

This was too much for Sue who thought that the battle was over. Her sobs abruptly cut out and she screamed: "You, you—you little nerd! Who are you to order me around? Why don't all of you stop picking on me! I wish I was dead, then you'd see. Yeah, then you'd all be happy. Just wait and see, I'll get a place of my own and leave you all flat!" She flung herself on the sofa and her sobs resumed.

This was the final shot and as always in these rows Kevin tasted defeat. He felt wiped out. His sister had won again. He watched Uncle rush to the sofa and kneel to caress the heaving back of the girl. She shrugged off his hand, then allowed it to calm her.

Kevin watched his Uncle. He was partly to blame for the girl's behaviour. He had spoilt her rotten. Even when he had been working and not living in the flat, when he visited it had always been with a little something for his "princess". And when he had come to live in the flat it had continued. She would play up to him and until she left school would clamber up on his knees to search his pockets for what she called "a lucky dollar". Uncle encouraged her until she began to believe she could get anything with a simper and a smile. Now she had snared Wiseman who also gave her attention and presents. The piece of Marxism which he had read came into his mind. He wondered what part productive labour played in the piece of feminine nature in front of him. Not much, he decided, as he watched his sister turn a sad little face to smile a trembly smile at her dear uncle.

This was the last straw and forgetting any idea of dinner, he retreated to his room. His young brother glanced up as he entered. "The row's over, is it?" he drawled.

"Home early for a change," Kevin retorted, attempting to play the big brother again.

Tommy scratched his huge mop of unruly hair, then his skin beneath his ex-army shirt. He lay stretched out on his brother's bed and stared up at him. One foot idly swung a thong which went flap-flap against his sole. Ignoring Kevin's tone and obvious tiredness, he drawled out: "Guess what, we were creamed in the election. The students are a conservative lot only interested in going to their classes. You know, it's the end of the Left Collective as a force in the Student Union. Doesn't matter though, the whole committee's a dead loss. We'll get rid of them one way or the other."

"So what," Kevin muttered. His head still pounded. He felt weak and feverish. All he wanted to do was get into his bed and forget everything.

"Hey, are you holding? How about a loan of ten dollars?"

Tommy's large brown eyes staring up at him reminded him of Margaret. Already she seemed a million miles away in time. "Where would I get ten dollars?" he muttered. If he had had ten dollars, he could have gone to the pictures with Margaret and avoided the row tonight. If, if, if! He ran his hand over his aching head. He could feel his throat constricting. His mouth gaped wide in an effort to get air. All he wanted to do was flop down on the bed and relax, but Tommy wouldn't let him be.

"What about your watch? We could try a hock shop?"

Kevin stared down at his naked wrist. His watch had been sold a week ago. He hid the truth from his brother as he replied: "That cheap thing. Anyway I need it to be on time for interviews."

"You getting an interview, that'll be the day."

"Oh God, just leave me alone!" he tried to shout, but could manage only a whisper , Why did all of them go on and on about him getting a job? Christ, he was trying, wasn't he? His head was splitting and his throat seemed to have closed. Suddenly he saw that Tommy was wearing his belt and rage came. "Hey!" he croaked, "that's my belt. Give it over! How many times have I told you to leave my things alone?"

His words trailed off. He stood swaying and glaring down at Tommy until he undid the buckle and pulled the belt off. He threw it at Kevin who caught it by the buckle. He held the buckle, then suddenly snapped the leather like a stock whip. Crack! A giant hand tightened around his throat. He choked for breath and felt himself falling to the floor. His limbs began to writhe. He felt that he was engaged in a struggle with a giant foe. He struggled on, but it was useless. From a great distance, he heard Tommy yell out. Somehow he knew that Mum, Uncle and Sue had rushed into the room.

Kevin was having one of his asthma attacks. There was little they could do to help him, but before he lost consciousness a cosy feeling came over him that he too was loved.

THREE

Kevin lay in bed all next morning getting over the effects of his asthma attack. His mother fussed over him. It irritated him. He brooded over his sister's slights until he felt his anger flooding back. He knew what he would do! He would go and confront the guy head on. But what could he say to him? His body tensed with his thoughts. His breathing quickened, but the air flowed smoothly through his throat. At least the attack was over. Uncle had said last night that the guy lived in one of those poshly done-up places near the Workshop. It would be easy to find. He would show Sue. It was Saturday and the shop was closed in the afternoon. He should be home. Why, Sue might even be there. If he could catch both of them together...

Quickly choking down his lunch and ignoring his mother's advice to stay in and rest, Kevin got up. He pulled on a clean shirt and jeans, then rushed out of the flat, before remembering that he had no money for the bus fare. He had to rush back and borrow two dollars from his mum. He just made the bus and flung himself on board. In Northbridge his haste lessened. Second thoughts came. It might be idle gossip? The old guy was sitting outside on the veranda of the boarding house. Kevin knew him and he pointed out Wiseman's house. A high wall screened the house off from the street. His finger jabbed out to press the button before he could lose his nerve. He waited and waited. Perhaps he wasn't home, he thought with relief. He was about to turn away, when the gate or rather the door in the high wall swung open. The smooth face of Mr Wiseman smiled politely at him. Although he had seen the face before, he felt disappointment. He had expected to find guilt, dismay, or defiance, but the grey-haired man in neat slacks and open-necked shirt did not look like the seducer of young girls. Bland grey eyes magnified by gold-rimmed thick lenses looked past him into the street. When the man spoke his voice sounded as smooth as his face.

"What may I do for you?" Mr Wiseman enquired, concentrating his owl eyes on Kevin's face. He looked away and felt an idiot.

At last he managed to stutter: "I–I'm Sue's brother."

"Oh," the man hesitated, then went on. "I don't think I've had the pleasure of meeting you. Please come in. I've been unpacking a few cheeses I stopped off to buy at Roe Street market ..."

Kevin passed through into what he considered a dank airless garden and then on into the front room which was small but furnished in a posh style he had only seen in magazines. His eyes flickered over oil paintings, soft leather chairs and fled along a Persian carpet. His eyes stayed on the floor. How was he supposed to act? What if the man's wife came in?

As if in answer to the last question, the man began explaining as if to an acquaintance: "We have a small house up in the hills overlooking the city. My wife likes it up there. It's so much better for the children too, you see, gives them a taste for nature."

"Uh," Kevin said, unable to find a single word in his head. What had happened to his rage? He felt his stomach turn over.

As if to give him a lead, Mr Wiseman said: "Have you come about your sister? She was supposed to be coming along here to help me with–uh–some urgent business, but she didn't look at all well in the store. I hope that she isn't sick."

Kevin scowled. He was not only out of place, but out of his depth. He wondered how Sue coped with the place, but then she had always been able to handle things better. Finally he managed to say: "No, no, she's not real sick, not that much, and she didn't send me, well, not exactly. I came on my own," he finished lamely. His eyes clung to the patterned carpet.

"Well, what is it; what can I do for you?" the man said somewhat sharply.

The carpet pattern became blurred. His legs began trembling. He had rehearsed this scene over and over in his mind, but that was one thing, this another. "It's only, it's only," he began, then found a rush of words. "It's only that my sister is so young. She's told me that sometimes you leave her in charge of the whole shop. She's afraid that if anything went wrong she wouldn't be able to cope. She works long hours too, and it's affecting her health. You saw that this morning. I just thought that I'd come along and let you know. " His run of words came to an abrupt end. His eyes flickered up to the man, then back down to the carpet.

Mr Wiseman's eyes actually twinkled behind his heavy spectacles, and he even tut-tutted—a sound Kevin had never heard before. "I say, she does seem very happy working with me. She is very bright and I know she enjoys taking charge of things. She'll go far, I assure you. You know how hard it is to find youngsters willing to and able to think about their futures and the future of the business, rather than some grubby little pop singer, or something like that?"

"But, well, it's just that she comes home so late these evenings. It's not good for a young girl to work so hard, or have so much responsibility ..."

"You have to start young these days to get ahead, young man," Mr Wiseman snapped. "Hard work never hurt anyone." He stepped closer and even touched Kevin on the shoulder. "I'll tell you something, in confidence of course. There's not many young people around like your sister. I have a lot of faith in her, shall we say, business acumen. So much so that I am planning to open another shop soon; I am grooming her to eventually take charge of it. Not right away of course. I'll get an older woman in at the beginning to show her the ropes, but when she's shown that she's able to handle it, she'll have complete control. One of the reasons why she's working so late at present is because she has to learn all the ins and outs of the trade—all the threads of the cloth," he smiled at his attempt at a joke, then finished off: "To put it bluntly, I need bright young things like her in my shops. It's good for business."

And Kevin found himself out on the street before realising that their little talk was at an end. He stood in front of the locked gate feeling like a galah. He had messed it up good and proper. Now the rest of the afternoon yawned in front of him. He should have stayed in bed. The old man was still sitting on the veranda, and he stopped and spoke to him about his Uncle. Suddenly he realised that Uncle would know about this visit. God, he hadn't thought that. Waving a hand at the old man, he rushed off. He'd go to the Albion Hotel. Elias and Paul might be there and he could get some advice or at least cadge a drink from them!

He ducked into the pub and waited until his eyes had adjusted to the gloom. The usual pack of no-hopers with their sluttish women lounged around the tables. With a shudder, he imagined himself being one of them in a few years. Drinking away his dole money and not caring about anything but where the next drink was coming from. Swear words hit at his ears and raucous laughter jangled his nerve ends. He was ready to get out, when he spied Elias and Paul sitting in front of a jug of beer at a corner table.

They saw him and beckoned him over. As he reached the table, Elias upended his glass and got to his feet. Paul flashed a smile at Kevin and nodded at the vacant chair.

"Just this minute, Elias has remembered that he should be studying," he gently mocked. "I was thinking that I'd be left all alone with these wetjelas, when lo and behold, I look up and there's Kevin Young to keep me company. Get yourself a glass. Use Elias's. He hasn't got any use for it now."

Elias bowed mockingly, said, "See youse," and went off.

"Arrh, the pressure of exams; makes you want to down a few and then plenty more," Paul exclaimed, glancing after Elias.

"Who knows, I might need a good lawyer one day?" He filled the glass for Kevin.

Kevin slumped in the chair, emptied the glass in a gulp, then refilled it from the jug. Paul eyes shifted from the door to a woman, then to Kevin. He gently began to chide him. "That yorga, Margaret, she's something, isn't she? And country fresh at that. Bet you can't guess who's caught her eye? Noretta told me that she thinks you're something: I don't know what. Maybe what the cat dragged in? Anyway you better watch out. She's mardong for you, and you better watch out. You know that Bayside mob—all cousins—and the girls have to find husbands away from home. So you better watch out and not trifle with her affections. As Elias might declare, if he was here: she's filled with good works and other things are on her mind."

The aftermath of the asthma attack and the meeting with Mr Wiseman had driven all thought of Margaret from his mind. Paul's words only irritated him.

"What's wrong, you mardong too?" the irrepressible Paul taunted, but at the same time he was careful to punch Kevin lightly on the arm. But the touch only caused Kevin to remember the man. He had done the same thing, and for one wild moment he wanted to return the blow—hard! Instead, he grinned and asked Paul for a loan of five dollars.

"Bro, you want five dollars from me?" Paul replied with a mock frown.

"You know how it is, I haven't got two cents to rub together. You got your student allowance yesterday."

Paul pretended a serious face as he did an elaborate search of his pockets. With a great show, he carefully pulled out a thin fold of notes. Slowly he separated a five dollar bill and passed it reluctantly across. He dragged out: "Alright, alright, have it, but only on one condition."

His mate, who had been cheered up by the performance and found it hard to keep a straight face, demanded, "What?"

"You take this other five and go and get the jug refilled!"

"Right on."

He went to the bar and while he was waiting to be served, a Nyoongah in his late twenties appeared at his elbow, and said: "Add another jug to that one, won't you, Kev? It's my shout."

It was Alex, the guy in charge of the Study Centre where Tommy went. He picked up the two jugs and left the guy to pay for them. He had plenty of money. As he was handing the five back to Paul, Alex came and dragged up a chair. He offered around cigarettes. Paul shook his head, but Kevin took one, though he seldom smoked. The dole wasn't enough to keep himself in smokes.

The man filled his glass and took a long gulp before setting it down. He leaned towards Kevin as he asked him how he was making out. His voice was rich and deep, which he used with great effect especially when he was addressing a crowd at a rally. It managed to project such confidence that it made most people bashful and on guard. Kevin felt this as he replied: "Nothing much." He shrugged off the man's searching gaze. In some ways he reminded him of Mr Wiseman, and he felt his irritation return.

"No job yet?"

"No job as yet."

"I hope that you're thinking about doing a course like Paul's doing," he said openly, and bringing Paul into the conversation so that he wouldn't feel left out of it.

"That's what I've been trying to get him to do," Paul volunteered.

"That'd be the best thing, but if you don't want to study, think about something else. I met this union bloke the other day. There's a job going on the roads. It's hard yakka, but you look strong enough. I could check it out for you; just say the word."

Kevin shrugged. His irritation grew. He felt that he had some sort of fatal disease and that everyone went out of their way to offer advice. Now Alex mistook his silence for thinking about it, and smiled. "Good, just think it over. It pays good too and you'll have more than a bob or two in your pockets. You'd like that, wouldn't you? Well, on Monday just come to the Centre and we'll arrange it."

He waited for a reply, received none, and went on: "Hey, Kev, what's bugging you? You look really green. What's wrong with him Paul?"

"Mardong," Paul laughed.

"Mardong," Alex laughed. "You want any help?" he grinned.

"It isn't that," Kevin said, wishing they would leave him alone.

"Well, what is it then—trouble at home? There's a lot of that around these days, mark my words. At the Centre I get kids who can't hack a home life any more."

"Arrh, I'm just feeling down, that's all!"

"Something must have caused it. If your family gets you down, just be like your brother Tommy, and come down to our centre. There's always something going to interest you there. Just ask Tommy, he'll tell you all about it. Anyway, you've been down there a few times and know for yourself. You can come again and get involved."

"Arrh, I'm not interested in that sort of stuff," Kevin replied, then blurted out his problems. "Everything at home seems such a mess and now my sister's playing up. I just don't know what to do about it. It'll get worse, not better."

"Maybe, maybe. You're in that Mia Mia housing complex, aren't you? That's a problem in itself that is."

"It's not only that–" and Kevin found himself relating to Alex all his worries. The trouble with Sue, Tommy, Uncle, even his mother's absurd attachment to the awful flat. He downed his beer and refilled his glass. The others did the same.

"Well," said Alex, "That's how it is all over. Things are not as good as they were. Once our families used to be tightly knit together. They were always there to fall back on, but now that feeling, that solidarity is beginning to get lost. You know, they put us in houses and flats too small to have anyone stay over, and then check up to see how many people are living there. Why, just the other day, one of our own people said publicly that if Aborigines wanted to live like that, they should go back to the reserve. Well, some day I hope that it works out and that you're not the only one with problems. You know, just the other day my wife, Pat, took our kids and went off East, just like that. She got some job in Canberra and decided that she was too good for me. Hell, now there's this gap in my life. I suppose I did neglect her a bit. I spend a lot of time at the Centre, but then my work comes first, and it'll keep me going now. I haven't got the time to mope about and feel sorry for myself. No, I'm too busy for that!"

Kevin accepted the proffered cigarette. He was learning new things all the time. He had known Alex as a grown-up who helped kids and that was all. It was the first time he had heard about his wife and kids. The man had always appeared so in control of his life. If this could happen to him, what chance had he of pulling through?

"So we've just got to go and make the best we can of it," Alex said softly. "Just go on and hope for the best, that's the way to go."

"Maybe, maybe," Kevin answered, still on the defensive. He knew Nyoongahs and how often what they said and what really happened differed. Maybe if he went to the Centre he could find out the true story? At least he could ask Tommy about it.

"Another thing, Kev, let me offer you a little advice. It's free," he grinned to allay any resentment. "It's hard to tackle things on your own. You have to realise that all our problems are linked into the system. You have to see the whole and find the answers there. It's then you find out that the whole mess has to be done away with, and that is what all of us together, as a mob, must work for. But we have to do it all together, and the Centre is a start. Think about it and if you want to come in and be with people you can trust, come in with us. We help each other too, and it'll be better than sitting around all by yourself feeling the system tugging you this way and that way."

Kevin didn't know how to take Alex's little speech. Somehow he knew that it wouldn't be as good as Alex said it was. He had been to the Centre a few times and had sat in on discussions. Of course they made sense, and of course the people there did help you with your studies, but he didn't know about the rest of it. At a loss, he hummed the words of a song he knew: "The system, the system, the stupid system..."

Paul refilled their glasses and the whole thing was forgotten. Someone called out to Alex and he drained his glass and left.

"What was he on about?" Kevin asked Paul.

"You know, bro, that's how some of them talk at the uni. Alex was one of the first Nyoongahs to go to uni and he must have learnt it from the rich kids. They talk about wrecking the whole rotten system, and then graduate and join the system. It's only someone like Alex who listens and believes that crap who ends up without a piece of pie. I bet they laugh at him from the shelter of their nice cosy professions."

"Yeah," Kevin agreed. "What can we do anyway?" His voice turned shrill as his resentment grew. "I get enough to eat, have a place to sleep and can't get a job. I have to put up with a sister calling me a bludger. I have to watch Mum who hasn't been the same since Dad died, and Uncle who's on the same kick as Alex, saving people in spite of themselves. At least he didn't learn about it in a university. He's just an ex-drunk spoiling other ex-drunks just like he's spoilt Sue rotten. Then blokes like Alex go on about the system, the stupid system, when they part of our problems. He's gotten Tommy onto some political thing. I've read the papers he prints. Before you know it, he'll lose his apprenticeship and all because of some fool thing Alex learnt from rich kids. I'm sick of all this garbage." He downed his beer, saw that the jugs were empty and said: "I've had enough of this place too!" He got up to leave and Paul asked: "Mind if I tag along?"

"Why not, why not?"

They went out into the bright sunlight and Kevin let his rage explode again: "They're all so ready with their good advice, but when the crunch comes they're nowhere in sight." Then his rage left him as he fell into the dumps. What was the use of anything? All that he could hope for was a good pass in that exam, so that he could get a government job. He had to get it, he had to!

He stared across the street, and suddenly recognised Ralph walking along. When had he been released? The black leather jacket had been exchanged for a business suit, but it failed to disguise the hood. Thank God, he thought, that Sue had managed to escape from his clutches. Why, she could have been working in a brothel by now. Ralph was just the type to become a pimp. But was Wiseman any better?

"Just where are you off to?" broke in Paul.

"Don't know—let's go and see Johnno." He hurried away from any chance meeting with Ralph. Johnno at least made him feel relaxed. He never demanded anything, and never offered advice. He was just the bloke to see, so cool and detached from the mess around him. Maybe it was the dope he smoked that made him apart from everything, but then he had his culture to fall back on. He wasn't trying to make it in the white world. Still, to get to him they had to take a bus to Freo.

They got off the bus and walked along High Street towards Parry Street. They reached a huge dilapidated boarding house crammed with lonely old men. Johnno had a room behind it. The passageway smelt of urine and medicine. They reached the kitchen, nodded at an old guy fumbling at a gas stove, then went through the back door and out onto a patch of concrete. To the right side, opposite the laundry, leaned his wooden bungalow. On the door had been painted a boomerang, red, black and gold, but this had faded with time into a rough curve. Through the thin wooden walls came the sharp tap-tapping of mulga sticks and the keening of an Aboriginal voice.

"He's in," Kevin told his mate. He knocked on the door in time to the rhythm so that Johnno would know it was friends.

It was a minute or two before the door was opened by the thin wiry man clad only in a pair of shorts and a floppy knitted head covering which hid his hair. He grinned widely at them and stepped back with a flourish and said: "Wulyu Karuwarra". Johnno was from Fitzroy Crossing and still had his language intact. He believed in using it as much as possible, and often his words were a mystery to the Nyoongahs from the south. Kevin knew that Wulyu Karuwarra meant "Good afternoon" and he replied: "Wangkikarra marna pirriyani".

"Ngana pa nyantu yini?"

"His name's Paul. He's at the university."

"Yuwayi, come in."

The doorway opened directly into a small neat kitchen. They went through into the larger room which had a double bed mattress bent along one wall, a wardrobe, table and two chairs. There was a cassette player and a pair of congo drums painted red, black and gold. Johnno was a good drummer and often got work to accompany bands. He made enough to make ends meet and to keep himself in Nyandi (herb) as well. He turned down the volume of the tape-player a fraction and said, "Yutanti", motioning with his hand so that they would sit down. He went off into the kitchen to brew up some tea. This was one of his rituals and would be served, as only tea should, in large enamel pannikins.

Kevin flopped on the mattress and glanced through the window. He was amazed at how much light flooded through without making the place unbearably hot. This may have been because of the morning glory plant which on his last visit had been cut down to its roots. Now it had erupted in a frenzy of growth to assert its land rights over the narrow space beneath the window and the high brick wall of the factory. The sun's rays bounced off this wall, filtered through the lush green leaves and tumbled coolly into the room.

"That stuff sure grows fast," he told Paul, nodding his attention at the plant which poked its purple flowers through the window.

"Sure does," Paul agreed. He was wondering about Johnno and his knowledge of his language. This touched him. Nyoongah had been destroyed long ago, and all he knew were a few words. He stared at a bright paper poster tacked on the wall. It advertised a concert, A Battle of the Bands, put on by Abmusic in aid of the Fremantle Nyoongah Association. It was tonight! Next to it a land rights poster showed a tranquil bush scene. On the wall gleamed the black, red and golden sun of the Aboriginal national flag.

Johnno returned from the kitchen with three large pannikins of steaming tea. He handed them out, then sat on the mattress and stared out at the plant.

The tape ended with a click and he got up to change it. The music of Coloured Stone, an Aboriginal band from Alice Springs, sounded out a poem of Oodgeroo Noonuccal's "No More Boomerang".

They sipped on the tea and after the track had finished, Johnno spoke. "Yara, yara," he said and unfolded a slow, slow smile.

"Yeah," Paul replied to say something.

"Kwup," said Kevin in Nyoongah.

"Rain soon come, then sun again, That's how it should be, a constant flow. See that plant, it got its land rights. It fills out its right space just as we all should, yu!"

Paul and Kevin acknowledged this in their language, "Kayar!"

Johnno smiled at them, then asked Kevin how he had been going. He said, "OK," as Johnno got to his feet and went to the wardrobe. He pulled out a bong and a cloth bag and took out something wrapped in tin foil. He opened it and shook some brown Nyandi into the palm of his hand, carefully removed the seeds and stuffed it into the small bowl of the pipe. "Pituri," he said as he passed the bong to Paul. Paul expelled all the air from his lungs. Johnno lit a match and applied it to the bowl. Paul sucked in slowly, and gave a first quick gasp which sent the ashes of the Nyandi hissing into the water container beneath.

"Yara, yara," smiled Johnno.

"Yalorn," smiled Kevin.

Johnno replaced the bong and passed it to Kevin. He inhaled the sweet smoke and then lit the bowl for Johnno. The ritual smoking over, the three lay back on the mattress and let the song of Coloured Stone's "Take Me Back To The Dreamtime" sweep them away into stillness. Kevin's problems receded into the far distance. They were so far, far away that he could contemplate them without becoming upset.

Johnno seemed to see them too. He said to Kevin: "Worries!"

"Worries," Paul stated.

"Only waiting around to see if I get that government job," Kevin replied, slowly pulling this particular problem back from the horizon. Another one came with it.

"Family's getting me down too," he added, then went on. "My kid brother's never at home and this worries Mum. My sister, Sue, is mixed up with some old gaddiya and this is a worry too. I don't know how to handle any of it! I saw that guy Alex today, just before coming here. He told me to forget about it and spend more time down at that Centre of his, but you can't forget your family, can you?"

"Ngajirta," agreed Johnno. "Family is everything." He was silent for minute, then suddenly said, "Listen, there was this old

Bibbulman who taught me this song. I teach it to you." He sang, "Buyal ngunda buyal/ yeerdee mandoo/ kaaning urbaa. This means 'South, brother, south, you must go. No, O teach you, till it run smooth'."

He got Kevin to repeat the words until he could sing them directly from the heart, then he taught him another short song: "Nandeegur kenj beebul woonanga/ yanee yanman yaan ee yanman, yaan ee yanman, yaan ee yanman yaan. That means," he explained to Kevin with a laugh, " 'the Bibbulman girl dances this and that way, this way and your way'."

The meaning of the lyrics annoyed Kevin. He protested that although it was good to learn some of the old songs, they didn't mean much to him.

"Who the shoe fits, let him wear it," Johnno replied with a grin. "Maybe gammon, maybe not?"

"My studies are gammon," Paul stated.

"Brainwash education to make us conform," Johnno agreed. "But some go that way, others go another way. Some even work for the Gubment, or to fix up the roads for the motor cars to take out our iron and minerals."

He put on another tape and Kevin looked towards Paul and asked, "But what to do, but what to do?"

Johnno began singing:

> *Captain on the rough sea,*
> *Captain on the rough sea,*
>
> *Singing here in my room,*
> *Singing here with my pipe in my hand,*
> *Singing here next to the sea shore.*
>
> *Watching the Freo women dance,*
> *Watching the Freo women dance,*
> *Waiting for the American captains,*
> *Dancing, dancing on the rough seas.*

He took his drum and began to beat:

Beating the drum, the drum,
Beating the drum, the drum.
For the Freo women dancing,
Dancing on the rough seas.

He finished off with a rattle-like crescendo, then went to brew another pot of tea. After, they had another smoke as the light began to fade into the softness of the early evening and the Fremantle Doctor shook the plant outside the window. Kevin grew aware of the reek of petrol fumes being blown along by the breeze. It constricted his throat, but another pipe released it and the reek turned sweet with his thoughts of his childhood country life.

Before they had ventured into Perth, they had lived on the outskirts of a small town. They lived in a dilapidated house in the middle of a wide paddock littered with old car bodies. Dad used to buy old car after old car. They were all that he could afford. When each one gave up the ghost they were laid to rest in the field and kept for possible spare parts, Dad bought what he could and the cars were of different makes and the parts rarely could be used. Over the years the car bodies accumulated. They were great fun to play in.

In those days, although wages were small, there was plenty of work for Dad in the surrounding farms and orchards. He was a good worker and everyone knew it. He was a big cheery man who never let anything get him down. Always he was coming and going and filling the house with his good humour. Mum had been happy then. She went about humming or singing and took time off from the housework to go fishing in the nearby river with the women from the other Aboriginal families living nearby.

The paddock was part of the floodplain of the river and the house stood in a corner made by a small creek entering the main stream. Towards the middle of the summer the creek stopped running and became a series of stagnant pools. That was a good time for the kids. They wandered from pool to pool, stopping to swim in the deeper ones. Even then, Kevin recalled, Sue was eager for any adventure. She would be the first to clamber up the trunk of a tree bending over a patch of water. She would perch on a high bough and taunt him to follow. Of course he had to, then he had to follow her in a dive head-first into the pool. She wouldn't allow any jumping. It had to be a dive. Tommy then was only eight. He had the job of minding him. He was not allowed to climb the tree and dive in, but had to enter from the bank. But his concern for his little brother did not prevent him from towing him out to the middle of the deepest pool and leaving him there to make his own way to the bank. Dad had taught him the same way, and it did work!

No-one had to throw Sue in. She took to water like a fish and loved swimming even more than catching gilgies. She enjoyed it as much as clambering up the huge old pine tree which stood in front of the foundations of a house which had been washed away. She would climb to the very top and sway there, screaming with joy. She had even made him go in the middle of the night to the remains of the old house, although it was haunted. She had laughed at ghosts and at him. "If I see that old ghost, I'll take this stick to him. See if I don't!" she declared.

The thing Kevin liked doing best of all was hunting for gilgies. Paddling through the shallow water at the foot of the banks of the pools and feeling the mud squelching up through his toes. He would bend over, grab hold of the matted grass undermined by the water and toss it onto its back on firm ground. Then he would push his fingers through the muddy roots to find the hard shell of a gilgie. He had to be quick and grab it before it had a chance to nip him.

He would get the other two kids to help him and they would heave up the grass mats for yards until they had filled a can with the fresh water crayfish. Then they ran home to Mum who put the can on top of the big rusty wood stove which was always kept burning. Like cats staring at a bird, they would sit around watching until the water began bubbling. It seemed magical, how the grey shells of the gilgies would turn a bright orange. Mum did all the hard parts, like taking the can off the stove, then tipping out the boiling water. There was no sink in the house and this had to be done outside. As soon as she had done this, they would grab at the gilgies, peel off the shells and eat the tails and suck the meat out of the claws. They had been boiled in water from the pool and always tasted delicious.

Kevin rested on the mattress feeling the memories of those days with a sadness he would feel at remembering a dead friend. Such sadness was mixed with the joy of those times. The crispness of the winter air, the hot stillness of summer days, the melodies of the plaintive songs his people sang, mixed with the barking of a distant dog calling to him as he lay through the last night before leaving his country house. Why had they decided to move to the city?

Uncle came on a visit with tales of plentiful work and easy living. He put the idea into their heads. Mum and Dad were concerned about the education of their kids. Schools were better in the city, and so they had left the country behind them and arrived in Balga. Dad found a job easy enough, but the local school was tough. He had to fight to survive kids that grew into the likes of Ralph. He had stuck at it and finished his schooling just in time to find all the jobs had gone.

He felt the city closing in around him again. Funny, but he had never had an asthma attack in the country. He coughed to clear his throat of petrol fumes. The continual roar of the city closed off the country from him. Only nineteen, and he felt completely useless. Would that Public Service job ever happen? Well, he would wait a little longer and then go and see Alex. Maybe he could get him into the CYSS retraining scheme? That way he could get job experience, but in what? Anything, as long as it was something. With steady work things could become as good as they were when Dad was alive. With a job he too could fill the world with huge mirth and love of life.

He began humming the words of the song Johnno had just taught him. "Nandeegur kenj beebul woonanga / yan ee yanman yan ee yanman yan ee yanman / yan ee yanman yan ee yanman yaan." Margaret glided into his mind as if he was singing her. It didn't annoy him. Instead he felt a little like he had felt recalling those country days. Such a warm person and good to be around. He remembered that Paul had told him that she was solid for him, and smiled. Paul most likely was having him on, but that didn't matter. He liked Margaret and would see her again—soon!

Night had fallen and the light had gone from the window. Johnno spoke through the darkness to tell them about the concert. "You want to come along? Come along, both of you. I'm playing with a band or two, maybe the whole three. Good cause though, so hope you got the boyo for the ticket. Only a couple of dollars, you know. Good night for all. Yan karlipa—let's go!" he urged them.

Kevin remembered that he had borrowed five dollars and an idea flashed in his mind. "How you getting your drums there, Johnno?"

"Not far, put them on my back and lug them along. Do it all the time."

"Hey, I might be able to give you a lift. I have a friend who'll enjoy the concert. She has a car and can come and get us."

"When Emu lost his wings he said, 'it happens like that'; when eagle grew his wings, he said, 'I can fly to the tree, but not to see the moon man. If it can happen, it must happen soon, wali?' "

"Wali—alright," Kevin agreed.

"I'll go and ring Margaret and see if she can come," he told Paul.

"Hey, see if Noretta can come with her," his mate replied.

"I'll do just that. Won't be a sec."

"Phone in the big house in passageway," Johnno told him.

"Yeah, I remember passing it on the way in," he replied, getting to his feet. Now, if only Margaret was there. It was Saturday night and she most likely had gone off somewhere, but there was no harm in trying. As Dad would have said: nothing ventured, nothing gained.

Kevin was overjoyed when she answered the phone and even more so when she said that she would love to come. Noretta had gone out, but Diana was moping about the hostel with nothing to do, and she would bring her. "She's really down in the dumps and could do with some cheering up," she told him.

"One time or the other we all have a touch of the blues," Kevin answered. "A concert is just the thing to lift her. You know, when the music starts, you can't hear yourself thinking."

Paul wasn't too happy that Diana would be coming instead of Noretta. She thought too much of herself. Kevin laughed and said: "Lot's of blacks'll be there, and some of it will rub back on her. She'll unwind soon enough."

"Wali—alright," Johnno laughed and palmed out an African rhythm as he tuned his drum skins.

FOUR

Kevin was relieved to find that it was only two dollars to get in. A bloke he knew called Bimbo was on the door and there might have been hassles getting past him without paying. Diana was really down in the dumps. Still, she volunteered to buy each of them a can of beer and this at least cheered Paul up. With a few quick jokes, he even had Diana smiling after a while.

The concert was being held in a large dance hall decorated for the occasion with the Aboriginal colours of red, black and gold. It was early, the first band was just setting up its equipment on the stage and they settled themselves at a corner table. A song began over the sound system; a local song, "Brown Skin Girl", which had received a lot of airplay over the Aboriginal radio programme. Margaret knew the words and sang softly along.

> Brown skin girl,
> Brown skin girl.
> Brown eyed girl,
> I love you see.
> I could live with you,
> All my life, I would love with you,
> Until I die, all my life until I die.
>
> Share your cries and share your sighs'
> Share your laughter and your smiles'
> Feel the pain and all the sorrows'
> Feel the slurs that stain your honour,
> While I watch the ripples of your hair,
> Watch the ripples of your hair,
> Of your brown hair across your brown skinned body.

When the song came to an end, Margaret said that it was her favourite. Kevin, happy to be with her agreed, though he thought it

soppy. Paul went off for more beer and they watched Johnno
positioning his drums on stage. Then "You Gotta Be Strong" by
Warumpi Band came on. Kevin felt the lyrics of the song and asked
Margaret for a dance.

As they reached the floor, the lights dimmed and a strobe light
began flickering. This got rid of any shyness and other couples
followed them onto the floor. They began jerking around him, and
suddenly he felt that the life was not only being choked out of him
but out of everyone else. Strangely this did not drive away his
mood. It was happening to everyone; they could all get together and
do something about it. Spots of light began circling the floor and
touching each face. They came from a sphere of mirrored glass
rotating slowly above the centre of the floor.

A new song began fast and furious. Johnno began pounding along
on his drums:

> *Rock your backs, rock your back,*
> *Drive them back, drive them back,*
> *Don't be slack, show them that you're black,*
> *Rock your backs and drive them back.*

"Hey, hey!" shouted Johnno over the microphone. "Rock you
blacks! Hey, hey, lively up you blacks and rock your backs, rock
your backs!"

Kevin danced opposite Margaret, not touching her, but wanting
to. Red and gold spotlights began caressing the dancers. Muscle by
muscle, he felt his body relaxing. Everything will be alright
tomorrow, tomorrow, tomorrow...

"I've never been to a dance like this before," Margaret told him,
as exhausted, they made their way back to the table. "Look there's
so many blacks here too. Why, it's a bit like home. They're
everywhere. We're everywhere! And gee, you know I hardly knew
that there were Aboriginal bands until I started listening to 6NR and
the Aboriginal programme. You know, they're just as good as any
white band, and they sing what we can relate to."

"Yeah, and a lot of it isn't that love shit," Kevin blurted out
before realising it. He looked at Margaret and was relieved to see
she seemed not to have heard him. His words must have got lost in

the loud music.

It was difficult to talk below a shout and so they sat quietly together, sipping on their beer, and watching Diana and Paul making fools of themselves on the dance floor. At last the band and Johnno were ready to play. They announced themselves as Makaratta and they featured a didgeridoo player up front. Johnno began a slow muffled beat behind the sweetly crooning voices of the band.

> *I passed over the land and saw our people crying,*
> *I passed over the land and saw our people crying,*
> *They need some place they can sit and live on,*
> *Some ground they can rely on.*
> *Many days they feel the pain and the strife,*
> *Of the earth being torn asunder (asunder),*
> *Machines tearing the heart of their crying,*
> *(drowning the sounds of their sighing).*

The didgeridoo droned on in a dirge-like solo, then the chorus was repeated and the song ended. In the sudden silence, the words of a white man sitting at a near table with an African shouted: "I like real black music, but not this Aboriginal crap!" Fists clenched all over the hall, then relaxed. The African glanced at Kevin and shrugged. He smiled back. No one would spoil his evening, not even that wetjela who would get what he deserved before the night was out.

The concert continued far into the night and the music got better and better. At about two in the morning it ended with all members of all three bands on stage singing behind a man from the Pilbara who sang a sad blues song of good night. Then they were expelled into the coolness of the morning still reeking with petrol fumes and noisy with starting engines. Margaret's car added its quota of sound and smell. She dropped off Johnno and his drums, then Paul and lastly Kevin. As he left the car in front of the Westhome block of flats, he realised that now she would know that he lived in such a place, but then did it matter? He hesitated at the side of the car, and she asked him to come and see her in the afternoon. She mentioned that her Dad was coming to the city for a meeting in the Council Hall, but after that she would be free. "Hey, bend down for a sec," she suddenly said. Not knowing what to expect, he did so and received a kiss right on the mouth. "That's for the lovely evening," she whispered. He turned from the car feeling that he was floating. When he entered his room, he saw that Tommy was still out. He shrugged and didn't let it bother him. For once he had enjoyed himself and nothing could spoil it.

FIVE

It was noon when he awoke. Tommy's bed was unslept in. He must have been out all night. Kevin lay there listening for any sounds. The flat was creakingly silent. Mum must still be at church. By the time he had showered and dressed, she was home and grilling chops for lunch. He didn't feel in the least hungry, and went into the kitchen to tell her not to worry about him.

"Where's Sue?" he asked.

"She's been to church with us, and stopped to get a litre of milk," Mum told him.

"She's behaving herself," he grunted, then told her that he was going out.

His mother didn't reply, but he turned at the front door and saw her sad eyes watching him.

Reaching the exit door of the building, he pushed it open and saw his sister walking towards it. She had a carton of milk clutched in one hand. He hid in a niche beside the doorway and watched her stroll across the lawn. She wore a pale pink skirt and a fluffy white blouse. As he stared at this, this woman, he realised that his little sister had grown up and looked much older than her seventeen years, In spite of himself his eyes went to her full breasts and moved down to her swaying hips. They jerked up to her face. Even on Sunday she had carefully made up her face. Where had she learnt that from? He recalled that she had done some sort of modelling course when she was sixteen and this explained her appearance.

Two young guys who lived in the block were kicking a football, though it was in the middle of the cricket season. They saw the girl, and the one holding the ball kicked it at her. Both raced after it as it bounced at her feet and almost collided with her. It was harmless horseplay. Kevin had done it himself. This time he saw red. The boys retrieved their ball and came towards where he was standing. As they passed, he heard one say to the other, "Bit of alright, isn't she?"

He felt his fist clenching. He wanted to smash the leer off their faces. His sister was too good for such bludgers! They raced up the stairs. Forcing himself to remain calm, he turned his eyes back to his sister. He watched as she strolled along, her hips dipping provocatively with each step. She must realise that her walk would attract guys like flies, he thought. At least, she had ignored the blokes when the ball had landed right in front of her and they had come charging towards her, but this meant that she could shrug off such things as everyday occurrences to be endured—until a guy came along who she liked!

When Sue reached her brother, she treated him as a smudge on the concrete wall. Like the young blokes before, he was beneath her notice. At least Kevin thought so. He called out: "Sue, Sue!"

She stopped just inside the doorway and turned a blank face towards him. Was he something to be endured too? He stared into that face, expressionless like a brown mask.

"Yeah," she said tonelessly, as if she was speaking to a stranger.

"What's come over you?" he grated out.

"What do you mean?" she replied. "What's come over you? I've been getting the milk." Annoyed with his spying on her, she turned towards the stairs.

He felt hurt, bewildered and resentful. What had he done to her? He felt like slapping some sense into her, but then, what good would it do? He had tried it before and gotten nowhere. "Hey, just hold on a minute, got something to ask you," he managed to say in a calm voice.

Her polite cold face waited. He imagined it recoiling from his slap. He might imagine it, but couldn't do it, Mum and Uncle would be down on him like a ton of bricks. Why, she had just been to church, and then they always took her side, didn't they?

"H–Has Mr Wiseman said anything to you? You saw him yesterday afternoon, didn't you?"

"Maybe," she shrugged. "What would he say anyway?"

"Don't know." He felt relieved that the man hadn't mentioned his visit to her. With that off his mind, he felt his fury growing. How could his sister treat him with such disdain? Why, didn't she remembered how they had played together? They had wrestled and fought too, just like a brother and sister. He felt like pointing out the scar on his head he had from a rock thrown by her. Now for her all that was over. They might never again giggle over silly things, or roam about together. His fury fell into depression. What was the use of trying to get through to her? "Alright," he told her. "I'm off now, got to meet someone, I'll see you when I get back." They turned from each other and went their separate ways.

As he reached the deli on the corner, he felt the need for a cigarette to calm his nerves. He remembered the ad on TV that only dags dragged, but so what, he felt like a dag. Suddenly he felt his whole body begin to tremble and his throat seize up as if an asthma attack was coming on. It was all the fault of Sue, all her fault. She had become a selfish tight little ball, so smooth that he couldn't grab hold. Worse, Tommy was going the same way too. They were getting beyond him and leaving him all alone to struggle on. He could hardly gasp out the words to buy a cigarette. It took most of the three dollars out of the five he had borrowed from Paul. He lit one and drew in the smoke. It seemed to loosen his throat. Thank God, he wasn't going to have an attack! The hostel was quite a long way away, and he decided to walk along the road for a while to settle his mind. He set off and began thinking of Margaret. They hadn't talked that much last night. The music had been too loud. He remembered the touch of her mouth on his. Her lips had felt so warm and soft. He yearned for the feeling of her body in his arms. But then this brought up the meeting with Wiseman and the vision of Sue in his arms. The trembling rage came back. A bus came along. He raced to the bus stop and flung himself on board.

Too soon, he dropped off at the corner of the street where the hostel was. Margaret's car was parked at the kerb. He hesitated beside it. He didn't really feel like seeing anyone. At last, he turned and went through the gate.

A cluster of people stood chatting at the entrance to the hall. Margaret had said, he recalled, that some sort of meeting was being held there. Oh well, too late to turn back now. As he approached, the girl and an older man detached themselves from the group and came towards them. The old guy was a country Nyoongah from his manner and clothing. Suddenly he remembered that Margaret had said her Dad was coming to the meeting. He stopped in confusion. What would he say? How to act? But the girl flashed her warm smile at him, then introduced her Dad. His tension lessened. The man had the same warm smile as his daughter—and the same slow deliberate movements of his own father. He had forgotten how easy country people were.

"So you're one of the Youngs from Pinjarra way. Knew Tom Young, your father, good man, one of the best in my book. Glad to know you," he extended his hand. "Know your uncle too. Does good work in his own way. Should be more like him."

Kevin was pleased to be put in his extended family. It felt good not to feel like a stranger. For the first time that day he smiled.

"Just been to one of those gabfests," Margaret's father told him. "Too much talk, but what else can you do? They're necessary, you know. We have to coordinate our efforts, pull on all together so that we don't keep doing the same thing over and over again. Pull together, that's the way to do things and get things done. And I had a chance to get down and see my little girl too. Miss her around the place, but what can you do? We need someone to keep the books straight, and in a few months she'll be home where she belongs. Another pair of willing hands with skills that we can use—that's what we need, willing hands with skills. Hard to find them, lucky when you do."

Kevin nodded in agreement, although on other occasions he had reacted to such sentiments with derision. There wasn't much time for more words, as the meeting had just finished and Mr Michaels wanted to be back in Bayside that night. They walked with him to his car, a big old Kingswood station wagon which reminded Kevin of his Dad's old cars. The engine clattered as he pulled away, and Kevin smiled remembering his father and the good old times.

"Let's go to the park across the street," Margaret said softly, breaking into his reverie. She too had been looking after her Dad's car with an absent-minded expression. Now as they crossed the street, she confided that she would be glad when she could go home. "I don't like this city life," she told him. "It's all rush, rush, and people never have time for each other. You know," she said wistfully, "I've even begun writing letters to my sister. Me, that's never written a letter before in her life. It's only that I get so homesick when I think of my family and friends. I get this lump in my throat and feel that if I didn't watch myself and say 'Hey girl, buck out of it' I could break down and cry."

With a sinking feeling, he realised that in a few short months, the girl would be gone. Perhaps she might write to him? He imagined Mum bringing him the letter. By then he could recognise her handwriting. It would be large, but neat. Mum would be surprised at anyone writing to him. All that he had ever received in his life were letters from Social Security containing his dole cheques and terse acknowledgments to job applications. Would he ever receive that letter he was anxiously waiting for, that letter from the Public Service?...

All his thoughts always reached the same conclusion. They came to an abrupt end on that government job. It was his future. It filled his mind as they passed into the park and stopped before a flower bed overflowing with gaudy blossoms. They were too colourful and too healthy. City plants ripe for disease to strike.

"It was real nice last night, wasn't it?" Margaret said, smiling down at the flowers as if they were patches of happy memories. "I forgot that I was supposed to be in by twelve, but someone was up and let us in without a fuss. It was good medicine for Di too. She's really chirpy today. She likes Paul. He makes her laugh. I forgot to ask you about that job yesterday. Heard anything from them? Maybe you should be thinking of something else. There's a few jobs going in Aboriginal organisations, but you got to have the proper skills. Dad was telling me that the Housing Co-op might be needing someone to keep track of the accounts, rents and mortgages—things like that. I'll just be doing the secretarial side of things, not the hard things like statements of accounts. So perhaps there'll be a job coming up there. If you were doing some sort of commercial course, I could put in a good word for you, but I suppose you want to stay in the city? People seem to get used to it, though I haven't. Why, even the air's stuffy and clogs your throat."

Kevin found himself saying how much he hated Perth and how it got him down. How he missed his old country home—and began describing things he missed. "You know," he said, "we lived in an old house right next to the river. I know now that we had it because there was the threat of floods and no white person wanted to live in it, but that didn't matter to us. I remember waking up one morning to find the brown water swirling under my bed. Us kids, me, Sue and Tommy, thought it was great. We paddled out the front door and found the whole paddock flooded. Dad's old cars looked like boats drifting over a wide lake. Nothing like that ever happens in the city. And I remember when sometimes Mum and the other women would catch a mess of fish, or Dad would bring home a whole sack full. The other Nyoongah families in the neighbourhood would come around for a feed of fish and a yarn. Dad made up fires in old petrol drums. The sides of the drums would grow red. It was best when it was cold. He put sheets of iron over the tops and the fish would be laid out to sizzle on them."

"Everyone sat around on logs and ate fish and drank beer or sweet wine. All us kids would be together, around our own drum, and sometimes we would dare each other to sneak a bottle of beer or wine. Sue was the best at daring and at sneaking. Then she would egg the kids to have a sip, and scream with laughter when a kid would screw his face up at the bitter taste. And the night would end with singing. Someone always brought along his or her guitar and would sing songs everyone knew and it would last to the dawn. Why, it was even fun if it rained. As soon as the first drops sizzled on the tin, everything would be snatched up and everyone would crowd into the big front room with its huge country fireplace and the party would be held there."

The girl had a faraway look in her eyes when he finished and she began talking about Bayside. "I love the ocean," she murmured. "The coast is real rugged at home. I like to wander along it and explore the little coves. It's not like the beaches around the city, there's not that many people to get in your way, and you can let the sea talk to you alone.

"You know, I found this cave at the bottom of a steep bank. I'm sure no one else knows about it, except, maybe, for a few old people. It's hard to find; I came on it by accident when the tide was out. At high water, the entrance is underwater, and that keeps it from being found too. You know, you push through a sort of slit in the rock and worm your way along a kind of burrow. After a few metres it opens out into a large chamber with those stalagmites and stalactites growing from the floor and ceiling. The floor is above the level of tide and is never covered. You know, it's my own secret place and I go back there when I want to get away from everybody. And cemented into the floor are the remains of these old camp-fires and—guess what—I found a stone knife. I've still got it at home and can show it to you, if you ever come down our way.

"You know what?" she whispered. "What I want to do is stay down there when the tide comes in. I can imagine what it would be like and maybe, you know, with those camp-fires it might be haunted, but I would like to do that, though with someone I liked."

Kevin listened to her, noticing how he towered over her. He hadn't noticed before, how small she was beside him. Then as he looked down, he realised that there was something familiar about her brown hair and even about the way she tilted her face up at him. What was it? Yes, she looked like Sue, resembling her in more ways than race. There was the same determined jutting of the jaw and the same eagerness in the eyes. He felt his eyes prick with tears and a lump form in his throat. The two were so alike, but so different. Sue had embraced city life with its hard morality which left her family out in the cold. Would she ever be able to find her earthen cave as Margaret had, and would she ever feel stifled by the city and long to escape? He didn't think so. She would stay and battle on. It was her nature and he should follow her example. Yes, he should, and then maybe he could reach her again?

As if catching a glimmer of his thoughts, Margaret suddenly asked him about his family.

He explained that his father had died some years ago and that his mother had taken it hard. Then, to avoid mentioning Sue or Tommy, he asked about her parents.

Her face turned serious and it looked quite plain. "I know how it is about your Dad, you see Mum died just over a year ago. Dad took it hard too. He was awful lonely until a few months ago. Now it's all changed and I'm so glad for him." She smiled her warm smile and her face became attractive again. "You see, he's going to get married again in a little while, as soon as I return from the city. Not to a stranger though, I've known her all my life and have called her aunt since I could talk. She's not really an aunt, just like one. She used to drop in to help after Mum died, and one thing led to another. She's a little younger than Dad, but that's alright. It'll be like having an older sister around. You haven't got a big sister, have you? Just Sue, and she's younger–?"

Kevin's face fell at the sound of his sister's name, then twisted into a scowl. Margaret stared at the flowers and didn't notice. She continued to talk. "When are you going to introduce us? I'd really like to meet her. I don't know many city girls. The ones at the hostel are all from the country." She glanced up at him for his answer, and was dismayed at his expression. What was wrong, she thought. He was a pleasant-looking boy, but not when he looked like that, She must have said something to offend him, but what? They walked around the park in moody silence.

The sun was still shining brightly, but the air as if affected by Kevin's mood had turned heavy, sullen with the promise of a storm. Somehow it affected the flowers. They lost their sparkle and looked like faded, plastic replicas. She tried to talk to Kevin, but received only a mumble in reply. She began to feel gloomy too. She felt rejected and wondered what she had done. At last she could bear it no longer and steered their steps back towards the hostel.

Reaching it, they stopped. "See you again soon?" and she managed a fluttery smile.

"Yeah, sure, ring you in a couple of days, sure to," Kevin mumbled brokenly. With a half-hearted wave, he turned and hurried away. She stared after him wondering what was the matter. If only he would tell her, maybe she could help him. It was such a shame that he was so moody!

SIX

The long-awaited, white but grubby government envelope at last lay in his hands. His name and address was typed in bold uppercase letters. He stared down at them. He hardly dared to open the letter, and discover his future. Then he noticed the date stamp. It had taken five days to cross over the city to Balga. Feverishly he ripped open the envelope and shakily unfolded the single sheet of paper within. Cold words informed him that he had been placed fifth in the examination and please would he present himself for an interview on Thursday at ten a.m. With a shudder, he realised that the next day was Thursday, and that Australia Post had nearly ruined his chances.

His mother had been anxiously waiting to open the letter. Her son had pinned all his hopes and dreams on it. With a surge of gladness, she watched Kevin's face change. "Mum, Mum! I've passed, I've passed! Got to front for an interview tomorrow."

"Never any doubt about it Kev," she replied. "You were always the smart one of the family." She sighed in relief. Over the past few months he had been such a strain on her. Now at last things were turning alright for him at least.

He spent the rest of the day immersed in dreams. His only knowledge of office routine had been gained through being briefly interviewed for jobs and in watching the people working behind the counter in the dole office. Now he imagined himself sitting behind a big desk importantly bent over a file of papers, or in standing behind a counter at the CES office. It was then that his vision began to falter. He recalled the false heartiness of the staff and the dread felt in approaching them. He really didn't want to have a job like that. He really didn't want to have someone trembling before him while he decided whether they were to stay on the dole or not. Or did he want to conduct job interviews and turn people down. Well, what sort of position did he want? He tried to imagine something different, but without the experience couldn't. The picture of himself sitting bent over the papers returned. What were the papers? Was he deciding some poor bastard's fate?

With an effort, he pushed such negative thoughts away. He would find out sooner, rather than later. He found his suit and examined it to see if it needed pressing. He brushed it and hung it up carefully. Now for his good shoes. He polished them brightly. Now a clean shirt. He didn't have one. He rushed to his Mum and found her washing one in the sink.

"This'll be dry by tomorrow," she told him. "You'll have to borrow one of Uncle's ties though. Tommy's been using yours as a belt."

That evening even Sue smiled when she heard the news and in the morning she wished him the best of luck before leaving for work. Kevin began humming as he dressed. His job prospect was already changing home for the better.

But Tommy saw it differently. "I hope you get the job, Kev, but if you don't, no worries, eh?"

"What do you mean? It's a real chance."

"Yeah, maybe, but you would be better off working for an Aboriginal organisation."

"I can still do that, when I get some experience."

"Oh, come on, you'll be some sort of pen-pusher marking government forms. In no time you'll be bored to tears."

"No I won't."

"We'll see."

"At least, I'll be getting in some money."

"Yeah, and then I'll be able to hit you for a loan when I need it," Tommy grinned. "So you better get this job, then we'll all be better off."

"Yeah, we will!"

"Anyway, Kev, Alex was talking about you the other day. Seems like once you were in the thick of things. Painting that peace dove on the war monument in King's Park was really something. He says that in time you could be a really good organiser. You might be wasting yourself going into a government job."

"Paul was telling me about Alex. He picked up all his ideas at the Uni and never dropped them. Who cares what he says? And you'd be better off getting on with your apprenticeship. That'll get you somewhere, farther than you'll get on the ideas of Alex."

"And then he mentioned something about that letter you sent to the Prime Minister... You know, Kev, they might remember things like that. You were in the land rights movement too. I bet they have a file on you!"

"Don't be stupid. They don't worry about kids. Uni students get up to all sorts of things and that's never held against them later. It's the same with me," Kevin replied, though he couldn't help wondering if it was true.

"Anyway," Tommy said, "best of luck and all that. See you tonight with that job."

Mum gave him five dollars for the fare into the city. He got onto the bus, feeling stiff and uncomfortable in his suit. He wondered if he would have to wear one every day when he was a public servant. The bus took him to St George's Terrace and he got off a few stops before his destination. He would walk the rest of the way. As he walked, he thought of the coming interview. What sort of questions would they ask? He didn't know, but there seemed little to worry about. He had passed his high school exams in all subjects, and had been placed high in the public service examination. He was very near the building now. He went into a shop and bought a packet of cigarettes, as Tommy had ripped off the other pack. This time the smoke instead of relaxing him made him a little dizzy and light-headed. There was a queasy feeling in his stomach which wouldn't go away, and to make matters worse his head began to throb. Still he had to face up for the interview and get through. He had to—so much depended on it, so much!

Flinging down his half-smoked cigarette and stamping on it, he entered the government building. The interviews were being conducted somewhere in the place, but where? At last he found a uniformed attendant and asked him. The man pointed at the lift and said, "Sixth floor, room 401." The rudeness annoyed him. The bloke could at least have managed to help him a bit more. Now Kevin felt his eyes beginning to smart at the corners. His legs trembled as he left the lift and walked down a long corridor in search of the room. At last he pushed through double glass doors and entered a large room. Ten young men and women sat there. This must be it! At the far end, next to a closed door, a young girl about his age sat pecking away on a typewriter.

She glanced up as he approached, then said in a voice which

exactly matched Sue's tone on Sunday, "Well?", and left Kevin floundering for an answer. He jumbled out his letter and dropped it on top of her machine. She extended long fingers to pick it up. She studied it slowly then said in a friendlier tone, much to his relief, "Wait a mo, I'll have to check this out inside." She left Kevin nervously clenching and unclenching his hands. At last, he hid them in his pockets. The minutes went by and still the girl had not returned. After a while he went to sit in a vacant chair beside one of the other guys.

"You after a job too?" he asked him.

"Y–y–yes, I am, b–b–but it's only a f–f–formality. Th–they j–j–just ask y–y–you a few questions, then assign y–y–you to a de–de–de–partment."

"That's good to hear," Kevin answered. He had the inclination to help the guy out with the words he stuttered over, but had let him go on. There were worse faults than stammering, and he did it himself sometimes when he was nervous, but never as much as this guy did. At least, he didn't have to worry about the interview. The exam had been the hardest part, and the interview was only a formality to assign him to a department to work in. At long last he was going to be employed and in a steady job too. He felt his body relaxing and his headache vanished. Even the queasy feeling left his stomach. Already he could imagine himself bringing home his first pay. Now Sue couldn't sneer at him for being a bludger. No, never again, and she would have to listen to him now.

At last the girl returned. She beckoned him over, held out his letter and said tonelessly: "I'm sorry, there's been a bit of a mix-up. You're not being interviewed today. We'll be in touch with you later."

"W–what do you mean?" Kevin said, stuttering in his anguish.

"Just what I said. These things happen, you know. I expect it'll get sorted out." She sat down and began typing.

"When will they get in touch with me?" Kevin demanded. They weren't going to put him off just like that. They weren't! "Well, I want to know!" he almost screamed. "Tell me!" he demanded.

Everyone was staring at him, but he didn't care. He could fell his body tensing and his breathing quicken. What bloody right had they to do this to him? He wanted to hit at all of them, first at the white face of the bitch in front of him, then at the others behind the closed door. They were the ones who were rejecting him. He ran past the frightened girl and into the inner office. Three grey old men in grey suits flung up white startled faces. They gaped at him. This drove him to a frenzy. "You get me down here and now you tell me that it's all a mistake!" he screamed. "Now you won't even interview me! There's supposed to be some sort of mistake and you'll get in touch with me later. I know your sort. Yeah, we all know your sort. You're all gutless wonders. Won't even face me—send out that girl to tell me. Well!"

He shouted out the last word, then his throat began constricting and he had to gasp for breath. The men looked at each other, and the senior one framed a reply: "Please calm down. There's only been a mix-up. Believe me, with the number of persons we interview this is always a possibility. Now, just calm down and leave quietly. I'm sorry, but we can't do anything about this today. We'll sort things out and get in touch with you shortly. I promise you."

"Yeah, you promise me, do you? Promises are for fools," Kevin managed to get out. They were all alike, smug and self-assured. It felt like a hand clutching at his throat. He managed to croak: "You're all the same." It was the end, he knew. His mouth stretched wide as he fought for air. He turned and tried to run from the office. He knew that it was all over, all over and he had failed once again. He felt himself fall writhing to the floor. Darkness closed over him. Now nothing mattered to Kevin, not even life itself.

SEVEN

Kevin came to in a hard white bed in a huge white room. He felt lost and forlorn. Very puny and brown, he lay there wondering where he was. A strong smell filled his nostrils. Gradually, he realised it was disinfectant. He was in a hospital ward. Lazy thoughts floated through his head. They anchored. They sunk into depression as memory returned. He had lost again. No government job! How would he cope now? Huddled in the bed, he tried to flee from all thought.

"Well, we've finally come around, have we?" a cheery no-nonsense voice grabbed at him. He was dragged back into the world of the living again. No job!

His eyes fell open. A nurse stared down at him. Mercilessly her voice kept at him. She took his details, name and address and next of kin. With a promise to bring the world to him, she left to get in touch with his mother. He closed his eyes and tried to shut out everything. A doctor came to examine him. "Asthma attacks, eh? Who's been treating you?"

Kevin told him.

"Well, there's not much we can do about it. You'll be ready to leave in the morning." He left and Kevin closed his eyes again. No, there wasn't much anyone could do for him. Lunch came to relieve him of his depression. He ate the tasteless food, then stared at the ceiling. There wasn't much anyone could do for him! At last, he managed to drift into sleep, came awake for tea, then drifted off again.

Early next morning his mother rushed in. She hugged him fiercely. For one long moment he felt the security of a small child. He needed his mum and the strength flowing from her arms. The feeling left and all he saw was a distraught women.

"What happened son, what happened Kev?" she asked in a trembling voice.

"I–I h–had one of my attacks during the interview," he replied in as trembling a voice. His stutter made him recall the stammering guy. He hoped that at least he had gotten a job. After all it was a formality, he had said. Yeah, some formality, Kevin thought.

"They won't penalise you for being an asthma sufferer, will they Kev?" his mum asked anxiously.

He stared up at her distraught face. A tearful weakness turned his bones to jelly. She really cared for him. How could he tell her the truth? No job, no government job—ever! Desperately he struggled to pull himself together. Finally, he thought that he could trust his voice. He said as cheerfully as he could: "It really went well, up to the attack that is. They said that they'll let me know what department I'll be working in. The interview was just a formality, j-j-just a formality, that's all. It's really great," he managed to say with a grin, and for a moment almost believed it himself. Almost, but not enough. Despair flooded his heart.

His mother looked at him with so much loving concern that he was ready to own up. He was saved by the nurse. She efficiently got him up and dressed. His mother signed a few papers and he was out. She took him to a taxi and home.

Home, he took refuge in his bed hoping against hope that it would prove all a bad dream. Morning reached noon and noon leaked into the afternoon which drifted towards evening. The day had been a stinker and his room was stifling. He lay there sweating under a sheet. From outside came the happy sounds of children playing under the swishing lawn sprinklers. How he wished that he was a young kid again. A country kid hunting around the edges of a cool pool for yabbies. He turned over and pressed his face into the moist pillow. His misery overcame him and he began sobbing. His chest felt filled with some sort of heavy fluid. His headache returned and began throbbing his head. He wished that he was dead. He had had enough. He dozed off with the setting sun and awoke in the middle of the night. Everyone must have gone to bed. Mum had left a plate of sandwiches beside his bed. He dozed off again, awoke to find Tommy eating the sandwiches, then dozed off again. The pitiless light of day flooded his room. He lingered on in bed until noon. His mother came in with the letter containing his dole cheque. He dragged himself up and dressed. He had to get out of the flat!

He cashed his cheque at the corner milkbar, then force of habit sent him to the CES office. His eyes examined red-bordered card after red-bordered card. There might just be something he could apply for? A card caught his eye. The city council wanted a gardening assistant. He wrote down the number of the card and went to the counter. A young guy behind the counter checked the number. He would never have a job like that. Never! He watched as the guy pulled out a slip of paper from a file drawer and went to ring up. It took some time. He came back shaking his head from side to side. They wanted someone with experience.

Outside the dole office, he hesitated. His eyes hugged the pavement. He felt worse than the day he had met Margaret here. What would she think of him now? And on that day when he first met her, he still hadn't a clue on how to spend the rest of the afternoon. He couldn't go and see her. She would be busy. Well what could he do? Why not go and see Elias and Paul. Maybe one or the other would go with him? He hoped it would be Paul. He was good at cheering people up.

Paul poked a furrowed brow through his doorway. His face held an absent-minded expression. He beckoned Kevin inside, then went to his desk. He began muttering over something he had written. At last he glanced up, but without his usual carefree grin.

"Sorry about this," he muttered, "but I've got an end of term paper to do. Just look at all the bloody books I've got to check–" as he gestured at the floor. About a dozen books lay open and they were almost covered by sheets of screwed-up paper. Kevin looked at the mess, apologised for disturbing him and left. That was the end of Paul for a while. He would have to go to the pub on his own. He walked along the road towards the bus stop and passed a school. In a place like that he had been taught all sorts of things, but never how to cope with life!

From across the street, he stared at the pub. A shabby bearded man lurked outside. He looked like a bushranger or an explorer. Kevin knew him as poet. He had written some verses about what he described as the plight of the Aborigines. Once, he had spent an evening listening to some bullshit about old Aboriginal men chewing their beards when angry. It had concerned some image in one of his poems. Kevin crossed the street and walked in front of the man. The poet who occasionally wrote verse about Aborigines stared right through him. Kevin pretended to chew furiously on an imaginary beard. The poet failed to receive the message.

He walked into the bar and ordered a pot of beer. As he was about to clasp it, someone grabbed him from behind and planted a wet kiss on the nape of his neck. Kevin leapt a mile in the air. He whirled to find Elias grinning at him. He managed a smile in return as he said flippantly, "What's up with you? Gone troppo, or something?"

"High spirits, bro, high spirits. Celebrating a coup against this dingy pub and its watery beer. Grab hold of your pot, and get over to the jukebox."

Kevin followed him to the table in front of the jukebox. He saw that Elias was drinking whisky.

"Listen to this," he yelled, rolling a coin into the slot of the jukebox and pressing a button. A song came on with a harsh black voice yelling over a simple rhythm.

> *Hey, hey, the payback—the big payback,*
> *Revenge,*
> *The big payback.*
> *Got to get some back,*
> *Need to get some back,*
> *The payback, the big payback...*

"My own personal record!" Elias shouted over the song. He flashed a jagged piece of metal at Kevin, then palmed it. "Was trying to get into the cash box and got into the sound box instead. Their records are so much crap, so I switched one for this. Bet you they won't even understand about the payback, eh? None of these wetjelas at least!"

"You mean, compensation?"

"Yeah, compensation and paying the rent for two hundred years. Hey, you've got the message. Give the man a prize from that fixed percentage, the big payback. Get yourself another beer."

He flung down a dollar, then changed his mind and scooped it up. He rushed off to the bar and came back with a double whisky. "Get that down you."

Elias was really speeding. Kevin was mildly shocked at him for drinking neat spirits. It wasn't like his mate at all. It was a different Elias he was seeing, or was it? He recalled the collection tins and the key for the jukebox. It was in character.

"Drink up, you got religion or something?" Elias roared at his slow drinking.

Kevin raised the glass of whisky and took a sip. He almost choked. It tasted revolting and made his throat feel as if another asthma attack was coming on.

"Good, huh, not like that watery beer!"

He nodded and took another sip. It still tasted as awful as claret.

"Get you some chips to go along with it," and Elias rushed back to the bar.

He took the opportunity to pour some of the whisky into his mate's drink. He hoped that it would pass unnoticed, but Elias saw that his glass was nearly empty and grabbed it for a refill.

"Been sucking on your mummy's tits for too long," he smirked, plonking down the whisky in front of Kevin.

Kevin flushed at the mention of his mother. Yesterday in the hospital he had really needed her. Feeling the scornful eye of his mate on him, he took a huge gulp of his drink. This time it didn't taste half bad.

Elias rattled on and he let the words wash over him. He was feeling dazed from the strong drink. At least it had had the effect of driving yesterday's fiasco from his mind. He wanted to tell Elias about it. Once or twice he tried, but couldn't get a word in. Now his mate began to ramble on about girls and one in his tutorial class who was going for him. He switched to Paul and the girl Diana. Kevin paid more attention. He stared at Elias; he looked more than a little merry. His eyes were red and moist. His fingers clenched and unclenched about his glass as his hysterical voice rattled on.

"You know, you know, just the other day, Monday it was, guess who I see in the street? He's supposed to be writing his term paper, you know, but there he is with this yorga, Diana, and they looked mardong, you know, real solid. That other one was along too, that what's-her-name, the one on the large side. You know, the one with the real nice smile? Margaret. Like to slip her one, maybe?"

"You mean Margaret Michaels?"

"Yeah, that yorga. You know that one for sure," he smirked. "Be a pal, and let me have a bit."

"What?", Kevin managed to say. Things were getting a little chaotic. He had another gulp of whisky.

"Are both of you like this?" Elias demanded, holding up two fingers entwined. "Well, nothing wrong with that. Why not, I say? Why not?"

"Oh shut up about her!" He finished off his glass.

"Oh, so it's true, is it?" Elias smirked. "She's special, is she?"

Kevin felt like punching him.

"Come on drink up. You have! Well, we'll just have another one, right bro?"

Kevin shrugged, and before he knew it Elias was up and back with full glasses. Elias slowed down on his drinking. He went silent for a while as he looked around the bar. "I was waiting for this yorga," he said. "Thought she would be here. She isn't, but I know where she lives. Not far from here. Drink up and we'll go and see her."

Elias drained his glass, but Kevin had the sense not to. He felt a little woozy, and stumbled when he got up. He recovered and carefully piloted himself into the street. As they walked carefully along, only lurching every now and again, he asked his mate: "You know, Elias, I didn't think you drank so much, and not whisky at that?"

"Habit I picked up from my Dad, you know," his mate replied. "A minister of religion he might be, but that doesn't stop him from communing with the spirits now and again. Besides, everyone drinks. I bet your Dad did too?"

"Only a few glasses of beer, or a little wine with his mates. He wasn't what you'd call a drinker. He had too much sense."

"Nor was my dear old adopted Dad. He drank strictly for medicinal purposes."

Elias led the way down a lane and out into a short street lined with terrace houses. He pushed open the gate of one and went to the door. He knocked loudly. An untidy woman opened it and laughed out a loud "hello". She led them down a grubby dingy passageway and into the kitchen. An old sofa nestled across from the gas stove. A kitchen table was littered with scraps of food and the sink overflowed with dirty dishes.

"Excuse the mess," she said with a short laugh, "but the front room's just as bad. Boy, did I hang one on last night." She pulled two glasses out of the sink, rinsed them under the tap, then filled them with red wine from a two-litre cask. "Get it down fast. It'll give you such a buzz, that you won't notice how foul it is."

She plonked herself down between them on the sofa, and asked Elias: "Who's your friend? I've seen him a few times at the Albion."

"Alex, another one of us students," Elias replied, giving Kevin an exaggerated wink.

"Hi, Alex, I'm Ann. I'm a part-time student at the uni too. Hey, you got that wine down quick, didn't you? You people can sure put it away. Help yourself to another, you're welcome."

Kevin refilled his glass. The grubby place and the woman made him nervous.

"Where's the kid?" Elias asked.

"I sent him off to Mum's for a few days. It'll give me a chance to tidy up the place." She laughed her short laugh again. "And get some things done."

"That means you're free to party?" Elias leered.

"Yup!"

"A good sort," Elias informed Kevin. "One of the best, with a heart as big as Uluru."

Kevin glanced at the woman between them. His eyes slid over her tired face and drooping soft white body bulging beneath her dressing gown. He couldn't help comparing her with Margaret, though the very idea made him uneasy. It just didn't feel right. The woman caught his eyes. She smiled, took his glass from his hand and lifted it to her pouting lips. He watched her large, pendulous breasts lift with her motion, watched them swing as she lowered the empty glass.

"Silly me, I didn't pour myself a drink. Fill this one up and get one for me too. Bring the cask over."

Kevin did so.

"You got a cigarette, love?" she asked, leaning back.

He fumbled in his pocket and found the forgotten pack from yesterday. He pulled it out with all the travesty of that day congealed around it. How stupid he had been. How stupid. No job. Suddenly he shrugged as he passed over the packet. It had never been on. Best to forget it and try for something new. Only a fool would hang on to yesterday's dreams. He drained his glass and refilled it. Ann demanded a light from him. He found matches, but his hand was shaking so much that he could hardly strike a light. She held his hand to steady the flame. He almost recoiled from the grip of her fingers. He was acutely conscious of her hip pressed against his side and of how the flesh seemed to sink in to accommodate his male hardness.

He talked to Elias across her. His eyes slid over her face and figure again and again.

Her thick blonde hair was pulled back in an untidy bun and her red puffy face was damp with sweat. Well, so was his for that matter from all the drink. Her body slumped between them fully relaxed and her head rested on the back of the sofa. He sat like that too, but Elias was less relaxed. He watched him nudge her in the side. She barely moved, then turned her face and planted a kiss on his lips. Elias laughed. The woman shot a quick questioning glance at Kevin.

With another laugh, Elias gave her a shove. With a little shriek she fell against Kevin, twisting her body so that her breasts flattened against his chest. Her face was uptilted. Kevin managed a laugh. He pushed her back against his mate and drained his glass. He leant forward to refill it and escaped from the pressure of her body.

To tell the truth, he was shocked to find himself in such a scene. He didn't believe in bunji-ing around. He knew that Margaret could never act like this woman with her wine-stained lips and tobacco-stained fingers. She was so different from the hungry bunji woman.

"The bedroom's tidier, and more comfortable," she suggested. She gathered up the cask and the cigarettes and went off.

Kevin looked at Elias. The drink had caught up with him and he lolled on the sofa, like a bag of chaff. "How'd you come across her?" he asked him.

Elias managed to come out of his stupor. "At the Albion. She's always there. Good sort, though. Wants nothing from you, but what she gets. When studying gets me down, come and see her." His words were slurred and he had trouble putting a sentence together. With a sickish grin, he lurched to his feet and staggered off to the toilet.

"That's better," he said coming back. With a gesture towards

Kevin, he went out of the room. Kevin reluctantly followed.

A wide bed filled most of the room. Ann lay stretched out on it. Elias had already fallen beside her. Both stared up at him with meaningful eyes. They made him feel nervous, and with his nervousness came his irritation. How had he let Elias drag him here, he thought.

"What's wrong with your friend?" the woman asked.

Elias stared up at him and his eyes turned mean. "Just a little virgin."

They both laughed, and then the woman patted the space beside her: "Really, well we can fix that. Rub-a–dub-dub, three in a bed is just what he needs."

They both laughed again, and Kevin felt shame. He would show them! Suddenly he felt his stomach rising. He clapped his hand over his mouth and raced out to the toilet.

It was the last straw. Carefully he washed his face and rinsed his mouth out. "Let Elias do what he wants to," he muttered to himself. He went past the bedroom and out. Shame and pride and relief struggled in his head. What would Elias say next time they met? "Who cares," he muttered to himself as he went along the street. At least vomiting had sobered him up.

He was going past a book shop when the cover of a book in the window caught his eye. The cover illustration was of a dark man with a stringy hairstyle similar to Johnno's. Must be about Aborigines, he thought, and on an impulse he went in. It had been marked down to three dollars and he bought the book. He could take it and show Johnno. At least he was a good listener, unlike Elias who loved the sound of his own voice.

He had to catch a bus in St George's Terrace and that meant going past the scene of yesterday's debacle. His steps slowed at the thought. It was late. Maybe he would go home instead. He hesitated outside a group of cinema houses. People were coming for the evening show. They all looked so well-dressed and happy that he felt shabby and sad. "Why couldn't everyone be happy?" he thought. Why couldn't everyone get a job and be well-off? Suddenly he felt the fingers of the city feeling his throat and seeking for a hold. No, not another asthma attack so soon after the other, he thought, and began breathing slowly and deeply. He tried to think of a scene which would relax him. He imagined himself ten years from now. Older and wiser and a full adult. He wore a suit, not city flash, and was on a visit to the town with his wife. She was short and dark with curly hair and came up to just below his shoulders. Walking arm in arm, they came towards the theatre to see a movie while they were in the city. He smiled down at her and she smiled up at him. He was just about to identify her face when a voice cut out the picture.

"Kev, how you going, bro?"

The voice startled him and he swung around with fists clenched, before belatedly recognising it. He gave a sheepish shrug.

"What's upset you?" Alex said, patting him on the shoulder. "You seemed just about to take a swipe at me."

The man's face was filled with concern and as always his voice was velvet. Kevin stared at him, at the old army jacket and the out-of-fashion flared jeans. Another one wearing his assumed poverty like a virtue. It didn't cut much ice with him. He knew how much the man made saving people. Alex for all his man-of-the-people stance was way above them, as far above as a university education. He would make a good mate for Elias. He was city, and Kevin didn't like the city and its ways.

"You going to take in a show?" Alex said into the silence.

"Just looking, that's all, just looking."

"See a movie you want to see?"

"Who can see movies on the dole?"

He wanted to get away from Alex before the man asked him about the job interview. If he knew anything, the news would be all over the community by now. Then he might smell the whisky and wine on his breath, put two and two together to make five, and decide that Kevin was walking down the same track along with many other Nyoongahs.

"You know, I was expecting you to come along and see me," the man said.

"Coming tomorrow. Been busy and didn't have the bus fare. My dole cheque's due, then I'll come."

"Good, I'll be expecting you. There's a new government support scheme..."

"I–I've got to rush. Mum's expecting me home for tea"— and he raced away.

"Don't forget, tomorrow!" the man called after him.

"Yeah!" Kevin turned and shouted back. Alex was smiling at a good-looking woman, he obviously had been waiting for. She was white!

Kevin decided to go home and found the Balga bus at the stop. A bloke in dark glasses hesitated at the entrance. "Need a hand?" Kevin asked. He guided the blind man aboard and received thanks.

This cheered him up and he could sit in the back seat and smile at the events of the day. "Elias, bunji man, meets bunji woman." He could grin about it now. Why she was really old, all of twenty-five, he thought. He would really kid Elias when he saw him again. Something was in his hand. He looked down and saw the book. He decided to give it to Margaret. It would be a good excuse to ring her up. It was about Aborigines! He began reading bits and pieces of it.

EIGHT

" 'And they came out onto the sea and Wooreddy recoiled from it, but Crow took him through the sand dunes until they came right to the edge of a cliff beneath which the sea boiled. Wooreddy watched the sea lash at the land, lash as it always had. He saw it in its fury had battered right through to create an archway through the land. The spray rose up to wet his face as they made their way along the cliff. They edged between the sea and the matted vegetation massed to protect the land. Then Waau led him down a path which was but a crack in the rock face. The ocean battered at Wooreddy, hurling wind and spray in an attempt to sweep him away and take him into its domain. Finally they stood at the base of the cliff from which the sea had been driven, if only for a short time. It seemed sacred ...'

"There's still more to come; but is it like the place where your cave is?" Kevin asked, wondering what had gotten into the girl since he had last seen her. He had phoned her, thinking that she would be pleased about the book he had found, but when she had come to the phone, she had replied to his cheery "hello" in a little girl's voice which made him want to hang up. He suggested that he ring back later, but she told him "no". Now in a stern voice, she snapped at his question: "No, it's nothing like the place. It's all wrong, wrong! Still, Kev, go on. I like listening to you read."

"And here is where they enter the cave," he said, finding the part.

" 'And he pushed Wooreddy toward a cave. He slipped on the slimy floor as he entered. The sea-smell filled his nose and reminded him of women. He saw fish swimming in rock pools, and his mind opened. He thought of the wonderful sights the women saw below the face, and of how men had been denied a whole world. He shuddered and stood within the light falling in through the cave mouth. Great spears fell from the roof. Great Ancestor casting down his shafts to keep Ria Warrawah at bay! But other shafts rose from the floor, and these united with the ones falling and formed a oneness. They met and there was no conflict ...' "

He stopped reading and waited for the girl's reaction. Her breath fluttered over the phone. Then she spoke, firmly and negatively: "No Kev, it's not my cave. It's all wrong–" Her words trailed off. Her voice broke and she began sobbing. It upset him. He had no idea what to say or do? Margaret always seemed so self-possessed, so sure of herself. Now here she was sobbing as if something awful had happened. How could he help her? "Just thought that you might like it," he said lamely.

"Oh, Kev, it's nothing to do with you. The book's lovely, honest it is. It's just, just that I had this typing test today, and I was so nervous, I mucked it up. You know how it is? And my Dad is counting on me. He expects me to get through the course quickly, and now I'll have to take the test again. It'll mean that I'll have to be away longer from home too." She continued softly sobbing over the phone. After a few minutes they trailed off and she apologised.

By that time, Kevin was close to tears himself, though he was also glad that the girl would be staying in Perth longer. He told her that everything would be fine, and before he knew it, he found himself describing the interview and what had happened. His story came out in a rush of words. He confessed that he didn't know what to do about it, but something was sure to turn up, then he lapsed into an embarrassed silence.

Margaret had recovered much of her brightness and confidence when she replied. "Kev," she exclaimed, "you should have rang me up. What are friends for? Here I was carrying on about a silly old test, that I'll pass next time, and you had a real chance and lost out. What can I say? Gee, what are you going to do now?"

"You know Alex? he's a guy who runs a Nyoongah Study Centre. I met him and he told me that there's a new youth scheme. I guess I can see him and find out about it ..."

Margaret's depression fled as she concentrated on Kevin's problem. She might suggest what she had before, but how would he take it? "Kev," she began tentatively, remembering how he had reacted, "you know how I mentioned that Dad needed someone to keep the books for him. Well, you might think about that. Of course, it won't be anywhere as good as a public service job, but it'll be better than being on the dole, and you would be working among your own people."

"What do I know about keeping books?" he exclaimed. "Don't

know anything about it at all."

"You could learn, couldn't you?" she snapped in reply. "You said that you were good at studying. It's not all that hard. There's this course just starting—"

"No, not likely! I'd be running away because I couldn't get a job in Perth."

"Why would it be running away? Once we had to run away from our homes in the country and come to the city, but now things are different. It wouldn't be running away, just returning, coming back to where you belong." She replied more sharply than she had intended, but these city Nyoongahs were all the same. They moaned about how they missed the country and hated the city, but when they had the chance to get away and back to their roots again, it wasn't on. They were good at shouting slogans, but what meaning had they without their won ground beneath their feet?

"I'll think about it," he said lamely.

"What's to stop you thinking about it, while you're doing the course? It's only for six months and right in the city too." She stated this in a voice implying some sort of ultimatum.

"Well, will I go and see Alex and ask him about it—"

"Why him? We have our Aboriginal Education Section. I could ring them tomorrow about it, that is if you really want to do it?" Again there was that suggestion of an ultimatum in her voice.

"Why not, why not, I'll give it a try," Kevin replied. The decision didn't hurt at all. "It'll give me something to do," he added.

"Then we'll see," Margaret stated enigmatically. "But we have to hurry and get you enrolled. The course starts next week, and there's forms to fill out."

"I'll do it first thing tomorrow." He felt annoyed at the girl. What did she take him for? A no-hoper unable to fill in a few forms? "You'll see," he exclaimed, "tomorrow I'll do everything, then later I'll think about that job if it's still going."

She decided that this was as far as she could get Kevin to commit himself. "Well, I'm glad that I've done something today. You know, Kev, I was really down before you rang. You've cheered me no end. It's good to have someone to talk things over with."

In spite of himself, Kevin felt a thrill go through him. No-one else had ever told him that he made them feel good. In fact, he remembered that with Sue it was the opposite. Well, he too was cheered up. Now he had something to look forward too, and even Mum wouldn't get upset for him not getting that job. "Hey," he said, "how would you like to celebrate tonight? There's a couple of good pictures on at the Carlton."

"I don't know, Kev. It's a work day, and that test really tired me out. Oh, why not, I need something to relax with."

"They're showing two black films," he explained, suddenly afraid that she'd change her mind again. "One of them's called *Two Laws* and is about Aborigines in the Northern Territory. You know, how they live, their history and struggle for land. The other one is *The Harder They Come* and was made in the West Indies. It's about this guy who comes to the city and what happens to him. My brother Tommy saw it last week. It's got lots of songs in it too."

"OK, OK," Margaret agreed with a laugh. "Let's see now, it's about half-past six. I'll be along in an hour to pick you up. Is that alright?"

"Yeah, I'm in the phone box just opposite our block of flats. I'll wait downstairs for you." He looked out and saw with dismay that a storm was about to descend on the city. "It might rain," he told her. "Hey, there's a flash of lightning. You hear the thunder over the phone?"

"It sounded loud, but I think it was right overhead. No need to worry about a little thing like that. At home we have these terrific storms. I love them. It'll be fun driving through it."

"Right, I'll be waiting in an hour. You know, I really like you," he confided into the phone. It was so much easier to say it from a distance.

"And I like you too," she answered in a soft voice, then hung up.

Kevin listened to the dial tone for a few seconds. He saw the dopey look on his face reflected on the glass of the phone booth and quickly hung up. As he stepped out, lightning seared the sky and a heavy clap of thunder made him bound into the air with a laugh. He raced towards the block of flats just as the first heavy drops of rain began tumbling down. An empty milk carton lay in his path. He gave it a swift kick. The wind swooped down and flung it high up against the wall of the building.

As he leapt into the doorway, Kevin laughed again. Things were at last looking up for him. He turned to stare at the rain teeming down. He smelt the fresh air of the country as the downpour scrubbed away at the heavy petrol smells. The wind roared, blowing away the last of the smog. A faint smell of eucalyptus came to his nostrils. At last things were working out for him, he thought as he bounded up the stairs to get ready. It would be fun to venture out on a night like this. A night so different from the stifling days of the past weeks.

NINE

That night, under the lashing storm, the city turned oddly beautiful. Its sharp angles and flat surfaces shone wetly, gleaming darkly bright. The scarlet, gold and emerald of the traffic lights flooded out over the dusky street surfaces. Kevin and Margaret felt that they were driving through a mystic fairyland. They enjoyed the movies, and found in them a feeling of togetherness. By the time, they emerged from the theatre, the storm had blown itself out, leaving everything clean and fresh. When Margaret dropped him off, they exchanged a soft kiss which made Kevin walk to the building in a rosy glow of warmth. It made him feel so good that he ignored Tommy's wet clothing strewn over the bedroom floor. His younger brother was fast asleep in his bed. To Kevin, this was a good omen. Unknown to him, his sister was still not home, nor was she the next morning. He listened to his distraught mother, and tried to calm her. After all, Sue had stayed out late before, though not all night! She usually returned from work anywhere between six and eleven. He knew this because he had often watched his mother anxiously waiting.

"Arrh, Mum, she must have got caught up in the storm, and stayed over at a mate's place," Kevin said, trying to console his Mum. His mother tried hard to accept his words. She tried hard, but thought the worst even though it had really been blowing a gale and Tommy had arrived home looking like a drowned cat. She nodded her head, but dread filled her. Her eyes grew redder than ever, and her woebegone face made her sons want to cry. They hated their sister for bringing down such grief. They hung about the flat wondering what to do.

Although they took Sue's staying out overnight hard, the truth of the matter was that they had been expecting it to happen sooner rather than later. This was not only because of Sue's behaviour, but the behaviour of the other girls in the block of flats. Sooner or later, it happened to each one of the younger girls, and nothing could be done. It was either accepted or argued over until one day the girl never came home again. Now the same thing had happened to them, and they were engaged in a predetermined ritual. They would act it out as other families had. At least they hoped so. Perhaps the only reason was because of the storm? It must be the storm! She must have stayed over with a friend. And how could she have let them know? They hadn't a phone. In fact there wasn't a phone in the whole block of flats and so, how could Sue have contacted them?

"She'll be at work now," Kevin said confidently. "I'll go and ring up the shop. No worries, eh Mum?" he grinned and raced off.

The public telephone was being used. He stood shifting his weight from foot to foot, watching the hot sun steaming up the last of last night's rain. It was going to be a stinker! Already the reek of petrol stank the air. His eyes bored into the back of the woman nattering away. He tried to shame her into hanging up. While he waited, his confidence in Sue having spent the night with some girlfriend slowly dissolved in the heat. The idea of her having spent it with Mr Wiseman replaced it. She most likely had spent the night at his place. He would bet on it! His wife had been at his house in the hills and that left the way free for him to work his dirty tricks. Yes, he would bet on it. That had happened, and as soon as he had tried the shop, he would go around to that old creep's house and confront him—but then doubts arose. What if the old guy was at the shop and his sister was not? Where would he search for her then?

At last the woman left the booth. He squeezed into the box stinking of cheap perfume and stale urine, picked up the tattered phone book and searched for the shop number. He found it, flung thirty cents down the slot, dialed the number and waited. Engaged! He hung up, stared out at the muggy street, then tried again. Still engaged! A woman came to the phone box. She glared at him through the glass. He hurriedly dialed the number again. At last, a few burrs, then a click. A posh female voice simpered: "Hello."

"Hello, hello, may I speak to Sue Young, please?"

"I'm sorry, she's not in this morning."

"Well, uh, is it possible to speak to Mr Wiseman?"

"I'm sorry, he's not available. He's not in either. You may catch him at the new shop," and the girl hung up without offering to give him the number.

Uncertainly, Kevin held onto the receiver. Where was the other shop, and how would it be listed in the phone book, if it was? The waiting woman began tapping on the glass. It distracted him so much he couldn't think. He left the receiver hanging and pushed past the woman. She gave him an angry glare and remarked: "Some people think that this is their private phone."

"Stupid old cow!" Kevin shouted, his confusion erupting into anger. What a bitch his sister was. She didn't care a damn for her family, for any of them, and he had so many things to do today. Wait till he found her!

Back at the flat, he found his mother sobbing on the sofa. Uncle was trying to comfort her, while Tommy sat glumly watching. No one seemed in control. He went to his Mum, wrapped an arm around her shoulders, and managed to say cheerfully: "Mum, Mum, it's alright. Nothing wrong. It was like I told you. Last night Sue went to a girlfriend's place after work. The storm came on and she decided to stay over. She's at work now. I just finished speaking to her. Mum, it's alright!"

His mother lifted her weeping eyes to gaze into his face for the absolute truth. "That's true, Kev, you're not lying to me?"

"No, Mum, I've just finished speaking to her. There was nothing to worry about at all," he assured her as brightly as he could. Now he had to find his sister and see that she got home that evening.

Relief flooded the faces of the other members of his family. Tommy whistled and went off to the bedroom. Kevin, frightened that he would fail to keep up the pretence, followed. Then he did need Tommy's help. "Tommy," he said to him, "I lied to Mum. Sue's not at work, nor is her boss."

Tommy stared at his brother. The crushed expression which sometimes replaced the scowl was on Kevin's face. It was a sign of defeat, and he didn't like it. You had to be tough and keep up the fight until you won through. No one gave you an award for stopping the struggle. "Don't take it so hard, Kev, I'll ask around and see what I can find out."

"But what if she's had an accident. Mum'll never forgive me for lying to her. I don't know—"

"Hey, get a hold of yourself. Might have, isn't have! I suppose there wouldn't be any harm in trying the hospitals, just in case."

"You'll do that, won't you, Tommy? I could never face Mum

again, not if Sue's really lying all smashed up in hospital. You know how bad the roads are when it rains. Why, we saw one accident last night ourselves. God, it might have been Sue!"

"Arrh, Kev, don't take on so. Let's do something instead of sitting around here all day imagining the worst."

Kevin watched his younger brother screw up his face as he pondered the situation, and couldn't help thinking that at last he was taking an interest in family affairs. Tommy gripped his shoulder and said: "Let's get some sense into the situation. This happens all the time. Go and talk to any of the families in the flats and you'll find that their daughters, if they have one or some, have stayed out all night at least once. It's the way things are."

"Yeah, I know that, but she isn't like the rest of the girls here. She's, well, different. Besides, she's only seventeen."

"I bet you'd be surprised to learn just how much she is like the rest of them around here. We're all alike and even went to the same school together. And seventeen is old these days. Now you're a man or a woman and ready to take your own life in your hands. Take it from me, that's how it is!"

"Is it?" Kevin replied in a crushed voice. He hung his head in surrender. Only yesterday, just last night, he had had the world on a string. He had finally come to grips with himself and made some decisions. Now this had happened, and he couldn't handle it. How could Tommy talk about being a man or woman at seventeen, when at nineteen, he found life so hard?

"Arrh, come on, buck up. Bet you anything, she spent the night with some boyfriend. I'll scout around and see what I can find out. You want to wait here till I get back?"

"No, I can't hang around here. I'll go and see that boss of hers. The dirty old bastard! He's not at his shop. They could be still at it, for all we know."

"Don't know about that, Kev, but suit yourself." He gripped his brother's arm hard. "But if she's has been with him pass along the word and we'll fix him. A few bricks through his windows will teach that bastard not to mess with Nyoongahs!"

"I'll knock his bloody head off!"

"Let's go!"

They left the flat after checking to see that Mum had cheered up.

Everything was OK and Uncle had already left for the workshop.

This time Kevin didn't hesitate outside Wiseman's house. He leant on the button of the gate bell until it opened. A dark-haired woman stood before him. Her fierce eyes threw him into disarray. He had counted on Wiseman and Sue being there. He had worked himself up for it, and now it seemed neither were there. It was all turning out bad!

"Yes?" the woman flung at him.

"I've come to see Mr Wiseman."

"You have, have you? What about?"

"I–I–I'm looking for my sister. I thought she might be here."

"Why should she be here?"

"S–she works for him."

"Does she? Well, I can tell you that she isn't here with me. I'm his wife and I know at least that."

Kevin's eyes clung to the face of the woman before him. It was a hard face with bitter lines running from mouth to chin. Where would he look now?

Mrs Wiseman swung around, then turned to Kevin again and said: "You might try his new shop in Subiaco. It's on the corner of Chapel and High Streets. He's getting it ready for the opening on Saturday." Then she asked in a flat voice underlined with tension: "What made you think you might find your sister here?"

"Only, only because she does a lot of work for him, and sometimes stays on to model dresses. She might have been doing that last night and got caught by the storm."

"Oh, I see. Well, if that grub wants to crawl around young girls that's his problem, not mine. How old is she?"

"Seventeen, going on eighteen."

"Underage—he wouldn't have the guts to do anything. Look, he's got too much to lose—though not me—let me tell you that." A whining kind of anger had entered her voice. "I don't care a damn what he does any more, just as long as me and the kids don't suffer for it." Then she was gone. A door slammed behind the gate with a clang like a cell door.

Kevin hurried to the city where he could catch the Freo train for Subi. He hoped that Sue was helping the man at the new shop. Wiseman had mentioned something about grooming her for it. If only she was there … ?

He got off the train and crossed the road to High Street. A huge old building had been remodelled into a shopping complex. He felt the air conditioning cool his body as he entered. He wandered around the brightly-lit space stopping at each shop. There were a lot of them. Small cubicles in which bored girls waited to serve the odd middle-aged woman with money to waste on posh dresses. He reached the central plaza and stared around. There was another level and he was about to go up, when a shop on his left caught his eye. It was freshly decorated and rows of dresses were pressed against one wall. He went and looked through the window and saw Wiseman supervising the arrangement of the goods. The door gaped open. He stepped in.

"Mr Wiseman!"

"Well, what is it? Can't you see that I'm busy," the man replied without glancing up.

"I'm looking for my sister. I thought she might be here?"

The man straightened up. His magnified eyes bulged through his gold-rimmed spectacles. "Why should she be here? She is at the other shop."

"I tried there. She isn't. And she didn't come home last night. Mum's worried and I'm trying to find her."

"She isn't there! I'll ring. She might have arrived late. You know these girls–" Mr Wiseman said in a friendlier tone, shrugging. He picked up the telephone, and listened. "You're in luck. Been after Telecom all week to get it connected." He dialled, nodded and spoke a few words, listened, then replaced the receiver. "No, she's not there, but the storm might have upset her. You know those skinny types—all nerves—then they come and go as they please these days. No discipline at all. I expect she'll be in tomorrow claiming that she was sick. It happens once a month with some of them. Well, nothing I can do about it. I've got to get this place to rights. You know, she'll be working here from Saturday. That's a step up for her, but then she is better than most."

He bent down again as if the conversation was at an end. Kevin's resentment exploded into rage. "You dirty old sod! It's alright for you to fiddle about with young kids. Well, your wife knows all about you. Just remember that if you've had anything to do with Sue's disappearance, we'll get you for it. Just see!"

The gold-rimmed spectacles flashed at the savage gesture Kevin gave before leaving the shop. But his rage only covered his impotence. He didn't have a clue where his sister might be. All that he could do was go home and see if Tommy had turned up anything. He leapt on a bus and glared out at the city. He changed buses and stared, almost grinding his teeth in hopeless rage at the people around him. He had had enough! Just let anyone get in his way. That bastard, that dirty old sod, he thought over and over again. Pigs like him had spoilt his sister, had fancied her and turned her head with talk of giving her this and that. Now because of it, Sue had grown too big for her knickers and thought she didn't need her family any more. It was the fault of bastards like that Wiseman. He'd get them all for it!

It was just after lunch when slamming the door after him, he entered the flat. At least his lies had settled Mum down and she had cooked up some sausages for lunch, but he couldn't bear to eat them. Dread of the future twisted his stomach.

"Where's Tom?"

"He's still out. Expect he's at classes, or work."

"Yeah, I forgot about that."

Finally he forced himself to eat some of the sausages so that his mother wouldn't become suspicious that something was wrong. After that he sat and tried to watch TV. When would Tommy return? Tiredness overcame him and he went to his room and flung himself on the bed to rest. There was a stuffy feeling in his lungs and his throat fought to take in air. He hoped that an attack wasn't coming on. That would be the last straw, that would. He drifted off into a nasty dream, to gasp awake when Tommy tugged at him.

His bleary eyes stared up into his brother's face. He watched the lips form a word and eject it—"Ralph!"

"That's impossible," he muttered from a blurred mind. Sue was above that level now. Why, she was going to get her own shop to manage. She wouldn't waste herself on such a creep. He recalled seeing the guy on the street and how he had changed. It wasn't so far-fetched after all. "How did you find out?" he demanded, fully awake.

"Just asked a few blokes around here. No secret that they've been going together. She must've been with him last night—"

"And now," Kevin broke in, quickly telling Tommy that Sue hadn't turned up for work.

"Well, at least we can hope so. Better than being in an accident. Anyway, if she had, we'd have heard about it by now."

"Yeah, the cops would have been around. I forgot that. Well, where does he live?" Kevin asked through clenched teeth.

"Don't know. He's moved out of the suburb. You'll have to see some of his mates."

"Yeah, they'll know. I'll do just that!" he shouted. "Shouldn't be that hard. You stay here and try and calm Mum if she starts getting upset. I'll get back as soon as I can. And with Sue," he added under his breath.

TEN

The pub was different from the time when he had caught Sue there with Ralph. The outside walls gleamed dully from a new coat of brown paint. Beside the door to the bar a poster splashed out that live music featured on Fridays and Saturdays. Something called "See-Through Girls" was there on Thursdays. He found that the interior had been renovated into a huge dim cavern squashed with tables and chairs. The saloon bar, or lounge, or what-have-you, was deserted and he went into the public bar. He ordered a beer and sipped it as he looked around. Two men were playing pool. A third one stood watching them. He walked to the man, stood beside him, then asked: "Seen Ralph lately?"

"Can't say that I have."

"You know, I'm a friend of Sue's..."

This broke the ice. "She's a bit of alright, though on the young side," the man answered, his eye on a shot being made. Two balls snicked into a side pocket. One of the players cursed.

"Just thought I might catch him here..."

"Little too early to catch anyone, mate. You might ask Rob," the man replied, jerking a thumb at one of the players. "He's a good mate of Ralph." And he called out: "Hey, Rob, you think Ralph'll be in later?"

"Don't know about that. Don't think he will at all. He lives in Scarborough now and it's a long way to come just for a beer. He'll be in on Friday though."

"This guy's looking for him. Says he's a friend of Sue."

The pool player glanced up and examined Kevin for a long moment before saying: "Try his flat. It's on Beach Road. New building, cream brick, almost next to that high-rise building going up. Don't know the number, but it's on the second floor." He bent down over the table and spun an eight ball into a corner pocket. "That's it—you owe me a dollar," he said to the other player.

"Thanks mate!" Kevin called out to his back. He drained his glass and left.

As he waited for a bus to Scarborough, he asked himself how come he hadn't known about it before. Everyone else except him and his family knew. It was no secret. But then Ralph was white and an outsider. If it had been a Nyoongah, everyone in the community would have known about it. In some ways this sticking inside the community was a trap. Once someone stepped out of it, no-one knew what they were about, until something like this happened.

He jumped aboard the bus and left it when it reached the beachfront. He made his way along the road, feeling the hot sticky sea breeze adding its discomfort to the day. He stopped before a cream brick block of flats. They must be the ones! He bounded up the outside stairs and reached the top level. A shrill burst of female laughter led him towards a flat. He recognised it as coming from Sue, but there was a different tone to the laughter. One he had never heard before.

The door to the back corner flat was ajar. Obviously they weren't expecting to be disturbed. He pushed the door wide. The first thing he saw was Sue sprawling in an easy chair. In an aggressive voice, he heard her demand: "Hey, put that what's-her-name, that Sydney singer's record on again." He saw that she held a cigarette between her fingers and that there was a half glass of wine on the low table to one side of her. "That one's a drag," he heard a man's voice declare as he entered the room.

Sue glanced at the door and saw Kevin standing there. Her face paled. Defiantly, she reached for her glass and took a sip. She was not alone with the owner of the voice. Three other guys lounged about. He saw that one of them was Ralph!

His chest heaved. Tears started at the corners of his eyes. Here was his little sister, sitting as relaxed as if she was in her own home. No-one had twisted her arm to get her there. She had come of her own accord, and not only stayed the night, but most of the next day. Didn't she care that her family would be upset; didn't she care that her brothers were running around all over town trying to find her; didn't she care about them at all?!

"Sue," he called out in a small quavering voice. So weak! Even his anger had deserted him. If only Ralph had been alone with Sue...

"Yeah?"

"You know, we were worried. Didn't know where you had gotten to. What're you doing here?"

"What do you think I'm doing? Sitting and enjoying the company. It's too hot to go outside, otherwise I'd probably be on the beach."

"Mum's worried sick about you. You could have let us know..."

"How? We're not even on the phone. How you reckon I could've done that? Sent you all a telegram, I suppose?"

"You could have come home this morning."

"Arrh, you know how it is. You go to bed late, you get up late."

Kevin clutched the door frame. The situation was out of control. He couldn't cope. How to handle his sister? This was the city Sue and there was no shame in her at all. No shame!

He stared at her as she lit up another cigarette. He listened as she asked one of the blokes to refill her glass. She was deliberately stirring him up. She raised her glass to her lips, keeping her eyes on his face as if daring him to react.

"Sue!" he called desperately. Then he felt his rage rising and getting out of control. He welcomed it as an ally. "Sue, you better come home now. I told Mum you were at work. She'll be expecting you for tea."

"So what! I'll come when I'm good and ready."

"You come now!" His body began trembling violently as he watched her stand up and stretch. She flashed a smile at the three guys. They all wore suits and must have plenty of money. The flat's rent must be a bit too. He became aware of his own scruffy appearance. It raised his rage to boiling point.

It was then that Ralph got into the act. He sneered a smile at him, and said: "Now Kev, why don't you relax? Have a seat and a glass of wine. Sue'll go when she wants to. No use hurrying her. She's old enough to make up her own mind."

"No she's not!" Kevin retorted. "She's only seventeen. I could get the cops in here." He spoke quietly. Somehow his rage had leveled off.

"Why, don't you just try, Kev? Why don't you just try? They'd laugh in your face."

In his new soft voice, Kevin spoke to his sister: "Sue, get your things together. Mum's expecting you home for tea. I want you there!"

His words flowed into a waiting silence. Sue calmly finished her drink, then butted out her cigarette. Kevin's low voice had made her aware that something awful might happen. The three guys were watching them as if it was a family drama on TV. Kevin moved further into the room. One thing he was certain of, he wouldn't leave the flat without his sister!

"I have to go," Sue said. She picked up her purse, then glared at her brother and snapped: "But not because of you—I don't want to hurt Mum!"

"That's alright," Kevin agreed. "None of us wants to hurt her."

"Yeah, well you don't go out of your way to help. All you do is rave and rant and carry on. Do this and do that. Well, brother, no more! Take care of your own side of the fence and I'll take care of mine."

Kevin felt his hand rising. He would like to slap her, teach her some manners, but didn't make a move. The situation was still tense. It felt as if a storm was about to erupt. He had to be in control. His sister pushed past him. He listened to her steps click-clicking along the walkway, and then down the stairs. "You know, she's just a kid, so leave her alone," he told the men.

"Come on, mate," Ralph sneered. "You heard her. She knows her own mind and it's a hot one at that."

"And you're a dirty little animal at that," Kevin said calmly.

"What did you say, you little prick?"

"This is what I said," and he leapt forward and slammed his fist into the man's smirking mouth. The other two sprang up to aid their mate. He fought them off in a cold fury. He got in another fist to Ralph's mouth. He grinned as he felt a tooth give. One of the others whacked him in the nose. He felt the blood begin to drip. It was three against one. The odds were against him. He was in for a good hiding. Ralph was whimpering and out of the fight. Later he would move in and put in the boot. He slammed the door behind him and raced for the stairs. Feet came after him. They stopped.

Safely out on the road, he wiped away the blood streaming from his nose. Something blocked his throat, almost choking him. He coughed, spluttered, then retched. A hard clot of blood and phlegm flew from his mouth. Air flowed freely.

Kevin felt like a hero, Ivan, in the film he had seen with Margaret. Just like Ivan, ready and willing to take on the whole world. "You can get it if you really want to." He heard the sound of Ivan's theme song sounding in his head. He rubbed his bruised fist cut across the knuckles from Ralph's teeth. He had fixed that bastard! He grinned in triumph. Let Sue find him attractive with a mouth filled with broken teeth! At last, this day had become his day. He would make the next days and the ones beyond his days too! He was winning through at last. "You can get it, if you really want to," he hummed as he went to the bus stand.

ELEVEN

"She'll be like new with a fresh coat of paint," Bill declares, running a rough hand over a discoloured wall. "Roof's in good nick and the floors as solid as jarrah." He gives a hard stamp which shakes the house.

"They built them well in those days," Kevin replies, staring around the walls. With a spot of paint, they would be, as Bill had said, like new. He follows the bloke through the rest of the place. They reach the kitchen.

"Wood stove that. Can't beat them for cooking up a stew. You'll never run out of wood either." He lifts his hand to scratch at the mop of grey hair. "Beats me why you want to live way out here though. Most people are moving the other way. Family used to live up here went off into one of your homes in the town. Seems to me, you being with the Co-op and all, you could get yourself a new house without any fuss."

"Not me, mate, not me! First come first served is our motto. Then I used to live in the city—now all I want is a little bit of peace and quiet."

"You'll get that around here. Heard you marrying the older Michaels girl. Family lived here for years. Have a stake in the place, you know? You become part of the family, no worries about you moving here as soon as you get it fixed. Give you a hand with the decorating," Bill adds with a sly smile. He pokes about in the stove. "Could do with a good clean-out. Glad some of you young ones are moving back into the old place. It'll give the mission a new lease on life."

As they walk back to his car, Kevin explains how they plan to have everything ready by their wedding date. As they walk along, he looks around at the cluster of houses that make up the settlement. Nyoongahs have been living here for over a hundred years, but only in the last year have they been given full title to the old mission. He looks at the chapel standing right in the centre of the houses. It bore witness to the time before, when the mission was managed by the

Church of England. Now it is rarely used as a chapel. Only when the odd missionary spirit arrives to give the people a rousing. Margaret suggests they get married there.

"Know, they tried to get us out about ten years back," Bill tells him in his deep slow voice. "You know, the Head of the Department of Aboriginal Affairs came down himself. He set fire to some of the houses. See, you can still make out where they stood. Then they wanted us out, and into the town to become part of what they called the 'general community', but we stuck it out. Now this place is ours for ever. We had to fight for this land, mate, had to fight for it. Now we have it," he ends with a soft note of satisfaction in his voice.

"Good place to bring up kids," Kevin says, glancing around at the bush.

"Bus goes right past here to pick them up for school in town," the man informs him. "Expect out here with nothing to do at nights, you'll have a whole mob of them about in no time."

Bill leaves him with a huge grin. Kevin smiles after him, then begins to think of his future. He wants his first child to be a boy. Easier to manage, he thinks, recalling Sue and those days of strife. On an impulse, he strolls down towards the sea. He edges around a stretch of water and keeps to a faint path heading over a hump of ground and down into a cove. On the rise, he can look down towards the beach where the ground has hardened into rock. Boulders lie there like giant emu eggs waiting to be gathered. "This is Aboriginal land," he tells himself, and feels at ease. A breeze rises, blowing from the southern ocean. It fumbles under his coat and tingles his skin. The air is so clean, so unlike the smog of the city.

He makes his way around the side of the curved breast of earth and scrambles down a bank onto the beach. The tide is going out, uncovering more of the land. A fishing boat chugs across the still water, smudging the sky with exhaust fumes. The put-put of the engine comes clearly to him as hard black dots of sound punctuating the quiet stillness. A bird warbles from his left. He glances up into the bough of a tall tree overhanging the bank and catches a glimpse of the songster. It is almost hidden in the leaves, brown and placid amid the olive green.

Around the curve of the shore there is a jumble of rocks heaped against a steep bank. As he comes closer to the pile, he makes out the two boulders hiding the entrance to Margaret's cave. The sand begins to yield under his feet and he moves closer to the water ...

The first time, Margaret leads him here. She pauses to point at a seagull. He looks at it, then turns to find her gone, vanished into thin air. He ducks around a boulder thinking that she is playing. Her hand beckons to him from a narrow gap in the bank. He squeezes through and crawls along a burrow-like tunnel. It suddenly expands into the cave. He sees that it is not like the one in the story at all, or for that matter, is it exactly like she has described it. There are no stalagmites or stalactites. Only a thick central pillar formed from mineral deposits. He points this out to the girl. She laughs and flashes her torch at the ceiling and floor. Tiny gleaming needles like glittering spear grass sparkle from the rock.

Kevin makes his way to a ledge set right at the back. On their last visit, they left a sleeping bag there. He finds it. It is still dry. This means that the cave is not flooded at high tide. He flashes his torch about. It might even be possible to have a fire down there. A distinct draft flows from the heap of rocks at the back towards the cave entrance, but this most likely would cease when the tide covered the cave mouth.

Margaret still wants to stay in the cave overnight. She has even suggested half jokingly that they spend their wedding night within the earth. Kevin shrugs at the suggestion. He finds it weird. Then they couldn't sneak off just like that. He sits on the ledge and switches off the torch. A shaft of light passing down the tunnel, but it is really not enough to illuminate the whole cave. It should be dark inside. Instead it is gloomy like the grey light of winter's evening. Must be some trick of the light, he decides before letting his mind drift back to his last months in the city.

Mum and Uncle disliked the idea of him leaving the city. Tommy flatly declared that it was crazy and Sue stared at him in astonishment. Mum spoke for all of them. She said that he was splitting up the family and that they should stick together. If they didn't, they were nothing and had nothing. Kevin had already confessed that he wouldn't get the Public Service job and when they continued to protest, he told them there was little chance of him getting a job in the city. Eventually, they came to accept his coming departure. Bayside was only five hour's drive away and it was not like leaving the state.

Relations between Sue and her brother remained tense. After her escapade, she regarded him with something like apprehension, as if she feared that he would step in and try to dominate her life. Kevin had no intention of doing this. During his last days in the city, her stance had softened, though a barrier still remained. On the very last day, she informed him that he had been right about Ralph and that the guy was back behind bars. "You wouldn't believe the half of it," she fluttered in her new nervous manner, then left it at that. Kevin was relieved that she was no longer interested in the bloke though he was still concerned about her. On reaching eighteen, Wiseman had kept his word and put her in charge of the Subi shop. The location and responsibility was bad for her. She acted like a much older woman and, worse, began to take on the persona of the shopping centre which had become quite fashionable. Copies of women's fashion magazines lay about the lounge and more and more she began to resemble the skinny models pictured in them. Her manner became very bright and brittle. She radiated a nervous energy which kept her hopping from one thing to another, like a Willy Wagtail pecking at seeds. Her comings and goings became more erratic than ever, but Mum kept her peace. She had decided that her daughter was grown up and had to learn her own lessons. She consoled herself with the fact that Sue had a good job.

Tommy also began to behave himself. Kevin suspected that Alex had given him advice based on the importance of the family in Aboriginal culture. Whatever it was, it had worked. Tommy began coming home earlier and doing some of his study in the lounge room.

The day after Sue's escapade, Kevin enrolled in the course without difficulty. He flung himself into study, trying to do everything as quickly as possible. What spare time he had, he spent with Margaret. They grew closer and closer. After a month, Kevin took her home to meet his family. Sue exchanged a few words with her, decided that they had little in common, then vanished into her room. Mum found the girl nice and uncomplicated. She reminded her of what she had been like when a girl. After dinner, Margaret helped her with the dishes and they had a good chat. When she left, Mum confided in Kevin that he couldn't have found a nicer girl. He replied that he wished Sue was like her, and the conversation came to an abrupt end. It was a bad blow when Margaret went home. Kevin moped around the flat for most of the day, then decided to see Elias and Paul. Both were knee-deep in paper, preparing their end of the year work. He caught a bus to go to Freo and see Johnno. Next day he was back at his studies. Three months to go!

Four days after she left the city, a letter arrived for Kevin. He received it very differently from the government one. Mum was all smiles as she waited for him to open it. Margaret wrote how much she loved being home for good; expressed the hope that he was studying hard; stated how much she missed him; then closed with love and kisses all round. From then on, they exchanged letters regularly. Her letters became filled with local gossip and activities. Each one gave Kevin more information on the town and the local Nyoongah families.

The National Aboriginal Day celebrations were a big event. Three of her letters covered the preparations (she was on the planning committee), the dance which was the highlight of the festivities (she handled the competitions) and the aftermath of the celebrations, mainly bill-paying. In another letter she described the local footy team and how it had fielded a team one man short, but had won the match. She hinted that there was always a place on the team for him. Over the months, Kevin became familiar with the local scene. When he arrived, he would not feel a complete stranger.

At last the course ended. On receiving his certificate of completion, he left for Bayside. Margaret met the bus. In front of everyone, she hugged him. Mr Michaels put him up at his place. He settled in without any fuss. The work was easy enough. It was what his course had prepared him for, but before he could become bored he was on the footy team and a couple of committees. Even before his arrival, he had been coupled with the Michaels girl and it came as no surprise to the community when they announced their wedding day. When Margaret told her father, he merely commented: "Wondered when you two would tie the knot"—and let it go at that. The following weekend they had gone to see the cave and stopped at the empty house. They peered through the dusty windows, and then and there decided to make it their home. They went to see the manager. He put them before the committee and there were no objections. The settlement was only a hour's drive from the town and this would be no trouble.

Kevin sits in the cave. It is almost time to make a move. His family are coming down for the wedding. This makes him a bit apprehensive, but he knows that everything will go off OK. His people too are country and know country ways. They mightn't understand him living in the settlement, though. Still, it really is a beautiful spot and so quiet and peaceful. Mum, he knows, will love it, and as for Sue? As for Sue, she might enjoy a quiet rest away from the shop. Tommy might prove a problem with his know-all city ways, but the locals would soon sort him out.

He gets to his feet. Over the past few months, he has filled out and his skin has become a rich Karri brown. The scowl is an expression of the past and his face is getting used to good humour. He squeezes back down the tunnel and stands on the beach looking at the clouds hulking on the horizon. They remind him of a city skyline. There is a menace of constant change about them. He strolls back past his future home to his car. Before driving away, he takes one long look around and fills his lungs with clean country air. His sense of victory is almost complete. Nothing can go wrong, and if it does, he will face it and win through again.

MIRNMIRT

JIMMY PIKE

When single woman likes a man, she draws this story in the mud with a stick. When woman talks about man, talks about love, she draws this story.

When someone talks, or a man sees that story, then he goes to the woman. Then they talk marriage. Mirnmirt is the marriage law.

When man has finished the law, done everything, he can marry. He has got to learn everything. There are two laws. One for the young boy, takes several months. One for the full man, takes five or six years.

When man come back from bush after manhood, woman waiting. They have a big feast and make man and woman red with clay.

Black Girl

Jimmy Chi

Black girl, black girl,
Won't you love me tonight?
Come over darlin' make everything right.

Black girl, black girl,
Won't you love me and then,
Come over darlin' and love me again.

I know, I know,
It's hard for you.
And you know darlin' it's hard for me too.

I know, I know,
I love you true.
Come over darlin' say you love me too.

Black girl, black girl,
Won't you love me tonight?
Won't you come over darlin' make everything right.

Black girl, black girl,
Won't you love me and then,
Come over darlin' and love me again.

Some day, some day,
We'll be alright
Just like it is on this shiny night.

Some day, some day,
We'll have it all.
'Cos you know darlin' you make me stand tall.

Black girl, black girl,
Won't you love me tonight?
Won't you come over darlin' make everything right.

Black girl, black girl,
Won't you love me and then,
Come over darlin' and love me again.

So love, so love,
Won't you say you love me?
We'll be together eternally.

So love, so love,
Won't you love me and then
Come over darlin' and love me again.

Black girl, black girl,
Won't you love me tonight?
Won't you come over darlin' make everything right.

Black girl, black girl,
Won't you love me and then,
Come over darlin' and love me again.

Black girl, black girl,
Won't you love me tonight?
Won't you come over darlin' make everything right.

Black girl, black girl,
Won't you love me and then,
Come over darlin' and love me again.

My Finke River Home

Herbie Laughton

There's a spot I know
Where the big tall river gum trees grow.
By a peaceful little valley is my home.
Oh I long to go back to Hermannsburg I know.
Take me back to where the old Finke River flows.

By a peaceful stream in the valley of my dreams,
I can hear sweet voices calling me it seems.
"Won't you come back home to the ones who love you so?"
Take me back to where the old Finke river flows.

Dream voices ever calling me,
Sweet dream voices calling me back home.
Calling me, calling me,
Sweet dream voice that's calling me back home.

Cross the Western plains by the old MacDonald range,
To the loved ones' happiness I used to know.
By a peaceful stream in the valley of my dreams,
Take me back to where the old Finke River flows.

Dream voices ever calling me,
Sweet dream voices calling me back home.
Calling me, calling me,
Sweet dream voice that's calling me back home.

When the sun dips down beyond the Western range,
I'll be back with my relations once again.
Where the camp fires glow and the friends I used to know,
Singing songs beside the old Finke River flow.

By a peaceful stream in the valley of my dreams,
I can hear sweet voices calling me it seems.
"Won't you come back home to the ones who love you so?"
Take me back to where the old Finke River flows.

Dream voices ever calling me,
Sweet dream voices calling me back home.
Calling me, calling me,
Sweet dream voice that's calling me back home.
Sweet dream voice that's calling me back home.

Brown Skin Baby

Bob Randall

Yaaawee, yaahaawawee,
My brown skin baby they take 'im away.

As a young preacher I used to ride
my quiet pony round the countryside.
In a native camp I'll never forget
a young black mother her cheeks all wet.

Yaaawee, yaahaawawee,
My brown skin baby they take 'im away.

Between her sobs I heard her say,
"Police bin take-im my baby away.
From white man boss that baby I have,
why he let them take baby away?"

Yaaawee, yaahaawawee,
My brown skin baby they take 'im away.

To a children's home a baby came,
With new clothes on, and a new name.
Day and night he would always say,
"Mummy, Mummy, why they take me away?"

Yaaawee, yaahaawawee,
My brown skin baby they take 'im away.

The child grew up and had to go
From a mission home that he loved so.
To find his mother he tried in vain.
Upon this earth they never met again.

Yaaawee, yaahaawawee,
My brown skin baby they take 'im away.

Here Comes the Nigger

Gerry Bostock

Gerry Bostock's Here Comes the Nigger *was first performed at the Black Theatre, Redfern, in 1976. Portions of the original playscript were printed in* Meanjin *in December 1977, although the entire text has never been published. The excerpt reproduced below is taken from a revised version of the play, transformed by the author into a draft filmscript.*

SAM:
But the government's spending millions of dollars on Aborigines. Why isn't something being done?

VERNA:
I'll tell ya why. Most of the money that's earmarked for blacks ends up in white pockets; it goes to pay the wages of the white bureaucrats who control the black affairs; hardly anything gets to the people who really need it. Just look at the money that's returned to Treasury every year because the bureaucrats say it isn't used; Millions of dollars! And if they do happen to fund Aboriginal development programmes they make damn sure there's a white man in control of the money; and if that white man mismanages the money and the programme goes bust, it's not him that gets in the shit, it's always the blacks who work in government departments. Them black bureaucrats are nothing but window dressing for the Government: shop-front niggers, good little jackey-jackies, little black puppets dancing to the white man's tune. Do you know what they remind me of? Coconuts: brown on the outside and white on the inside!

SAM:
They're not all sell-outs. Not all of them have been bought off. Some of them get out and meet with the people. Some of them try to do things as best they can.

VERNA *(smiles):*
Yeah, sure they do. They visit Aboriginal reserves and communities, they shoot in for a day or two in their big, black government cars. But do they live with the grass-roots people, and experience conditions for themselves? No they don't! Instead, they stay in the nearest posh hotel where they can go to buffet luncheons, and have room service with hot and cold running white girls. And why not? They've got their expense accounts. If they can't get their little white girls to give it away, they can always pay for it; and if that doesn't work they can always accuse the girls of being racist, appeal to their guilt complex. Why should they worry about the blacks? They've got it made, the bastards!

(He places a comforting arm around her.)

SAM *(softly):*
It's okay kid. You're home now.

(She sobs uncontrollably.)

JIMMY:
Anyone for a charge?

*(Billy looks broodingly as Jimmy hands out the beer.
Cut to Odette.)*

ODETTE:
Enjoying yourself, Sam?

SAM:
I always do. How about you?

(Sam flinches as a half filled can of beer, flung by Billy lands at their

feet. Billy stands out and confronts Odette.)

BILLY:
Bitch! You bloody shits. You can't leave us alone, can ya...!

(She is obviously surprised by the attack but remains calm.)

BILLY:
Ya rip us off every chance ya get, don't ya! Ya've been kickin' us in the teeth for two hundred bloody years an ya still doing it, and we still have to put up with it!

ODETTE:
I'm not responsible for anything my father or my forefathers did to your people, and I'm certainly not responsible for anything that happened tonight.

BILLY:
You're not responsible? That's a cop-out and you know it. You are responsible! You're responsible for the two thousand black lepers in this country, you're responsible for the infant mortality rate of black babies being amongst the highest in the world, you're responsible for every old aged pensioner in this country who has to rummage through garbage cans to get something to eat, you're responsible for every unemployed person who has to steal to survive. Us blacks are the minority, we're two percent of the population. You're the majority; you can make changes so don't sit there and say you're not responsible for everything that happens in this country, so don't give me that cop-out about not being bloody responsible!

(Verna prods Johnny. Billy holds up his hands for silence.)

BILLY:
Awright, you fellas. Give him a go.

LUCY:
Come on, brothers. Show these buggers what ya made of!

SAM:
I don't know?

BILLY:

> The white man settled this vast country;
> Cleared the land;
> Built a great nation democratic and free,
> And they looked after you, their friends,
> Our brothers, the Aborigine.

(During the recital Billy walks in among the crowd using all the emotion at his command.)

BILLY *(cont.)*:

> They had to protect you, care for you,
> They gave you a home
> Or you would have died of disease
> Or starved if they left you to roam.

(From time to time Billy directs his recital at individual blacks as well as Odette.)

BILLY *(cont.)*:

> They educated you, employed you
> And gave you a trade
> They fed you and looked after your health
> You had it made
> They gave you a life of ease and leisure,
> Your only want was for more pleasure
> And they fought two bloody wars
> For that happy treasure.

(Verna and Ari seem anxious about the two brothers. Sometimes they are seen in the background, and sometimes the camera cuts to them, capturing their concerned facial expressions.)

BILLY *(cont.)*:

> These are the lies
> Of our white Judas brother;
> He has taught us deceit
> And contempt for one another
> And watched amused
> As we grovelled for fresh air
> Under his racist care;
> Derelict and abused.
> What about our infant mortality!
> Where is his morality?
> This patronising white
> Has murdered our people in hateful spite
> And bloody thirst
> Because we lay claim to this land first!

(Two blacks hang on Billy's every word. From time to time they make the odd comment but generally remain silent.)

BILLY *(cont.)*:

> Our land, our culture and our women
> He rapes with a lecherous grin,
> While society turns its back on his immoral sin
> And whispers an apathetic sigh
> While our people are left to starve and die.
>
> He stares and glares and loves to gloat
> This white beast frocked in an angelic cloak
> Who laughs at our woeful plight
> From which we have no respite
> And no weapons to fight his aggressive might.
>
> How long must we wait for justice
> And freedom to be won?
> The time has come
> to fight this racist-scum!

Rise up Black children
And tell society what it's all about.
Stand together
And stamp black persecution out.
Remember our infant mortality!
Wake up to reality
The fascist monger
Has murdered our people by racism and hunger.

Society has cast you aside
And you've been made to hide
And grovel in the gutter
And all you've done is sit and mope
And mutter
About life without hope.

Rise up Black Children
With your anguish cry
And from the rooftops
How your babies die
From government neglect
And society's inaudible outcry.

For years our land
Has been subjected to pillage and rape;
While our people faced corrupt politicians,
Police persecution
And government red tape
And whites who care not for our plight;
The time is coming for us to fight!

Rise up Black Children
And stand as one,
Shoulder to shoulder 'til freedom's won;
Brace your back,
Dig in your heel
And if need be,

Prepare for the onslaught of cold steel!

Rise up and face society's might,
For justice for our people
And for our birthright,
Our land!
This land
In which we've suffered aggression
And known nothing but oppression,
By our conquerors,
The invaders
Who have lowered us
To the blackest depths of depression.

Prepare, Black Children,
For the Land Rights fight,
Our cause is true,
Our aim's in sight,
Unite, my people, unite.

Come on, Black Children,
Rise on your feet!
Get out of the gutter and onto the street;
United together, hand in hand,
Heads raised high we stand
Then, march as one,
Surging forward and onward
For justice, for freedom and for our land!

(The blacks applaud and shout comments of approval.)

BILLY:
That's your poetry, Sam. Keep writing
that sorta stuff, brother.

SAM *(thoughtful):*
Yes, but that one's just a little bit strong.

(Billy gives up and sits down. Verna rises and walks slowly over to Sam as Billy rips open a can of beer.)

VERNA:
A bit strong? A bit bloody strong! They're your words, Sam not Billy's. You wrote *Black Children*, not him. A bit strong, ya say? Good God, man. You've been mixin' with whites too long!

ODETTE:
Now, just a damn minute. You've got no right to talk to him like that...

VERNA: *(coldly)*
You shut ya white mouth or I'll get Mother Palmer and her five daughters *(gesticulates)* and shove them down your throat!

(She turns to Sam.)

VERNA *(softly):*
Now, look here, bundji; this warraluman, this whaa-zhin of yours says I shouldn't talk to you like this. I'm talking to you like this because you're Billy's brother, and I love you just as much as he does. You know how we feel, how most blacks feel about white society; *Black Children* expresses exactly how we feel and you wrote those words. Don't lose sight of that. Don't lose your values or change your way of thinking 'cause some whaa-zhin spreads her legs for a couple of minutes and shows you a good time. Don't change because of that.

BILLY *(rising):*
Anyway, it's a party time! Who wants to hear a blackfella yarn? *(pause)* This is a schoolboy yarn. It's a true story, too. It happened to me when I was going to school; as a matter of fact, it was the first day I met Ari. Remember that, Ari?

(Cut to Ari who seems uneasy and turns to Sam.)

BILLY *(cont.):*
Ari and me was at one end of the schoolground when we heard this big commotion all the gubbah kids were making. Ya see, it was playtime and all the gubbahs formed themselves into this big procession; just like little soldiers. Everyone was marchin' and singing an clapping their hands; just havin' so much fun me and Ari decided to join in with them.

We raced over to some garbage tins. Ari picked up a tin and a stick and I grabbed two tin lids, then we joined the gubbahs—and there we were, me and Ari: I was clangin' these two lids together as hard as I could, and Ari was beltin' shit outta the garbage tin with his stick—an we were singin' "Wallah-wallah-blackfella, wallah-wallah-blackfella, wallah-wallah-blackfella..."

(Billy moves around the room clapping his hands and emotionally chanting. The crowd, with the notable exception of Sam, Ari and Odette stamp their feet, clap their hands and pick up the chant.

SUPERIMPOSE children in a procession in a school yard singing the chant. INTERCUT facial CLOSEUP of Sam and WIDE ANGLE of children. VOICE OVER of party crowd's chanting comes up and takes over from the children's track.

CUT TO WIDE ANGLE. Billy and his followers chant.)

BILLY:
Wallah-wallah-blackfella, Wallah-wallah-blackfella, Wallah-wallah-blackfella.

(Billy raises his hands for silence. The chanting stops and he goes over to Sam.)

BILLY *(softly):*
And you know what, my brother? When we looked everyone was laughing at you—'cause you was the blackfella, Sam. You was the blackfella.

(CLOSE to Sam. FAST INTERCUT between Sam and the jeering children, ending with Sam sitting rigid as the party crowd look on. FADE OUT.)

INTERIOR. DAY. FLAT.

The bed sitting room is small, comfortable, and economically furnished. Against the far wall, beneath a wide curtained window is a double bed covered with a Batik bedspread. Against the right hand wall is a small book-shelf with assorted books, magazines and a framed photograph of Odette's parents; a small stereo and assorted records; a small tape-recorder and cassettes; above are two posters of reproductions of famous paintings and two glass-framed Norman Lindsay prints; in the corner is a settee. The floor is covered by sea-grass matting. In a corner by the far and the left-hand wall are two bean bags. Built in to the left hand wall is a wardrobe, next to which is a door leading to the bathroom. The kitchen, situated in an alcove by the left of the front door, is separated from the main room by a serving bench; on the bench is small glass fish-tank containing two goldfish, a large corked bottle containing earth and a tropical plant. In the centre of the room is a small table with a lace table cloth and two chairs.

(Sam sits at the table reading a Braille book and Odette is on the settee reading and making notes.
SOUND FX TELEPHONE.)

SAM *(looking up)*:
Are you going to answer that or what?

(She continues to read as she rises.)

ODETTE:
You just keep working.

(She crosses to the phone and Sam goes back to his book.)

ODETTE *(answering phone):*
Hullo? *(uncomfortably)* Hi, what are you doing in town? How did you get my number? I'm sorry. I'm fine. How are you? *(pause)* No, that's no good ... Look, where are you? I'll drop by. *(looks at her watch)* About half and hour, okay? Right see you then.

(CLOSE TO Odette. She hangs up and appears thoughtful. Sam looks over to her.)

SAM:
Everything okay?

ODETTE *(pondering):*
Huh? Oh yes, everything's just fine.

(She goes over and sits next to him.)

SAM *(smiles):*
One of your old flames, hey?

ODETTE:
Huh?

SAM:
On the phone? Was that one of your old boyfriends?

(She pats his hand.)

ODETTE:
I have to go out for awhile. Can we finish this lesson tomorrow?

SAM:
Is our date still on for tonight?

ODETTE:
I don't know how long I'll be *(looks at her watch)*. Why don't I meet you at the railway station and we can go on from there?

SAM:*(Rising. He closes the book and puts it on the bookshelf.)*

Good. I'll walk you to the corner.

ODETTE:
Thanks. I'll get my coat...

Bran Nue Dae

Jimmy Chi and others

Bran Nue Dae *is the first Black Australian rock opera, the product of a collective of Aboriginal talent living in the area of Broome, Western Australia.*

ACT 2   SCENE 1

SONG: *"Tourist Dollar"* (Rosie)

("Tourist Dollar" playing as party arrive in Broome; continues to play during dialogue driving into Chinatown, and as they stop the car and enter hotel.)

> Bikini clad tourist down on Cable Beach
> Cutting bread showing off her cheeks
> Hey little tourists try some local meat
> Satay or bunja all that you can eat.
>
> If you lay down you'll stay down
> So hard to get up
> He'll walk all over you.
> Time has come to play their sucker game
> If you hang back you'll lose track of where
> they are going,
> He'll get you one by one
> No time to relax and fade away.
>
> *(Chorus)*
> Tourist dollar makes me rich and comfortable
> Tourist dollar make me belly fat

Tourist dollar staircase to the moon
Tourist dollar don't come back till June.

And in this place that we call Chinatown
You look so amazed as you wander around
But the "Chiffa's" all gone now
It's just lattice and tin
All I want for you is to fill my till.

And the caravan parks all lead to the bay
Pumping crap out every day
While I'm not sure what's really on my plate
But it must be OK the traffic's going oneway
Don't you want a ride
All you need is Huey's uncle's eyes.

(Chorus: Tourist Dollar
Repeat verses 3 and 4
Chorus: Tourist Dollar)

SWEET WILLIAM:
Hey boy, we're coming into Broome now.
Yeh, that's the lights over there. You can see that place where I bin
used to live before. We better hit the Roebuck I think. Yeh, yeh here
we are, come on!

(Pull up alongside pub)

MARIJUANA ANNIE:
What's the Roebuck?

SWEET WILLIAM:
That's where all the people drink. Band playing there, you can hear
them, I think. Sound like woman singing. He got good voice. I
wonder who that is ... *(They go inside)* Oh chrije! That's him. That's
the woman now I bin tell you about! That's him, there now look! He
singing! Ah I feel funny!

UNCLE TADPOLE:
Oh don't worry. Come on, my boy, you gotta friend him up and try grabbem!

SWEET WILLIAM:
But I feel big shame. I'm dirty and everything like that.

UNCLE TADPOLE:
Ah don't worry we all dirty!

MARIJUANA ANNIE:
Hey far out! wow, wow, this is my scene. Check out the band ... Slippery get me a drink. Willy come on, show me around. Willy and I'll go smelling around for a joint.

(Until song finishes, Willy makes his way over to Tadpole. Song stops and Uncle Tadpole introduces himself to Rosie.)

UNCLE TADPOLE:
Hullo, my girl. My name Tadpole. Steven Johnson, Tadpole and this one here my boy. I think he like you too. And I just wanna tell you that I think you singing good. That's good, that's deadly!

ROSIE:
You wanna have a go old man?

UNCLE TADPOLE:
Oooh, you give me a go....oooh yeh.
No you better let my young boy have a go with you but I'll have a go with singing.
I'll findem this womans. I'm good singer.
I used to sing before in choir.

ROSIE *(to band member):* Hey Bro! old man want to get up and play. Sing us a song what you reckon? *(To Uncle Tadpole)* You know these blokes ?

UNCLE TADPOLE:
Oh those young blokes I know your mothers. I can see what kind you look. You know this song? Here I'll sing for you and you follow me. I know how to sing. And grab tarts around this country. Yeh like this ... with a-one, a-two, a-three, uh uh!

SONG: "Is You Mah Baby" (Tadpole)

>Is you mah baby
>Is you mah baby
>Is you ?
>Is you mah baby
>Is you mah baby
>Is you ?
>When I'm in your warm embrace
>I feel part of the human race
>Oh !
>Is you mah baby
>Is you mah baby
>Is you ?

>Is you mah baby
>Is you mah baby
>Is you ?
>Is you mah baby
>Is you mah baby
>Is you ?
>You get under mah skin
>Take off you jowiij and let me in
>Oh —
>Is you mah baby
>Is you mah baby
>Is you ?

>Is you mah baby
>Is you mah baby
>Is you ?
>Is you mah baby

Is you mah baby
Is you ?
You wipe me off my face
Let's multiply the Aboriginal race
Is you mah baby
Is you mah baby
Is you ?

(Sweet William and Rosie take care of their business. Willy is shy. Rosie is more precocious. After Uncle's song she gives William a kiss and goes back to the stage to sing.)

SONG: "Somebody's Dreaming" (Rosie)

Somebody's Dreaming
Oh don't you.
Somebody's heart is
Breaking in two.
If you should love that someone
Who loves you true
Then let that someone love you too.

Deep in the dark I
Call out your name
I see your face reflected
On the window pane
If you should love that someone
come back again
and ease this yearning sad refrain.

(Interaction between her and William during song. Marijuana Annie and Slippery taking up large and meeting all the relatives of Tadpole. Tadpole is by now surrounded by women and in his element.)

SONG: "Stalebait" (Tadpole)

(Tadpole breaks into song and dance routine in beer garden,

initiating the whole pub to join in dance routine. As the song ends
he leads them out still dancing.)

I tell you I ain't foolin'
I not that kind of guy
She really stopped my dreaming
Shot me right between the eyes.
I knew I had it coming
but she don't hesitate
why should she keep me waiting
when the train is running late.

I knew I shouldn't worry
I knew I shouldn't stay
However she just took me
On a road that doesn't pay.

I told her it was naughty
I told her it was nice
She was a red hot curry that
I found amongst my rice.

So maybe when I'm older
I'll be more self assured
and take with me these memories
to that heavenly reward.

For though I'm getting older
I smile upon the day
When she gave me a present
and after she just say.

You just stale bait
You just stale bait
I been there before
Stalebait you just stale mate
I bin there before.

So don't despair you young men
I know you'll sometimes find
when someone comes and gives you
a draught of heady wine
then you will be happy
then you will understand
and always think so fondly of
the girl who made you man.
She'll take you oh so coyly
she'll play with you a while
she'll strip you to your body
then leave you with a smile.

And after its all over
there's no way you can repay
the girl who came between the sheets
and turned night-time into day,
'Cos
You're both stalebait
You're both stale mate
You've been there before.

(Everybody jumps into their cars looking for party arranged for Cable Beach.)

End of Scene

NGURRA WANJULAJARRA
(land all over the world)

JIMMY PIKE

Mountains and cloud and land.

This means that wherever you go you will still find mountains like this.

Aboriginal Land-Claims Not Excessive in the Land of the Great Fair Go

Rob Riley

Aboriginal people still occupy a wrong position in the minds of the majority of Australians, a fact confirmed by the Australian National Opinion Poll commissioned by the government and hidden from public view for nearly eighteen months.

This is the first government in two hundred years that has taken the trouble to gather statistical proof of what was quite obvious.

But having gathered the proof and having been told what should be done, the Hawke Government has cynically turned a deaf ear to the words of its ANOP researcher, who, shocked at the level of racism in this country, said forcefully in the report "If a pro-Aboriginal, pro-Land Rights campaign is not launched now the situation will become quite irretrievable. We have never recommended so strongly that a government campaign is needed in any area."

The researchers also stated that a "campaign is definitely, if not desperately, needed. This is a point that we cannot emphasise enough."

The Prime Minister is on record as saying that the government would not proceed with a campaign to educate the public about the validity of Aboriginal needs and aspirations on the grounds that "you cannot manipulate public opinion in Australia, a fact for which we should be eternally grateful." In fact he indicated that the Australian public's compassion in the area of Aboriginal affairs had diminished.

His argument fails for a number of reasons, and leads to the conclusion that this is not a genuine opinion but a deceitful way of avoiding an issue which he and his government refuse to confront with positive action.

If public opinion cannot be manipulated by education, why has the government committed $100 million to a campaign based on a very expensive and slick public relations strategy? The results of the Australian National Opinion Poll clearly show that public relations campaigns do have a marked effect on public opinion.

The poll points out the much higher profile of Aboriginal land rights as a result of the Western Australian Chamber of Mines campaign. This campaign was a deliberate attempt to reinforce negative attitudes towards Aboriginal people—an appeal to prejudice. Indeed, the Minister for Aboriginal Affairs, Mr Holding, consistently attributes much of the blame for the lack of public support of land rights to this campaign and that of the mining industry generally.

The effectiveness of this campaign in Western Australia was so profound that it moved Mr Hawke to unilaterally declare that one of the Government's basic principles of land rights (Aboriginal control over mining on their land) was just "not on".

It is largely because Australian society is permeated by soft prejudice and because twenty per cent of Australians are strongly prejudiced that our people are still bashed to death in jails, why some communities have trachoma rates as high as ninety per cent when major preventative treatment required is a decent water supply, why Aboriginal people are still living on the rubbish dump at Cairns and why the majority of Aborigines are still without even a tiny piece of their stolen land.

The truth of the matter, and Mr Holding well knows this, is that welfare dependency, as a strategy to improve the quality of life of Aboriginal people, is not effective.

The dilemma which Aboriginal people face today is a direct result of the process of colonisation, the loss of our economic base and with it the right to self -determination and the lack of recognition of indigenous rights of Aboriginal people. In comparison with the rights which are afforded indigenous peoples in other parts of the world the Australian Government applies a double standard.

The achievement of justice based on land rights is a prerequisite to effective repair of the damage done to our culture. Land rights is not the panacea, but it provides the scenario for further positive development and involvement by Aboriginal Australians in peaceful coexistence. This fact seems to be recognised by a narrow majority of Australians even in the present bleak political climate.

The ANOP found that fifty-six per cent of people surveyed believed that "land rights will help Aborigines keep their culture and help the survival of their race". Yet the Federal Government has backed away from a commitment to effective justice in favour of leaving the issue to the States to deal with, except in the case of the Northern Territory, where it plans to take the knife to the legislation itself. This perpetuates the process of cultural genocide that Aboriginal people see as part of this "hidden agenda" of past, present and future Australian Governments.

The States should remain bit players in this national drama. It is a national issue. It is the Australian Government not the State Governments which is the logical and legal inheritor of the crime of dispossession inflicted on the Aboriginal people by the British Crown.

With the severing in 1985 of the last legal ties binding Australia to Britain, the Australian nation has now fully come into its inheritance, the shameful legacy of brutal conquest.

History is plain—the British Government ducked international responsibility for its crime by passing the responsibilities of the Crown to the Commonwealth of Australia—the referendum of 1967 further underlined the Commonwealth's responsibility. Yet the Commonwealth continues to avoid the resolution of indigenous rights in this country by allowing the States to reduce this national crime to a series of regional problems.

Will the Australian Government argue that it is the States which have usurped our rights to original ownership?—an argument which would lead to the logical conclusion that this is not one nation, but a confederation of convenience between seven countries. This is an absolute nonsense.

The Australian Labor Party constitution, platform and rules claim to recognise both the rights of private ownership of property (Article 5 of the constitution) and the prior ownership of Australia by Aboriginal people (Article 17). There is a logical and moral contradiction in the way the ALP has put these principles into effect in its policies.

In failing to negotiate once and for all a just settlement with the

Aboriginal people, the Australian Government has denied both these principles. By accepting that the States have a right to stand in the way of the legitimate rights of our people, the ALP has endorsed the right of thieves to retain stolen property—justice denied is regarded as being of no consequence because it has been justice delayed too long. Might ultimately is right.

Does this fit with the image we project of a country where justice is a central pillar of national identity? The land of the great fair go?

What we are seeing is a return to the misnamed "law of the jungle", the best exponents of which have been the "civilised" and technologically strong colonising nations. If Australia accepts the law of the jungle by denying the Aboriginal people's right to justice and our rights to our property it puts itself in an extremely vulnerable moral position in the world.

Does a technologically superior nation like Japan, or a land-starved, over-populated country like Indonesia, have an intrinsic right to invade Australia?

Even on the basis of self-interest and political expediency the nation should be careful in weighing up the stakes when choosing a moral position on a people's right to sovereignty.

The demands of Aboriginal people for justice are not excessive. The lands won back, and likely to be won back, through land rights might be extensive, but they are also the harshest and least comfortable parts of the country—the deserts and wetlands where few white people can survive without an air-conditioned life-support system.

No land rights proposals have suggested that ordinary land owners will be dispossessed of land and none have.

In recognition of our original rights of ownership Aboriginal people ask for the Labor Party to honour nationally, as a national Government, its promise of five principles through a straight-forward implementation of these principles into national law without indulging in a deceitful and cowardly sleight of hand by passing responsibility to the States.

The Australian Government has gone only half-way in espousing five just principles and then retreating from them with obvious cowardice and political deceit.

Not only are we being sold out politically, but Aboriginal

organisations throughout the country are being subjugated administratively by the Department of Aboriginal Affairs. For example, the insertion of Section 13 into the department's conditions of funding for Aboriginal organisations.

Aboriginal organisations have consistently sought to work closely with the Government and the department to collectively counter the re-emergence of hard-line racism in this country. Instead of accepting this offer the Government has undermined the credibility of national organisations and embarked upon a campaign of personal vilification of those Aboriginal people who, with the best intentions, have dared to question the government line.

The Government, with a mandate from the Australian people, clearly has two sets of values which it applies with regard to the rights of indigenous people.

The position which is being developed with resolve by Aboriginal Australians is that there is no half-way mark, nor can there be compromise, between justice and oppression.

Through the formation of this National Coalition of Aboriginal Organisations, demands may be made at international forums for the establishment of a panel of eminent persons (South Africa re-visited) to investigate the lack of justice afforded to Aboriginal Australians.

Restore Dignity, Restore Land, Restore Life

Pat Dodson

Address to the Catholic Commission for Justice and Peace, Sydney, August 25, 1986

I want you to try two exercises in imagination. The first is this. I want you to imagine you are black. An Aboriginal Australian. The time is the present. And I want you also to imagine that the white invasion is just about to occur.

How would you be living your life? About three days in every week would be devoted to gathering your food. Hunting, collecting—a bit less in places of plenty, a bit more in the hard country. The rest of your time would be spent socialising, or in religious observances of different kinds. As to your knowledge of the land, your country you would know every tree, every rock, because in the Dreamtime the great ancestors came this way. And they are still here. They live. They must be revered, appeased, paid attention to. It is they who cause conception as a woman walks near. When the child is born he calls that part of the country "Father".You would husband the land. You would burn the grasses to promote new growth and to make sure that the delicate balance of nature that has been created has been preserved.

There is a rich and complicated legal system which is administered by elders and to which all are bound. The blind, the lame, the mentally defective are all to be looked after. Your spiritual and religious life is as rich as your material life is simple. The children are more deeply loved than perhaps any children on earth. Until puberty and initiation they can do no wrong. They are cuddled not chastised. They learn from love and from example. The children grow in security and confidence. They are tutored in the life of the spirit, in respect of the elders and kinship and the ways of the country.

Into this world comes the white invader. Their first act is to say that the land is terra nullius, that no-one owns the land, that it is not used. They knock down the trees, and blast the places sacred to you. They fence around the best water for their cattle. When you resist they shoot and poison your people. Thus begins the Australian Civil War. It can also be called the two hundred years war because it still continues. They still say that they know more than you about land and what your wants and needs are. They say it is important to fence it, to graze it, to mine it. You have difficulty in understanding how they could make such a preposterous claim to ownership. And only you call the land your father. If a whiteman stumbles into the hard country without water he will die. If the land is taken from you or if you are taken from the land your spirit will perish just as surely. Your body becomes like a drought without mercy on the land and your spirit without life blows across it.

In time the white people repent. For a very short time they have pangs of conscience. They pass one of their laws. You know about these white laws. How different they are from your own. The black man's law is straight: it never changes. How come the white man's law always changes?

But now, they say: "You come to us. You prove to us that you have always owned the land and we'll give it back to you." They want us to be grateful, but that is hard. Land according to black laws cannot be given or taken away. You belong to the Land. Your birth has not severed the cord of life which comes from the Land.

But we come to them. No, they say, you can't have the land which we own. You can only have the land which no white man wants. The Land Council helps you. You go to the Land Commissioner. You tell of your love, duties and relationship with your land. You tell of your brutal eviction and sorrows for your country and your people. You bear the secrets of your soul to total strangers. You are given back the land which no-one wants. The land you cannot leave. The country you call father.

Then you hear about mining companies. They want to dig for gold, uranium, for other minerals. The pang of conscience of the white people has passed. They want to change their law, to make sure the miners cannot be stopped from coming on to your land. How come you gave that land to us and now you take it away? Give a thing, take a thing, a white feller's play thing. How come the white man's law always changes? You hear the Territory Government say that they are acting in the interests of all Territorians. You hear Mr Hawke and Mr Holding and Mr Evans say that mining and water and sewerage and national parks and conservation are in the national interest. And you know that the civil war still goes on.

My country is northwest Australia. We are fish eating people. I was born Banaga near Broome, Minnira Ida, and that is my country, Minnira Ida to Yelen Brenan. The black people of Western Australia have been given no rights to their land at all. That is not because the principle changes or because there is a different moral standard. Principle and morals don't change. Or according to black law they don't.

The blacks of Western Australia have no right to their land because the mining companies don't want them to, and because there are no votes in it. By present indications there is no such thing as principle in politics. Politics is about votes and about power. The blacks are easy pickings. They have no princes or parliaments. Everyone has an equal say. The only constraint is the law that was handed down from the Dreamtime, a law that will never change. Up against the fast words and the money of the white politics the blacks don't stand a big chance. My *Rai* is Miayada, the Pelican, not Wanngarri, money or stone.

What would you do now if you were a black Australian in 1986? Not much you can do. You don't have control of votes. You haven't got the reserves of money that a mining company has. You can't use your investments to influence politicians and make their consciences change.

The position ought to be different for Christians. The moral ground ought to be theirs. The testaments are studded with exhortations to hold to principle. "What does it profit a man if he gain the whole world...?" What is there to say to a government which says "To hell with principle. Our country needs money. We will amend the Land Rights Act. That will get us more money."

They might be right. We might get more money. Frankly I doubt it, but we might. If we do, we pay a price. We sacrifice our black people at the altar of expediency. We break faith with them yet again. We remove the opportunity for them to make their own contribution to the country in fidelity to our tradition and unique cultural genius.

One could be forgiven for thinking that the high moral ground should be taken by our leaders. We should expect them to say we will right the wrongs of the past. We will restore to Black Australians the land which has always been rightfully theirs. We will not presume to interfere with how they run their affairs, any more than we would for any other Australian.

There is no special advantage in passing judgment on our politicians. That is a needless luxury. Let us do only two things. First, direct our legislators not to pass these cruel and heartless amendments to the NT Land Rights Act that do not respect our wishes. Secondly, restore to the ancient owners their dignity, their land, their life.

The Year of Mourning

The Sydney protests against the Bicentenary which took place on 25-26 January 1988 were historic events which captured the attention of the world. Over 30,000 marchers, both Aboriginal and non-Aboriginal, protested against the celebration of 200 years of European occupation of the continent. The following excerpts are taken from a verbatim transcript of the speeches delivered at the post-march gathering.

GARY FOLEY: Confusion, chaos, happiness and joy, and solemnity and dignity ... we're about to begin.

I'd like to start off by welcoming everybody here today. It's so magnificent to see black and white Australia together in harmony. It's what we've always said could happen. This is what Australia could be like and what better, what better occasion for us to come together in this sort of spirit than on the two-hundredth anniversary of the invasion. What we're saying here today, and what's very clear, and what will be very clear to Bob Hawke and to people all over the world when they see their television screens tonight and tomorrow, is that *we have survived.* We have survived, and we are here today to call on the Australian Government to give us justice, to give us the opportunity to attain our economic independence so that we can be free and dignified as people in our own land, and decide for ourselves our own future in this country. And then all of us in this country can work towards creating a truly egalitarian and racially harmonious country for the future and, perhaps, in another hundred years, we can all come together and have a good party together.

We have numerous messages of solidarity and support from all over the world. Just before I call on the Reverend Charles Harris to open proceedings formally for the afternoon, I'd just like to read a couple of them.

> On behalf of the Fretilin External Delegation, I wish you success in your struggle for land rights. Having our beloved country, East Timor, invaded and occupied by the Indonesian armed forces for over twelve years now, and fighting for our national independence, makes us feel closer to your struggle for land rights and survival of your people. In this historical event we join our voice to yours, so long live the struggle for land rights and sovereignty. To resist is to win.

And that's from the Fretilin representative in Australia.

> The Federation of Italian Migrant Workers, and their families, in Sydney recognise the culture of Aboriginal people is the foundation upon which we together must build the future of Australia. In doing so, we actively support your demands for land rights and other fundamental rights. Until such rights are officially recognised we cannot hope to attain an Australia that is truly multicultural and egalitarian. We stand together in solidarity.

From the Palestine Information Office in Canberra:

> On behalf of the Executive Committee of the Palestine Liberation Organisation, the Palestinian community of Australia and New Zealand, and myself, I would like to extend to our Aboriginal brothers and sisters our support and solidarity with your legitimate struggle and your demand for land rights. There are many things in common between the Aboriginal and the Palestinian people; as you have been dispossessed of your land the Palestinian people have been dispossessed and have been denied their right to live in their own country. We wish you all the very best in your struggle. Long live the solidarity between our two peoples.

Now that I hope we've settled down a little bit, I'd like to call on the man who I've watched go through a lot of heartbreak and agony over a long period of time; who has worked, if you'll excuse the term, his little black moom off to try and bring this thing together and be the magnificant success that it obviously is. I'd like to introduce to you the Reverend Charles Harris. Thank you.

REVEREND CHARLES HARRIS: First of all I would want you to join me in prayer. Let us pray.

God of the Dreamtime, you who are with us for these 40,000 years or more before 1788, you who gave us our ceremonies, and the law, and our stories, and our sacred sites. You who gave us our Dreaming, you who gave us this land. You were with us then, you are with us now. You march with us today as we march through the streets of Sydney in the march for freedom, justice and hope. You were with us through the last 200 years of onslaught, of terrorism, and of apartheid that has been administered to our people in this land. And you have helped us and enabled us to survive through the odds that were great against us. We pray that you will avenge your people, the Aboriginal and the Islander people. Show to the world, today, the evil deeds of those who came and robbed us, raped our land and our people, murdered and lied to our people. Expose them to the world today. Look and see the chains of oppression that keep your people, the Aboriginal and Islander people, in bondage. Hear the cry, and the call, and the plea for justice to be done in this land. Show the people that you are a God of justice and Lord be praised the God of the Dreamtime. Bring freedom, bring justice, and bring hope.

It's a great feeling to have marched today with the Aboriginal nation in the streets of Sydney. You young people out there can tell your children and your grandchildren about this because this week has been an historic week in this country. It has been a week where Aboriginal and Islander people have come together to lay their claim for freedom, justice and hope for their people. It has been this march that has caused the Aboriginal and Islander people to plead to the nation that exists here that we want justice to be done. In justice we call for land rights, for equality, for sovereignty, and for a treaty and for compensation. We call for these things that are included in the justice package and we want this nation to know that, we want the Government of this nation to know that, and we want the world to know that.

For too long the Aboriginal people and the Islander people have been victims of gross injustice. For too long the Aboriginal people and the Islander people have been manipulated and oppressed. For too long our children have been victims of racism in schools and in the public places of this country. For too long the Government has set the agenda for our lives and for the lives of our children. For too long we have been victims and manipulated here and there, and for too long we have been treated less than migrants and immigrants and foreigners in our own land. This is the time when we, as the original owners of this land, will begin to assert and begin to exercise our sovereign rights and our sovereign powers. We are the sovereign people of this land. We are the original owners of this land. And we say to the Government of this nation, we say to this nation that we want to be part of the negotiating body that negotiates the affairs of this country and particularly, the affairs of the Aboriginal people.

The thing that motivated me to become involved in the struggle was a guy who I pay deep respect to at this time of mourning, and we marched a few moments ago in a march of mourning, and I would like to here take time out to pay my respects to one of the greatest leaders of the Aboriginal community. I refer to him as the Dr Martin Luther King of the Aboriginal people and that is Pastor Don Brady. He has died now but I'd like to show my respect to him at this point of time. If it wasn't for him I would not be here today. He was the one that taught me, he was the one that led me into the struggle back there in Brisbane. As I sat with the people in Musgrave Park and saw the people drinking themselves to death out of a sense of sheer hopelessness, it was out of that feeling of sense of hopelessness, and it was out of that fear, the fear of death so to speak, that the fire of radicalism burned in my being. I am sometimes termed the "Radical Pastor" or the "Radical Minister", but I say that you can't be a Christian today and be a conservative because nobody is going to listen to you.

We want the Government to take a stand and see that the original owners of this land should be given the ownership that is entitled to them and the compensation that is due to them for dispossessing them of their land, of their tribal land, and of their culture; the culture that was here in existence for 40,000 years and was almost eradicated and almost totally destroyed in the short period of 200 years. That, to me, is a crime. That, to me, is a shame on this nation, and on the government of this nation. We here today are gathered to show solidarity across the board.

You white people that are here, you white supporters, we are wanting you to sign a pledge of continuing support to the Aboriginal struggle, to be genuine about your support, and to stand along side the Aboriginal people, because you know as well as I do that the thing that is happening only about two kilometres away from here, the"celebration", is a farce. It's hypocrisy. We call you, we call upon you to be upright and standing along side the Aboriginal people in your support for them. We thank you for your support today and we are so happy to have you here.

I'd just like to share with you some proposed steps as to where we go from here.

One of the things that we should be looking at as the Aboriginal people, we should be looking at setting up our own democratic processes where we begin to get the grass roots people involved and begin to empower them at the grass roots level. Empowering the powerless, because the people at the grass roots seem so powerless as to what happens in Aboriginal affairs across this nation. There needs to be power imparted to the people at the bottom rung of the ladder and the people at the grass roots are those people. They feel so powerless and if we can empower them then we will be a force to be reckoned with in the world. So we have to get the grass roots people involved. We have to get them to elect their leaders and the leaders must be responsible totally and fully to those people at the grass roots. *Not* to the Government as many of our leaders are today. They are responsible to the Government and they have neglected their people, the people at the grass roots. And so we need to set up our own democratic process where the people at the grass roots are involved in the struggle and involved in the decision making process in Aboriginal affairs.

The second thing I would like to propose is the revitalising of our Aboriginal spirituality. We, as a people, are a spiritual people, we come from a spiritual culture, we have a spiritual background and that is the very basis of our existence—our spirituality. As we develop that we can have a firm foundation on which to carry our struggle forward in this land of Australia. The Government's method has been to make us fight and struggle against their odds on their terms. Now we can never win on their terms, in their way, because the odds are so great against us and they have the machinery and the equipment to defeat us all the way down the line. We've fought for 200 years and if we can establish our spiritual base as a people and let the elders be part of the establishing of this spiritual base, then we will have a strong foundation to launch our attack, to launch our struggle, and to launch our fight against oppression and against racism and against all those things that destroy us as a people.

The third thing is to establish a summit conference where we call together the leaders of this nation, Bob Hawke and other leaders of this nation. People of the calibre like Justice Michael Kirby where we sit and talk to these people. We want to begin to become part of the negotiating body and we want to begin exercising our sovereignty.

Those are three proposed steps that I would like to offer the Aboriginal people here as to where we go from here. Thank you very much.

GARY FOLEY: Moving right along folks, I'd just like to make a couple more announcements. Moving through the crowd this afternoon will be people selling *Land Rights News*. There's one hundred thousand copies been printed by the Northern Land Council and we urge you all to buy a copy, especially those supporters of the Aboriginal people who may never have read a copy of it before. So when you see people moving through the crowd with that, please purchase one. That's one way in which you can give further indication of your support this afternoon.

And, also, at some point this afternoon there will be people moving through the crowd with buckets. They're not portable toilets ... they're for the collection of money and the people who will be moving around will be raising money to help cover the costs of the people who have come from interstate and from all over Australia to be here today.

I'd like to send a special call to all the different mobs from all the different parts of Australia and I'd like you mob to give them all a big cheer as I call them out. First of all there's the Top End mob from the Northern Territory—let's give them a welcome. And, of course, we've got the Central Australian mob—we'll give them another welcome as well. And we've got people here from the Kimberleys—let's give them a cheer. And the people more further south in Western Australia here as well—welcome. We've got people here from South Australia—let's give them a rousing hand. There's also a bunch here that are very special to me because I've spent a long time living amongst 'em for the last ten years, that's the Victorians. Let's give the Victorians a big cheer. And, of course, we never forget 'em ... how can we? The Tasmanians—let's give them a welcome. And I'm getting abused here because they reckon I've forgotten Queensland—how can you forget Queensland? Welcome you Queenslanders. Not only that, from all over the rural areas of New South Wales people have been bussed in and driven in for the last week or so. Let's give a special welcome to our own from out the bush of New South.

OK folks. Moving right along here. I'm going to read a few more messages before I call for the next speaker who will be Galarrwuy Yunupingu if you're around mate. In the meantime, while we're waiting for Galarrwuy to get here, got a message here from New Zealand:

> We walk with you today to honour your time of mourning.
> We walk together united in the struggle against oppression
> and in the fight for self determination. In solidarity.

That's from the Maori people of Aotearoa, better known to some of you as New Zealand. Let's give the Maori people a big cheer too. Thank you.

I'd now like to call on one of the most important Aboriginal leaders in Australia, the Chairman of the Northern Land Council, Mr Galarrwuy Yunupingu. Let's give him a big welcome. Thank you.

GALARRWUY YUNUPINGU : Thank you very much crowd. It's nice to see black and white together on a very important day. Isn't it beautiful? Give a clap for yourselves in a hope that this kind of relationship should start from today onwards and established properly.

And with that relationship, I would like to point out some of the important points. I never seen so many faces, both black and white, at any funeral *ever*, and this is the biggest crowd I've ever seen to mourn the injustice of the past in the hope that there will be a better future for all of us in this nation. My point on the behalf of all Aboriginal people, and the Aboriginal people that we represent here, is only a part of Australia. I only wish that all Aboriginal people who are still sitting in their communities and hoping that they would be here, we'd almost take over all of Sydney if they were here.

But, nevertheless, our presence, we hope that the message will get through to the present Government, under the Government, whoever is in power to control the nation and its future. The gathering here is expressing one simple message—that Aboriginal people in the last 200 years have survived. And we will survive. And let me say we have been here, we are here, and we will be here. And there is no stronger message from this crowd, and from the crowd who are still at home, to tell the Government that very simple message and make the Government, today and in the future, that that message is clearly heard from this gathering.

People of this nation have asked a lot of questions and one question is: "Why is Aboriginal people trying through their struggle for land?" The land, as I know that was taught to me by my elders in my day of living since I was born and that education is life; the land is a total life to Aboriginal people of this land. That understanding is being tried to make clear to the people who has not yet understood, or tried to understand, what Aboriginal people is talking about. This gathering is passing on a message to the Government and they are simply just a few yards away from here ignoring and saying "happy birthday" to Australia. And while they are calling out "happy birthday" to Australia, every black man, and a white man who is practically thinking clearly, thinking and supporting the cause of Aboriginal people's struggle, we are saying that that is *all wrong. Aboriginal people have lived more than 200 years. This continent is older and it doesn't deserve a birthday party any more. The gods who have created everything that is on this land make 200 years look like a shit.*

The Queen's representation are being made to this nation at this very moment and they are the rulers, they are the powers. But we know that this land is more powerful than the man first landed here on the behalf of the kings and the queens, that this land is stronger than the rulers who rule this particular land. *The land is the force, the victor, and the oldest, the most ancient, in the world today. And the Aboriginal race of this country, the oldest race in the world.* And through all that understanding, we are expressing that and giving that message across to the people who are still ignorant what this land is all about and what Aboriginal people believe. I only hope that the next 200 years is the years as we make them, year after year to meet the next 200 years is somewhat that simple people, and Aboriginal people are very simple people, to make and to meet the next 200 years with the guidance of justice. Justice and well being for both white Australians and Aboriginal Australians. To meet the next 200 years with unity. It is very clearly understood with the guidance of good leadership among the Aboriginal communities who have met here, with the understanding that this march, and this gathering, is to unify *all Australians* so that what we have to fight for Aboriginal people to achieve in the next 200 years is justice and peace and self-determining powers given to Aboriginal people. On the basis of that core value which is more close to our heart and to our minds—*the land.* The land that Aboriginal people were pushed away from. We want our ceremonies, we want our language, we want our stories told to our children, we want to sing, we want to dance. And why do we do it? *We want to talk to our land and the land to talk to us.* And that is very important as the message. We don't celebrate here the Bicentennial or we are wiping out that bad history that cannot be wiped out unless there is justice and unity on this land.

And my last point. Aboriginal people have come all around Australia in a hope ... in a hope that a man in a powerful position like the prime ministers, the governor generals, and Queen's representatives and whatever, who've got ears to hear and eyes to see really open up what this is all about. We hope to establish a future for Australia and that future is very simple and clear; *white Australians together with Aboriginal Australians and then we are all Australians*.

Thank you.

GARY FOLEY: Moving right along. We realise it's hot out there, please be patient with each other. If you see someone beside you about to collapse from the heat or anything, help each other. That's part of what we're here for. We're all here to help each other. Ultimately this is what Australia is going to be like.

I just got a little announcement I'd like to make here. Somebody just told me that 2UE has been reporting that there's about ten to twenty thousand people here. Here is a classic example of the way in which the Australian media tells lies. I would have thought there's a minimum of fifty thousand people—would you? So all you media people out there take notice. If you saw this march coming up Elizabeth Street you'd know that this is the biggest march in this city that I can remember since the Moratorium days. Perhaps even bigger. It's an indication of the feeling of the Australian people. The last time in the sixties when they had crowds this big it forced the Government to pull the troops out of Vietnam. Let's hope we can force Bob Hawke to do something about Aboriginal people this time around.

*   *   *

I'd now like to call on the Chairman, Chairperson of the New South Wales Aboriginal Land Council, Mr Tiga Bayles.

TIGA BAYLES: Well, firstly, I'd like to thank the organisers of the "long march" for doing a pretty good job. All the people involved, all you people here. I think what we have achieved here today certainly does justice to our people that have fallen in defending Aboriginal land in the last 200 years. We certainly have done justice to our people. I'd like you to all put your hands together for the effort that has been put into this and the achievement that we have reached today.

The main tools of government, State and Federal Governments in this country, is mainstream media. Look at what Murdoch does. Doesn't do anything for our struggle. Whether you're working for peace in this country, international peace, whether you're trying to save the environment or whether you're standing up against the oppression and injustice of the people in this country, the Murdoch press does nothing for us. So it's obvious the mainstream media is the main tool for the governments of this country.

They have been able to turn the tide since the late seventies through until now. They have turned public opinion against Aboriginal people in their demands for justice, in their demands for the recognition of land rights, but it's quite plain to see that the work that Aboriginal people and their non-Aboriginal supporters have been putting into the struggle in the last few years is paying off. Who would ever have thought that we would have this number of people here today. It just goes to show that people are starting to question this society, people are starting to question the Government, and people are starting to recognise the legitimacy in the demands of Aboriginal people.

We do suffer atrocities in this country and, fair enough, maybe we cannot hold some of you people here today responsible for what has happened in the past, but what is happening here today—deaths in custody, leprosy in our communities, tuberculosis, trachoma, hepatitis, these diseases, the pox, venereal disease, or whatever you might call it—these diseases you do have a responsibility in, and it can be you people that put pressure on the Government in this country to stop these diseases. Some of these diseases have been eradicated in Third World countries, but there we are in Australia, we still suffer. It's time it was stopped. I think if we start to look at the situation as a people's struggle and don't think of it as: "Oh, we've got to do something for the bloody blacks again." There's no need to think of it like that. You think of it as doing something for yourselves because when Aboriginal people, when our rights are recognised, we then go on to make sure that oppression and injustice stop right throughout this society. The exploitation of people stops and it has got to be a joint effort, it has got to be a fight with people joining up together, it has got to be a combined effort.

I think there is enough evidence staring us in the face that we can see the need to change. You think about what White Australia is celebrating today—200 years of colonisation, the 200 years since they invaded Aboriginal land. And some of the people seem to expect Aboriginal people, the indigenous people of this country, to participate in the birthday party. *What bullshit.* That would be like asking the Jewish people to celebrate an anniversary of the Holocaust. That's what they're asking us to do. So it's obvious a lot of you people understand that parallel and our situation, our feelings.

Some of the evidence is staring you in the face, the demand for change in this society. You think back. They established this country 200 years ago with people coming in to establish a penal colony, to establish a jail system. That was 200 years ago. They came here to build jails. They're still building the bloody jails. Three years ago they built Parklea, it might have been four years ago ... it was only recently. Before 1990 we're going to see another new jail built. The mentality hasn't changed. They're still building jails, they're still locking people up, they're still dehumanising people be they black, white or indifferent. So it's quite obvious there's a need for change and it's going to be people like yourselves that will play a major role in changing this society and this system.

I think that's about all that I can say. Once again thank you very much, but let's see it as a people's struggle. Don't see it just as doing something for us blacks, you are doing something for yourselves. But, first and foremost, the indigenous people; our sovereignty must be recognised, land rights has to be recognised, national land rights—*meaningful* land rights, not token land rights— and we have to push on from here to see that we can implement some form of Aboriginal government, that Aboriginal people are in a position to be able to make the decisions regarding our affairs. We are sick of non-Aboriginal people making decisions about our affairs. I think we should utilise this situation. Let's not just go home and say: "I've had a bloody good day. Let's wait till next year and see how next year goes." Let's push on from here. Support Aboriginal people in their demands for self-government, self-determination, self-management, self-sufficiency, because if we are self-sufficient we don't need your taxpayers' dollar. We manage on our own. We're sick of being on welfare. We don't want a handout system, we're sick of it. So if you can support Aboriginal people, in turn we can make this a better country because we make your dollar go around further. But we must have self-sufficiency, self-management, self-determination for Aboriginal people first.

Thanks very much. We appreciate your support.

*   *   *

GARY FOLEY: You are probably getting a bit sick of all the male speakers up here some of you. I'd like to introduce Karen Flick.

KAREN FLICK: My name is Karen Flick. I'll be brief because non-Aboriginal history in this country is brief. I've come here just like everybody else has come here to commemorate those who have passed by, those whose spirits are still here, to mourn, to celebrate, everything.

We are Black. We are here. This country is, always was, always will be, Aboriginal land.

Still You Keep Asking Asking

Nimbaliman

This is my grandfather's country—
We've been here from the beginning—
And yet you come to argue with us—
You've kept asking and asking for a long time—
Still you come at us—
What are you going to give us?—
You can offer us nothing!—
And you still keep asking, asking—
and pushing all the time—
Thinking that we'll crack and give you our land —
Then you come to get rich and we'll be poor—
What rubbish!—
How stupid of you—
you and your tricks—
WE don't play games, not like you—
We see it all so clearly, so don't argue with us any more—
This has been your tactic for a long time—
like you did at YIRRKALA—
Then you approach us and start talking—
and keep running after us with your promises—
Really do you think we're so silly or mad?—
We watch each other from a distance—
We've had enough talk—
now you white people listen to us—
You think that by pestering us—
we'll become confused and lose our senses—
You must think we're idiots!—
How bloody wrong you are—
We don't long for your stuff—
Keep it, we don't want it—

We'd rather be poor—
At no time in the future do we want you to approach us again—
Look at this film and understand—
Don't keep coming back year after year—
Why would we give in?—
We understand how you behave—
you and your dirty tricks—
You would make a road, then explore and interfere with the place—
bring sickness upon us all—
Then your doctors would come to operate on us, to chop us up—
Because there are great dangers and illnesses in these places—
WE understand this—the need to be careful and not disturb the place—
We want to live in a healthy place—
This wouldn't be your way—you'd disturb and mess up the land—
Then the spirits of the place would settle us all—
You're too ignorant to know this—
We Aborigines know these things—
You're white people and we're Aborigines—
Don't come and argue with us again. Let it rest here, please—
That's it.

Abbreviations used in Bibliography

Alternative Publishing Co-Operative, Ltd	APCOL
Australian Government Publishing Service	AGPS
Australian Institute of Aboriginal Studies	AIAS
Australian National University Press	ANUP
Fremantle Arts Centre Press	FACP
Melbourne University Press	MUP
Oxford University Press	OUP
University of Queensland Press	UQP

Bibliography

Traditional Aboriginal Texts

Bennell, Eddie, and Anne Thomas. *Aboriginal Legends from the Bibulman Tribe*. Rigby, Adelaide, 1981.

Berndt, Catherine and Ronald M. 'An Oenpelli Monologue'. *Oceania,* vol. 22, no. 1, 1951.

Berndt, Catherine. 'A Drama of North-Eastern Arnhem Land'. *Oceania,* vol. 22, nos 3 and 4, 1952.

_____ *Land of the Rainbow Serpent*. Collins, Sydney, 1979.

Berndt, Ronald M. *Djanggawul*. Routledge and Kegan Paul, London, 1952.

Berndt, Ronald M. *Love Songs of Arnhem Land*. Thomas Nelson, Melbourne, 1976.

Bunug, et al. *Djugurba: Tales from the Spirit Time*. ANUP, Canberra, 1974.

Cairns, Sylvia. *Uncle Willie Mackenzie's Legends of the Goundirs*. Jacaranda Press, Brisbane, 1967.

Capell, Arthur. 'Some Myths of the Garadjeri Tribe, WA'. *Mankind,* vol. 4, nos 2-4, 1949-50.

_____ 'Cave Painting Myths: Northern Kimberley'. *Oceania Linguistic Monographs*, Sydney, 1972.

Charles, John, et al. *Ruwa Kuyingal Yanu (Going Hunting)*. Summer Institute of Linguistics, Darwin, 1973.

Glass, Amee, and Dorothy Newberry. *Tjuma: Stories from the Western Desert*. Aboriginal Arts Board, Sydney, 1979.

Gordon, Tulo. *Milbi: Aboriginal Tales from Queensland's Endeavour River*. ANUP, Canberra, 1980.

Gulpilil, David. *Gulpilil's Stories from the Dreamtime*. Collins, Sydney, 1979.

Harney, Bill. *Tales from the Aborigines*. Robert Hale, London, 1959.

Heath, Jeffrey. *Nunggubuyu Myths and Ethnographic Texts*. AIAS, Canberra, 1981.

Hercus, Luise and Peter Sutton. *This is What Happened: Historical Narratives by Aborigines*. AIAS, Canberra, 1986.

Johnson, Colin. 'A Snake Story of the Nyoongah People'. *Long Water*, (eds) Ulli Beier and Colin Johnson, 1988, pp. 32-36.

Jones, Elsie. *Kilampa Wura Kaani: The Galah and the Frill Neck Lizard*. Disadvantaged Country Area Program, Wilcannia, 1978.

Lucich, Peter. *Children's Stories from the Worora*. AIAS, Canberra, 1969.

McConnel, Ursula. *Myths of the Mungkan*. Melbourne University Press, Melbourne, 1957.

Marawili, Wakuthi. *Djet: A Story from Eastern Arnhem Land*. [Trans. by Dundiwuy Wunungmurra] Thomas Nelson, Melbourne, 1977.

Milinbilil. *Walking by the Sea: The Story of Gurrmirrinju Land*. Milingimbi Literature Production Centre, Milingimbi, Northern Territory, 1976.

Nangan, Joe and Hugh Edwards. *Joe Nangan's Dreaming*. Thomas Nelson, Melbourne, 1976.

Parker, K. Langloh. *Australian Legendary Tales*. Angus and Robertson, Sydney, 1953.

Ragett, Obed. *The Stories of Obed Ragett*. APCOL, Sydney, 1980.
_____ and June Napanangka Walker. *Wati-Jarra-Kurlu*. Yuendumu School, Yuendumu, 1979.

Reeves, Wilf. *The Legends of Moonie Jarl*. Jacaranda Press, Brisbane, 1964.

Robinson, Roland. *Aboriginal Myths and Legends*. Sun Books, Melbourne, 1957.

Roe, Paddy. *Gularabulu: Stories from the West Kimberley*. (Ed.) Stephen Muecke, FACP, Fremantle, 1983.

Roe, Paddy, in Krim Benterrak, Stephen Muecke and Paddy Roe. *Reading the Country*. FACP, Fremantle, 1983.

Roughsey, Dick. *The Giant Devil Dingo*. Collins, Sydney, 1973.
_____*The Rainbow Serpent*. Collins, Sydney, 1975.
_____and Trezise, Percy. *The Quinkins*. Collins, Sydney, 1978.

Siddon, Pompey. *Wangki Jiljigangkajaa Mayarujangka (Stories of Desert and Town)*. Summer Institute of Linguistics, Darwin, 1978.

Skipper, Peter, *Nganpuri Pujman (The Bushman)*. Summer Institute of Linguistics, Darwin, 1978.

Smith, W. Ramsay. *Myths and Legends of the Australian Aboriginals*. George G. Harrap, London, 1930.

Tjapangarti, Tutama. 'Three Stories'. *Long Water*, (eds) Ulli Beier and Colin Johnson, 1988, pp. 37-52.

Tjilari, Andy. *Pitjantjara Translation Series. Book 105*. Institute for Aboriginal Development, Alice Springs, 1975.

Unaipon, David. *Native Legends*. Hunken, Ellis and King, Adelaide, n.d.

_____ 'The Story of the Mungingee'. *The Home*, February, 1925, pp. 42-43.

_____ 'How the Tortoise got his Shell'. *Dawn*, vol. 3, no. 11, 1954, p. 9.

_____ 'Why All the Animals Peck at the Selfish Owl'. *Dawn*, vol. 4, no. 4, 1955, pp. 16-17.

_____ 'The Voice of the Great Spirit'. *Dawn*, vol. 8, no. 7, 1959, p. 19.

_____ 'Why Frogs Jump Into the Water'. *Dawn*, vol. 8, no. 7, 1959, p. 17.

_____ 'Love Story of the Two Sisters'. *Dawn*, vol. 8, no. 9, 1959, p. 9.

Utemorrah, Daisy et al. *Visions of Mowanjum—Aboriginal Writings from the Kimberley*. Rigby, Adelaide, 1980.

Vanbee, Amy. *Manga Yurrantinya (The Girl Who Nearly Drowned)*. Education Department, Perth, 1978.

Von Brandenstein, Carl G. *Narratives from the North West Kimberleys*. AIAS, Canberra, 1970.

Walker, Kath. *Stradbroke Dreamtime*. Angus and Robertson, Sydney, 1972.

Woolagoodja, Sam. *Lalai Dreaming*. [Trans. by M. Silverstein and A. Huntley] Aboriginal Arts Board, Sydney, 1975.

Worms, Ernest A. 'Djamar, the Creator: a Myth of the Bad (West Kimberley), Australia'. *Anthropos*, 1950.

_____ 'Djamar and His Relation to Other Culture Heroes'. *Anthropos*, 1952.

_____ 'The Poetry of the Yaoro and Bad, North Western Australia'. *Annali Lateranensi*, vol. 21, 1957.

Autobiography and Life-Stories

Bropho, Robert. *Fringedweller*. APCOL, Sydney, 1980.
_____'The Great Journey of the Aboriginal Teenagers'. *Limit of Maps*, Spring/Summer, 1985, pp. 19-25.
Cohen, Bill. *To My Delight: The Autobiography of Bill Cohen, a Grandson of the Gumbangarri*. AIAS, Canberra, 1987.
Chesson, Keith. *Jack Davis: A Life-Story*. Dent, Melbourne, 1988.
Clements, Theresa. *From Old Maloga: The Memoirs of an Aboriginal Woman*. Fraser and Morphett, Victoria, n.d.
Davis, Jack. *The First-born and Other Poems*. [The poems are prefaced by a brief autobiography taken from tape recordings] Angus and Robertson, Sydney, 1970.
Dhoulagarle, Koorie. *There's More to Life*. APCOL, Sydney, 1979.
Goolagong, Evonne. *Evonne! On the Move*. Dutton, Sydney, 1975.
Kennedy, Marnie. *Born a Half-Caste*. AIAS, Canberra, 1985.
Lamilami, Lazarus. *Lamilami Speaks: An Autobiography*. Ure Smith, Sydney, 1974.
Langford, Ruby. *Don't Take Your Love to Town*. Penguin, Ringwood, 1988.
Mathews, Janet. *The Two Worlds of Jimmie Barker: The Life of an Australian Aboriginal 1900-1972*. AIAS, Canberra, 1977.
Mirritji, Jack. *My People's Life: An Aboriginal's Own Story*. Milingimbi Literature Board and Aboriginal Arts Board, Sydney, 1978.
Morgan, Ronald. *Reminiscences of the Aboriginal Station at Cummeragunga and its Aboriginal People*. Friends of the Author, Melbourne, 1952.
Morgan, Sally. *My Place*. FACP, Fremantle, 1987.
_____*Wanamurraganya: The Story of Jack McPhee*. FACP, Fremantle, 1989.
Nangan, Joe and Hugh Edwards. *Joe Nangan's Dreaming*. Thomas Nelson, Melbourne, 1976.
Palmer, Kingsley and Clancy McKenna. *Somewhere Between Black*

and White: The Story of an Aboriginal Australian.
Macmillan, Melbourne, 1978.

Perkins, Charles. *A Bastard Like Me.* Ure Smith, Sydney, 1975.

Rose, Lionel. *Lionel Rose: Australian. The Life Story of a Champion.* [As told to Rod Humphries] Angus and Robertson, Sydney, 1969.

Rosser, Bill. *Dreamtime Nightmares.* AIAS, Canberra, 1985. Republished, Ringwood, Penguin, 1987.

Roughsey, Dick. *Moon and Rainbow: The Autobiography of an Aboriginal.* A.H. and A.W. Reed, Sydney, 1971.

Roughsey, Elsie. *An Aboriginal Mother Tells of the Old and the New.* Penguin, Ringwood, 1984.

Shaw, Bruce. *My Country of the Pelican Dreaming: The Life of an Australian Aborigine of the Gadjerong, Grant Ngabidj, 1904-1977.* AIAS, Canberra, 1981.

_____*Banggaiyerri: The Story of Jack Sullivan,* AIAS, Canberra, 1983.

_____*Countrymen: The Life Histories of Four Aboriginal Men,* AIAS, Canberra, 1986.

Simon, Ella. *Through My Eyes.* Rigby, Adelaide, 1978. Republished, Collins/Dove, Sydney, 1987.

Smith, Shirley, C., and Bobbi Sykes. *MumShirl: An Autobiography.* Heinemann, Richmond, Victoria, 1981.

Tucker, Margaret. *If Everyone Cared.* Ure Smith, Sydney, 1977. Republished, Grosvenor Press, 1983.

Unaipon, David. *My Life Story.* Aborigines' Friends' Association, Adelaide, n.d.

Ward, Glenyse. *Wandering Girl.* Magabala Books, Broome, 1987.

West, Ida. *Pride Against Predjudice: Reminiscences of a Tasmanian Aborigine.* AIAS, Canberra, 1984.

White, Isobel, Diane Barwick and Betty Meehan. *Fighters and Singers: The Lives of Some Australian Aboriginal Women.* Allen and Unwin, Sydney, 1985.

Selected Non-Fiction and Essays

Bandler, Faith. *Turning the Tide: A Personal History of the Federal Council for the Advancement of Aborigines and Torres Strait Islanders*. Aboriginal Studies Press, Canberra, 1989.

_____ and Len Fox. *The Time Was Ripe*. APCOL, Sydney, 1983.

Briscoe, Gordon. 'History and "Oral History"?: An Historical and Epistemological Viewpoint'. *Black Voices*, vol. 4, no. 1, July, 1988, pp. 14-22.

Buchanan, Cheryl. *We Have Bugger All! The Kulaluk Story*. Australian Union of Students, Carlton, Victoria, 1974.

Carmody, Kevin. 'The Bitter Cake'. *Social Alternatives*, vol. 7, no. 1, March, 1988, pp. 3-6.

Gilbert, Kevin. *Because a White Man'll Never Do It*, Angus and Roberson, Sydney, 1973.

_____ *Living Black: Blacks Talk to Kevin Gilbert*. Penguin Books, Harmondsworth, Middlesex, 1977.

_____ 'The Aboriginal Question'. *Social Alternatives*, vol. 2, no. 2, August, 1981, pp. 34-35.

_____ 'An Aborigine Speaks on Treaty 88'. *Arena*, no. 78, 1987, pp. 9-10.

Glass, Colleen and Archie Weller (eds). *Us Fellas: An Anthology of Aboriginal Writing*. Artlook Books, Perth, 1987.

Langton, Marcia. 'Urbanizing Aborigines: The Social Scientists' Great Deception'. *Social Alternatives*, vol. 2, no. 2, 1981, pp. 16-22.

Miller, James. *Koori: A Will to Win*. Angus and Robertson, North Ryde, 1985.

Pepper, Phillip. *You Are What You Make Yourself to Be: The Story of a Victorian Aboriginal Family 1842-1980*. Hyland House, Melbourne, 1980.

Perkins, Neville. *Aboriginal Australians Yesterday and Today: An Aboriginal Overview*. Interim Central Australian Aboriginal Rights Community Council, Alice Springs, 1973.

Riley, Rob. 'Aboriginal Claims Not Excessive in the Land of the Great Fair Go'. *Land Rights News*. vol. 2, no. 1, November, 1986, p. 17.

Rosser, Bill. *This is Palm Island*. AIAS, Canberra, 1978.

Sykes, Bobbi [Roberta B.]. 'The New White Colonialism'.
Meanjin, vol. 36, no. 4, December, 1977, pp. 421-427.
_____ 'Black Australians: Aboriginal Australians: Aborigines'.
Filmnews, vol. 8, April, 1978, p. 5.
Sykes, Roberta B. *Incentive, Achievement and Community*. Sydney
University Press, Sydney, 1986.
_____ *Black Majority*. Hudson, Hawthorn, Victoria, 1989.
Thaiday, Willie. *Under the Act*. North Queensland Publishing
Company, Townsville, 1981.
Thanacoupie. 'Was This Time Set Aside?'. *Aspect*, no. 34,
August, 1986, pp. 91-104. [Special issue edited by Ulli
Beier: *Long Water: Aboriginal Art and Literature.*]
Walker, Kath. 'Highjack'. Ulli Beier (ed.). *Aspect*, no. 34,
August, 1986, pp. 82-87.
Watson, Len. *From the Very Depths: A Black View of White Racism*.
Quaker Race Relations Committee, Surrey Hills, New South
Wales, 1973.

Poetry

Bostock, Gerald. *Black Man Coming*. Gerald L. Bostock, Fitzroy, 1980.

Corpus, Aileen. 'Different Shades'. *Identity*, vol. 2, no. 7, January, 1976, p. 25.

_____'Another Black Bird'. *Identity*, vol. 2, no. 8, April, 1976, p. 23.

_____'Five Poems'. *Meanjin*, vol. 36, no. 4, December,1977, pp. 470-473.

Davis, Jack. *The First-born and Other Poems*. Angus and Robertson, Sydney, 1970. Republished by Dent, Melbourne, 1983.

_____*Jagardoo: Poems from Aboriginal Australia*. Methuen, Sydney, 1978.

_____ *John Pat and Other Poems*. Dent, Melbourne, 1988.

Dingo, Ernie. 'Five Poems'. Ulli Beier, (ed.) *Aspect*, no. 34, August, 1986, p. 67.

Fogarty, Lionel George. *Kargun*. Cheryl Buchanan, Brisbane, 1980.

_____*Yoogum Yoogum*. Penguin, Ringwood, 1982.

_____*Kudjela*. Cheryl Buchanan, Spring Hill, Queensland, 1983.

_____*Ngutji*. Cheryl Buchanan, Spring Hill, Queensland, 1984.

_____*Jagera*. Cheryl Buchanan, Spring Hill, Queensland, 1988.

Gilbert, Kevin. *End of Dreamtime*. Island Press, Sydney, 1971.

_____*People Are Legends*. UQP, St. Lucia, 1978.

_____'To My Cousin, Evonne Cawley'. *The Bulletin Literary Supplement*, 18 September 1980, p. 2.

_____'Accessories After the Fact', 'Baal Belbora', 'Tree'. *Social Alternatives*, vol. 2, no. 2, August, 1981, pp. 10, 47, 71.

_____, (ed.) *Inside Black Australia: An Anthology of Aboriginal Poetry*. Ringwood, Penguin, 1988. [Contains poetry by over forty Black Australian authors, including Gilbert.]

Johnson, Colin [Mudrooroo Narogin]. 'Colin Johnson Replies to
   Adam Shoemaker'. *Westerly*, vol. 27, no. 4, December,
   1982, p. 80.
_____*The Song Circle of Jacky, and Selected Poems*.
   Hyland House, Melbourne, 1986.
_____'Three Poems from India'. Ulli Beier, (ed.) *Aspect*, no. 34,
   August, 1986, pp. 88-89.
Johnson, Eva. 'Differences', 'A Letter to My Mother',
   'Remember?'. Susan Hawthorne, (ed.) *Difference: Writings
   By Women*, Waterloo Press, Waterloo, 1985, pp. 34-36.
Moolenbroek, Lesley van. *Collected Works*. Cheryl Buchanan,
   Spring Hill, Queensland, 1984.
Narogin, Mudrooroo [Colin Johnson]. *Dalwurra: The Black Bittern*.
   Perth, The Centre for Studies in Australian Literature, 1988.
Ngitji Ngitji [Mona Tur]. 'This My Land'. *Identity*, vol. 2, no. 7,
   January, 1976, p. 25.
_____'Spring Rain'. *Identity*, vol. 3, no. 4, January, 1978,
   p. 23.
_____'What Now Aborigine?'. *Identity*, vol. 3, no. 6, April,
   1978, p. 23.
Rankine, Leila. 'The Coorong'. *Social Alternatives*, vol. 2., no. 4,
   1982, p. 9.
Sykes, Bobbi. 'Prayer to the Spirit of the New Year'. Rosemary
   Dobson, (ed.) *Australian Voices*. ANUP, 1975, p. 9.
_____*Love Poems and Other Revolutionary Actions*. The
   Saturday Centre, Cammeray, NSW, 1979.
   Republished, UQP, 1988.
Tjapangati, Tutama. 'Wangka Tjukutjuk'. *Overland*, no. 80, July,
   1980, p. 32.
_____'Aladayi'. *The Bulletin Literary Supplement*, 1 November
   1983, p. 64.
_____'Tjanake Pite'. *The Bulletin Literary Supplement*,
   1 November 1983, p. 65.
Tjupurrla, Nosepeg. 'Pangkalanga Dreaming'. *The Bulletin Literary
   Supplement*, 1 November 1983, p. 65.
Victorian SEMP and Ethnic Relations Team. *Aboriginal Voices*.
   Heinemann, Richmond, Victoria, 1978. [Anthology of
   Aboriginal creative writing, including poems by Davis,

Walker, Duroux, Maris, and Utemorrah.]

Utemorrah, Daisy. 'Mary's Plea'. *Identity*, vol. 2, no. 3, January, 1975, p. 27.

Walker, Kath. *We are Going*. Jacaranda Press, Brisbane, 1964.

_____ *The Dawn is at Hand*. Jacaranda Press, Brisbane, 1966.

_____ *My People—a Kath Walker Collection*. Jacaranda Press, Milton, Queensland, 1970. Revised edition, Jacaranda-Wiley, Milton, 1981.

_____ 'Minjerriba', 'Credit and Loss', 'Blue Crane'. *Meanjin*, vol. 36, no. 4, December, 1977, pp. 443-445.

_____ 'China ... Woman'. Ulli Beier, (ed.) *Aspect*, no. 34, August, 1986, p. 90.

Walker, Robert. *Up, Not Down Mate! Thoughts From a Prison Cell*. Catholic Chaplaincy to Aborigines, Kuralta Park, South Australia, 1981.

Ward, Glenyse. 'Wandering Girl—A Life Story'. *Long Water*, Aboriginal Artists Agency, Sydney, 1988, pp. 26-31.

Watson, Maureen. 'Black Child', 'I, Too am Human'. *Meanjin*, vol. 36, no. 4, December, 1977, pp. 545-547.

_____ *Black Reflections*. The Education Information Retrieval Service, Wattle Park, South Australia, 1982.

Woolagoodjah, Sam. 'Lalai (Dreamtime)'. *Poetry Australia*, no. 58, March, 1976, pp. 4-9.

Worrumarra, Banjo. 'The Man'. Helen Weller, (ed.) *North of the 26th*, The Nine Club, East Perth, 1979.

Novels

Bandler, Faith. *Wacvie*. Rigby, Adelaide, 1977.

Bandler, Faith and Len Fox. *Marani in Australia*, Rigby/Opal, Adelaide, 1980.

_____ *Welou, My Brother*. Wild and Woolley, Sydney, 1984.

Clare, Monica. *Karobran: The Story of an Aboriginal Girl*. APCOL, Sydney, 1978.

Johnson, Colin [Mudrooroo Narogin]. *Wild Cat Falling*. Angus and Robertson, Sydney, 1965. Republished, Sirius Edition, Angus and Robertson, Sydney, 1979.

_____ *Long Live Sandawara*. Quartet Books, Melbourne, 1979. Republished, Hyland House, Melbourne, 1987.

_____ *Doctor Wooreddy's Prescription for Enduring the Ending of the World*. Hyland House, Melbourne, 1983.

Maris, Hyllus, and Sonia Borg. *Women of the Sun*. Penguin, Ringwood, 1985. [Novelisation of television dramas]

Narogin, Mudrooroo. *Doin Wildcat: A Novel Koori Script*. Hyland House, Melbourne,1988.

Weller, Archie. *The Day of the Dog*. Allen and Unwin, Sydney, 1981. Republished, Pan Books, Sydney, 1982.

Willmot, Eric. *Pemulwuy: The Rainbow Warrior*. Weldons, Sydney, 1987. Republished, Bantam Books, Sydney, 1988.

Drama

Bostock, Gerald. *Here Comes the Nigger*. [Excerpts from the first draft in *Meanjin* vol. 36, no. 4, December, 1977, pp. 479-493]

Davis, Jack. *Kullark* and *The Dreamers*. Currency Press, Sydney, 1982. *The Dreamers* republished in *Plays from Black Australia*. [Intro. Justine Saunders] Currency Press, Sydney, 1989, pp. 1-71.

_____ *No Sugar*. Currency Press, Sydney, 1986.

_____*Honey Spot*. Currency Press, Sydney, 1987.

_____*Barungin: Smell the Wind*. Currency Press, Sydney, 1989.

Gilbert, Kevin. *The Cherry Pickers*. Burrambinga Books, Canberra, 1988.

Johnson, Eva. *Murras: Plays from Black Australia*, Currency Press, Sydney, 1989, pp. 79-107.

Maris, Hyllus and Sonia Borg. *Women of the Sun*. Currency Press, Sydney, 1983. [Television drama script]

Maza, Bob. *The Keepers*. *Plays from Black Australia* Currency Press, Sydney, 1989, pp. 167-229.

Merritt, Robert J. *The Cake Man*. Currency Press, Sydney, 1978.

Utemorrah, Daisy. 'Mugugu'. *Identity*, vol. 2, no. 3, January, 1975, p. 11.

Walker, Kath. 'Tail of Platypus'. *Identity*, vol. 2, no. 2, September 1974, pp. 31-32.

Walley, Richard. *Coordah*. *Plays from Black Australia*, Currency Press, Sydney, 1989, pp. 109-166.

Short Stories

Aboriginal and Islander Teacher Aides. *Cape York School Readers*. Aboriginal Training and Cultural Institute, Balmain, 1982.

Aboriginal Students. *Stories*. Aboriginal Training and Cultural Institute, Balmain, 1982.

Brennan, Gloria. 'Unwritten Policy'. *Identity*, January, 1974, p. 26.

Chee, Raymond [Archie Weller]. 'Dead Dingo'. *Identity*, vol. 3, no. 1, January, 1977, pp. 28-30.

_____'Stolen Car'. *Identity*, vol. 3, no. 3, July, 1977, pp. 29-33.

_____'The Storm'. *Identity*, vol. 3, no. 9, January, 1979, pp. 26-27.

Davis, Jack. 'My Brother Harold'. *Identity*, vol. 1, no. 10, April, 1974, p. 29.

_____'Deaf Mute Mother'. *Identity*, vol. 1, no. 10, April, 1974, p. 33.

_____'A Day'. *Identity*, vol. 2, no. 1, July, 1974, p. 15.

_____'The Contest'. *Identity*, vol. 2, no. 2, October, 1974, p. 27.

_____'The Bridge Dwellers'. *Identity*, vol. 2, no. 3, January, 1975, p. 30.

_____'The Stone'. *Identity*, vol. 2, no. 4, April, 1975, p. 25.

_____'Heat'. *Identity*, vol. 2, no. 7, January, 1976, p. 26.

_____'Pay Back'. *Identity*, vol. 2, no. 7, January, 1976, p. 28.

_____'White Fantasy—Black Fact'. *Identity*, vol. 3, no. 6, April, 1978, pp. 27-29.

Johnson, Colin. 'A Missionary Would I Have Been'. *Westerly*, no. 1, March, 1975, pp. 5-11.

_____'Safe Delivery'. *Westerly*, June, 1976, pp. 6-7.

Morgan, Sally. 'The Letter'. *National Aboriginal Day Magazine*, 1986. pp. 24-25.

Randall, Bob. 'Mother'. *Identity*, vol. 1, no. 7, July, 1973, p. 20.

_____'Minjilung: The One Who Came With the Sun'. *Identity*, vol. 1, no. 7, July, 1973, pp. 30-36.

Walker, Kath. 'The Tank'. *Identity*, vol. 1, no. 1, July, 1971, p. 35.

_____'Koo-Poo—A Story for Children'. *Identity*, vol. 1, no. 4, April, 1972, p. 30.

_____ 'The Turtle'. *The Cool Man, and Other Contemporary Stories*. Angus and Robertson, Sydney, 1973, pp. 66-70.

_____'The Rosary Beads'. *Identity*, vol. 2, no. 2, October, 1974, p. 29.

Weller, Archie. *Going Home*. [A collection of short stories] Allen and Unwin, Sydney, 1986.

Selected Literary Criticism

Ariss, Robert. 'Writing Black: The Construction of an Aboriginal Discourse'. Jeremy R. Beckett, (ed.) *Past and Present: the Construction of Aboriginality*, Aboriginal Studies Press, Canberra, 1988, pp. 131-146.

Arthur, Kateryna. 'Fiction and the Rewriting of History: A Reading of Colin Johnson'. *Westerly*, vol. 30, no. 1, March, 1985, pp. 55-60.

Beston, John. 'The Aboriginal Poets in English: Kath Walker, Jack Davis and Kevin Gilbert'. *Meanjin*, vol. 36. no. 4, December, 1977, pp. 446-469.

_____ 'David Unaipon: The First Aboriginal Writer (1873-1967)'. *Southerly*, no. 3, 1979, pp. 334-350.

Bostock, Lester. 'Black Theatre in New South Wales'. *New Dawn*, vol. 4, no. 4, pp. 13-14.

Brisbane, Katharine. 'Looking Out from Australia—New Directions in Australian Theatre' *Island Magazine*, Spring,1984, pp. 36-40.

Dale, Leigh. 'Lights and Shadows: Poetry by Aboriginal Women'. David Brooks and Brenda Walker, (eds) *Poetry and Gender*. UQP, Brisbane, 1989, pp. 73-82.

Davis, Jack. '*The Dreamers*'. *Meanjin*, March, 1984, pp. 44-48.

_____and Bob Hodge, (eds). *Aboriginal Writing Today: Papers from the First National Conference of Aboriginal Writers Held in Perth, Western Australia, in 1983*. AIAS, Canberra, 1985. [Contains papers by the Berndts, Davis, Johnson, Gilbert, McGuinness and Walker, Bandler, Bostock and Watego]

_____and Adam Shoemaker. 'Aboriginal Literature: Written'. Laurie Hergenhan, (ed.) *The Penguin New Literary History of Australia*, Penguin, Ringwood, 1988, pp. 27-35.

Doobov, Ruth. 'The New Dreamtime: Kath Walker in Australian Literature'. *Australian Literary Studies*, vol. 6, no. 1, May, 1973, pp. 46-55.

Dugon, Margaret. 'Black Voices, White World'. *The National Times*, 16-21 January 1978, p. 38.

Ellis, Rose, 'Black Writing: A Critical Reflection'. *Hermes*, vol. III, no. 1, 1987, pp. 80-83.

Ferrier, Carole, 'Black Women's Prose Fiction in English: A Selective Bibliography'. Part One: *Hecate*, vol. XIV, no. 1, pp. 104-111. Part Two: *Hecate*, vol. XIV, no. 2, pp. 110-125.

Gelder, Ken. 'Aboriginality'. Gelder and Paul Salzman, *The New Diversity: Australian Fiction 1970-88*. McPhee Gribble, Melbourne, 1989, pp. 205-242.

Goodwin, Ken. 'The Uniqueness of Recent Writing—Aboriginal Writers'. *A History of Australian Literature*, Macmillan, London, 1986, pp. 263-267.

Headon, David. 'Beyond the Years of the Locust: Aboriginal Writing in the 1980s—Part Two'. *Meridian*, vol. 7, no. 2, October, 1988.

Healy, J. J. 'Literature, Power and the Refusals of Big Bear: Reflections on the Treatment of the Indian and the Aborigine'. Russell McDougall and Gillian Whitlock, (eds) *Australian/Canadian Literatures in English: Comparative Perspectives*. Methuen, North Ryde, 1987, pp. 68-93.

Hodge, Bob. 'A Case for Aboriginal Literature'. *Meridian*, vol. 3, no. 1, May, 1984, pp. 83-88.

Johnson, Colin [Mudrooroo Narogin]. 'Guerilla Poetry: Lionel Fogarty's Response to Language Genocide'. Ulli Beier, (ed.) *Aspect*, no. 34, August, 1986, pp. 72-81.

———— 'Theatrical Fringe Benefits'. Ulli Beier and Colin Johnson, (eds) *Long Water*, 1988, pp. 1-19.

Jones, Philip. ' "A Curve is a Line and a Line is a Curve": Some of the Truth about David Unaipon'. *The Sydney Review*, no. 14, July, 1989, p. 8.

Kaine-Jones, Karen. 'Contemporary Aboriginal Drama'. *Southerly*, vol. 18, no. 4, pp. 432-444.

Langsam David. 'Jack Davis and Marli Biyol in London'. *Australian Society*, August, 1988, pp. 41-42.

McCallum, John. 'Black Theatre: Robert Merritt's *The Cake Man*'. *Meanjin*, vol. 36, no. 4, December, 1977, pp. 474-478.

McGregor, William B. 'Writing Aboriginal: Oral Literature in Print'. *Meridian*, vol. 8, no. 1, May, 1989, pp. 47-56.

Muecke, Stephen. 'Discourse, History, Fiction: Language and Aboriginal History'. *Australian Journal of Cultural Studies*, vol. 1, no. 1, May, 1983, pp 71-79.

_____'On Not Comparing: Towards an Aboriginal Aesthetic'. *The Age Monthly Review*, vol. 5, no. 7, November, 1985, pp. 8-10.

_____'Aboriginal Literature: Oral'. Laurie Hergenhan, (ed.) *The Penguin New Literary History of Australia*, Penguin, Ringwood, 1988, pp. 27-35.

_____'Aboriginal Literature and the Repressive Hypothesis'. *Southerly*, vol. 4, 1988, pp. 405-418.

Narogin, Mudrooroo. 'The Growth of Aboriginal Literature'. *Social Alternatives*, vol. 7, no. 1, March, 1988, pp. 53-54.

_____'Missions Mixed Blessings'. *The Age Saturday Extra*, 16 April 1988.

Nelson, Emmanuel S. 'Black America and the Aboriginal Literary Consciousness'. *Westerly*, vol. 30, no. 4, December, 1985, pp. 43-54.

_____, (ed.) *Connections: Essays on Black Literatures*. Aboriginal Studies Press, Canberra, 1988. [Contains essays by Watego, Headon, Muecke and Shoemaker as well as a keynote address by Sykes]

Newman, Joan. 'Reader-response to Transcribed Oral Narrative: *A Fortunate Life* and *My Place*'. *Southerly*, vol. 4, 1988, pp. 376-389.

Oxford, Gillian. 'The Purple Everlasting: The Aboriginal Cultural Heritage in Australia'. *Theatre Quarterly*, vol. 7, no. 26,

1977, pp. 88-98.

Rutherford, Anna. (ed.) *Aboriginal Culture Today*.
Kunapipi, vol. X, nos. 1 and 2, (special issue). Dangaroo Press,
Sydney, 1988.

Shoemaker, Adam. 'Aboriginal Drama: A New Voice in Australian
Theatre'. Joost Daalder and Michele Fryar, (eds)
Aspects of Australian Culture, Abel Tasman
Press, Adelaide, 1982, pp. 28-33.

_____ *Black Words, White Page: Aboriginal Literature 1929-1988*.
UQP, St Lucia, 1989.

_____ 'Build Bridges—Don't Burn Them'. *The Weekend
Australian*, 21-22 October, 1989, p. Weekend 7.

Tacey, David, J. 'Australia's Otherworld: Aboriginality, Landscape
and the Imagination'. *Meridian,* vol. 8, no. 1,
May 1989, pp. 57-65.

Thomas, Sue. 'Connections: Recent Criticism of Aboriginal
Writing,' *Meridian,* vol. 8, no. 1, May, 1989,
pp. 39-46.

Tiffin, Chris. 'Look to the New-Found Dreaming'. *Journal of
Commonwealth Literature*, vol. 20, 1985.

Walker, Kath. 'Aboriginal Literature'. *Identity*, vol. 2, no. 3,
January, 1975, pp. 39-40.

Watego, Cliff. 'Aboriginal Australian Dramatists'. Richard
Fotheringham, (ed.) *Community Theatre in Australia*.
Methuen, Sydney, 1987, pp. 69-76.

_____ 'Being Done to Again'. *Social Alternatives*,
vol. 7 no. 1, March, 1988, pp. 32-34.

_____ 'Backgrounds to Aboriginal Literature'. *Black
Voices*, vol. 4, no. 1, July, 1988, pp. 42-55.

Webb, Hugh. 'Black Words on a White Page'. Sneja Gunew and
Ian Reid, (eds) *Not the Whole Story*, Local
Consumption Publications, Sydney, 1984.

Weller, Archie. 'Portrayal of Aboriginal Men in Literature'. *Social
Alternatives*, vol. 7, no. 1, March, 1988, pp. 55-57.

Whaley, George. 'A City's Place of Dreaming: Black Theatre in
Sydney'. *Theatre Quarterly*, vol. 7, no. 26, 1977,
pp. 98-100.

Notes on Contributors

As the works in Paperbark *are frequently not created by individual authors, the construction of a Notes on Contributors section is problematic. Where entries do not appear here it is either because the writings are the product of a collective community voice or because no biography was available to the editors.*

Tiga Bayles
Tiga Bayles has for many years been actively involved in working for positive changes on behalf of the Aboriginal people. He is one of the co-ordinators of Radio Redfern in Sydney.

Gerry Bostock
Gerry Bostock is a member of the Bandjalong tribe, and was born in Grafton, New South Wales in 1942. He became involved in street theatre and the political struggle surrounding the Aboriginal Embassy in Canberra in 1972. Since then he has continued the writing of plays and poetry, co-directed an important documentary film, *Lousy Little Sixpence* (1981), and is doing further production work for television both locally and internationally.

Gloria Brennan
Gloria Brennan was a Wongai from Western Australia. She was a graduate of the University of Western Australia and worked for various organisations before moving to Canberra, working for the Department of Aboriginal Affairs and the Public Service Board, before her tragic death from cancer in 1985. She is remembered as a major figure in Aboriginal politics and culture.

Robert Bropho
Robert Bropho has been an activist for many years in the Swan River Community of Western Australia. His book, *Fringedweller* (1980), was an important contribution to the production of a politically-engaged oral history.

Jimmy Chi

Jimmy Chi is from Broome, where he works as a songwriter and musician. He is a driving creative force behind the Aboriginal rock opera, *Bran Nue Dae*, scheduled to premier at the Festival of Perth in 1990.

Pat Dodson

Pat Dodson was born in Broome, and belongs to the coastal peoples of the north-west. After being ordained as a Catholic Priest, he left the church and became an active member of land rights organisations. Until recently he was chairman of the Central Land Council.

Ellen Draper

Ellen Draper is from Moree, New South Wales. 'Old Cobraboor' is her first published story.

Jimmy Everett

Jimmy Everett [Mawbana Pleregannana] was born on Flinders Island, Tasmania in 1942. He is a writer of poetry, stories, articles and plays and has also been an Aboriginal Arts Board administrator and a political activist.

William Ferguson

William Ferguson was born in 1881 at "Waddi", Darlington Point, New South Wales on the banks of the Murrumbidgee River. His whole life was spent tirelessly campaigning for the Aboriginal people. On January 26 1938 he—together with Pastor (later Sir) Douglas Nicholls and Jack Patten—organised a Day of Mourning to protest against 150 years of unjust and callous treatment of Aborigines.

Karen Flick

Karen Flick has worked for a number of Black Australian organisations, including the Central and Northern Land Councils. She currently lives in Darwin.

Gary Foley
Activist, spokesperson, actor, organiser and educator, Gary Foley is one of the best known Aborigines in Australia. He has worked for many years on behalf of Black Australians in film, television and in Aboriginal political and service organisations.

Lydia George
Lydia George is from the Torres Strait Islands and is at present a student at the University of Technology, Sydney.

Reverend Charles Harris
Born into poverty in Ingham, Queensland, Reverend Charles Harris has been a Uniting minister since that church's inception. He worked for eight years with the Aborigines of Musgrave Park in Brisbane and says that his whole life has been motivated by love and compassion for his people. He is the former president of the Uniting Aboriginal and Islander Christian Congress and was co-organiser of the Sydney Protest Gathering of 26 January 1988.

Leanne Hollingsworth
Leanne Hollingsworth is from Cairns, and was a trainee teacher in the AITEP (Aboriginal and Islander Teacher Education Programme) at James Cook University at the time of writing her piece for this volume. She now works in Townsville.

Ruby Langford
Born on the Box Ridge Mission, Coraki, on the North Coast of New South Wales in 1934, Ruby Langford grew up in Bonalbo and attended high school in Casino. A qualified clothing machinist, she has nine children whom she raised mostly by herself, both in the bush around Coonabarabran and in Sydney. She tells the story of her life in her 1988 book, *Don't Take Your Love to Town*.

Gordon Langford
Ruby Langford's son "Nobby" has not yet broken away from the white injustice system. Although he is in prison, he has become an accomplished painter and some of his work is scheduled to tour with the First Koori Perspective show in 1990.

Herbie Laughton

Herbie Laughton is a well-known musician from Alice Springs.

Hyllus Maris

Hyllus Maris was born in Shepparton into the Yorta Yorta tribe and lived and worked in Victoria until her untimely death in 1986. A sociologist and a prominent activist, she founded the first Aboriginal school in that state: the Worawa College in Frankston. In addition to writing poems and short stories, she collaborated with Sonia Borg on the script (and later the novel) of *Women of the Sun* (1983), an outstanding television series which reexamined aspects of Black Australian historical contact with Europeans.

Sally Morgan

Sally Morgan was born in Perth in 1951 and completed a BA degree in Psychology at the University of Western Australia in 1974. She also has postgraduate diplomas in Counselling Psychology and Computing and Library Studies. Renowned both as a writer and as an artist, she achieved immediate best-seller status with her first book, *My Place* (1987) and received the 1989 Australian Human Rights Award for her second, *Wanamurraganya: The Story of Jack McPhee* (1989).

Ngitji Ngitji

Ngitji Ngitji was born in Pitjantjatjara country in the north-west of South Australia. Her "whitefella" name is Mona Tur. She writes poetry and prose, and is a teacher and translator of Aboriginal languages.

Oodgeroo Noonuccal

Oodgeroo Noonuccal, previously known by the name of Kath Walker, is a major poet and a lifelong activist for her people. She was born and grew up on Stradbroke Island in Moreton Bay, Queensland, and at thirteen left school to work as a domestic. In the 1950s she began writing poems, and *We Are Going*, the first of several poetry volumes, was published in 1964. It has been reprinted many times. She is also the author of a collection of traditional and children's stories, *Stradbroke Dreamtime* (1972). Both her poetry and prose have been published widely throughout the world in English and in translation.

Jimmy Pike

Jimmy Pike is from the Great Sandy Desert in north-west Australia, and is a member of the Walmatjarri Community of Fitzroy Crossing. He has had huge success as an artist and as a designer for *Desert Designs* fashions.

Bob Randall

Bob Randall works in the Aboriginal Education Unit at the University of Wollongong. As well as being a song-writer he has published prose in a number of magazines.

Rob Riley

Rob Riley is from Perth, Western Australia, and is a former Chairperson of the NAC. He has also worked for the Department of Aboriginal Affairs in Canberra.

Paddy Roe

Paddy Roe is a Nyigina man who lives in Broome. He is a community and ceremonial leader, and his oral narratives have been extensively anthologised.

David Unaipon

Born in 1872 at the Point McLeay Mission in South Australia, David Unaipon is acknowledged as the first published Black Australian writer: his *Native Legends* appeared in 1929. One of the best-known Aborigines of his era, Unaipon was famous as a spokesperson, an inventor, an organist and a preacher as well as an author. He died in 1967.

Archie Weller

Archie Weller was born in Subiaco, Western Australia, in 1957. As one of the younger Aboriginal writers, he has made a name as a novelist (*The Day of the Dog*, 1981), a short-story writer (*Going Home*, 1986) and has co-edited with Colleen Francis-Glass an anthology of Aboriginal writings, *Us Fellas* (1988).

Banjo Worrumarra

Banjo Worrumarra is a community elder of the Bunaba people from the Central Kimberleys. He is a poet and the custodian of traditional and historical narratives, one of which—the "Pigeon Story"—is being made into a feature film.

Galarrwuy Yunupingu

Chairman of the Northern Land Council for many years, Galarrwuy Yunupingu has been instrumental in the Aboriginal fight for land rights.